Australian Edition

HR for Small Business

FOR

DUMMIES

A Wiley Brand

by Paul Maguire

FOR

DUMMIES

A Wiley Brand

HR for Small Business For Dummies®, Australian Edition

Published by
Wiley Publishing Australia Pty Ltd
42 McDougall Street
Milton, Qld 4064
www.dummies.com

Copyright © 2014 Wiley Publishing Australia Pty Ltd

The moral rights of the authors have been asserted

National Library of Australia
Cataloguing-in-Publication data:

Autho:	Maguire, Paul
Title:	HR for Small Business For Dummies / Paul Maguire.
Edition:	Australian Edition.
ISBN:	9781118640302 (pbk.)
	9781118640401 (ebook)
Notes:	Includes index.
Subjects:	Personnel management — Australia
	Organisational behaviour — Australia.
Dewey Number:	658.3

Cover image: © iStockphoto.com/Rubberball

Typeset by diacriTech, Chennai, India

Printed in Singapore by
C.O.S. Printers Pte Ltd

10 9 8 7 6 5 4 3 2 1

Contents at a Glance

Introduction 1

Part I: Getting Started: So, You Need to Staff Your Small Business 5

Chapter 1: Looking at the Big Picture — Before You Employ 7
Chapter 2: Building a Recruitment Strategy for Finding the Right Person..............21
Chapter 3: Sorting the Good from the Not So Good........................41

Part II: Getting the Ground Rules and Paperwork for Hiring Right 59

Chapter 4: The National Employment Standards 61
Chapter 5: Modern Awards and Pay........................87
Chapter 6: Calculating the Real Cost of Employment 111
Chapter 7: Hiring: The Importance of the Employment Contract 137

Part III: Putting the Employment Relationship to Work 153

Chapter 8: Making a Good Impression: Orientation Programs 155
Chapter 9: Performance Expectations: the Wage–Work Bargain 171
Chapter 10: Pay Increase? You Must Be Joking!........................185

Part IV: The Non-Discriminating Employer 199

Chapter 11: Managing Workplace Conflict........................201
Chapter 12: A Journey through Australian Workplace Rights and EEO........................219
Chapter 13: Harassment and Bullying — Gee, Can't You Take a Joke?........................237

Part V: A Healthy Workplace Is a Happy Workplace 247

Chapter 14: Safety at Work Is Everyone's Responsibility 249
Chapter 15: Workers Compensation and Rehabilitation........................265

Part VI: The End of the Employment Relationship *283*

Chapter 16: Resignation of Employment 285

Chapter 17: Employee Dismissal: A Matter of Fairness 299

Chapter 18: Termination, Change and Redundancy 319

Part VII: The Part of Tens *337*

Chapter 19: Ten Ways to Build a Successful Employment Relationship 339

Chapter 20: Ten Things You Should Never Do At Work 349

Index *355*

Table of Contents

Introduction *1*

About This Book 1
Foolish Assumptions 2
Icons Used in This Book 2
Beyond the Book 3
Where to Go from Here 3

*Part I: Getting Started: So, You Need to Staff Your
Small Business* *5*

Chapter 1: Looking at the Big Picture — Before You Employ 7

Understanding Your Reasons to Employ Staff 8
  Analysing what you really need 8
  Putting workflow design to work 9
Your Recruitment Strategy: The Key to Successful Employment 10
  Describing your ideal employee 11
  Investment in staff can be profitable 12
Checking Before You Buy Saves Heartburn Later 12
Getting the Paperwork Right 13
  The importance of an employment contract 14
  Without rules, there's chaos 14
Managing the Employment Relationship through the Highs
  and Lows 14
Pay, Pay and Pay Again: Remunerating Staff 16
Making Sure Everyone Behaves Themselves 17
  Anti-discrimination in the workplace 17
  Bullying makes for an unhappy workplace 18
  Health, safety and workers compensation 19
Ending the Employment Relationship 19

**Chapter 2: Building a Recruitment Strategy for Finding the
Right Person** 21

Calculating the Investment in Your Staff 22
  Comparing costs with revenue 22
  Increasing revenue through adding staff 24
  Employing more doesn't necessarily mean more profit 24

Designing a Job that Suits Your Business 25
    Analysing the job 26
    Considering the form of employment 28
    Deciding when you want staff to work and for how long 33
Describing the Job: Creating a Position Description 36
    Setting out useful headings and information 36
    Outlining your key selection criteria 40

Chapter 3: Sorting the Good from the Not So Good **41**

Being Prepared with Key Selection Criteria 42
    Selection criteria versus the job description 42
    Using a scorecard 44
Finding and Selecting Applications 46
    Opening up the field of candidates 47
    Creating a short list of suitable candidates 48
    Providing feedback 50
Interviewing Techniques 101 50
    The engaging interviewer 50
    A bit like speed dating: Asking the right questions 51
    Really useful assessment tools 52
    Don't go there! Topics to avoid 54
A Fit and Proper Person 56
    Health issues 56
    Criminal record checks 57

**Part II: Getting the Ground Rules and Paperwork
for Hiring Right 59**

Chapter 4: The National Employment Standards **61**

Understanding the Basics of National Minimum Standards 62
    Maximum hours of work 62
    Request for flexible work arrangements 64
    Parental leave 66
    Annual leave 68
    Personal/carer's and compassionate leave 70
    Community service leave 72
    Long service leave 74
    Public holidays 76
    Notice of termination of employment and redundancy 79
Recognising the Special Case of Western Australia 83
    Working out constitutional corporations 83
    Understanding the Western Australian features 84

Chapter 5: Modern Awards and Pay 87
  Modern Awards and You..88
    Finding out which award applies to your business.................88
    Getting to know your award 89
  Minimum Wages, Allowances, Penalties and Loadings............................99
    Modern award minimum wages 99
    National minimum wage...100
    Employees with disabilities...101
    Allowances...101
    Shift loading, penalty rates, casual loadings and overtime..........103
  Juniors, Apprentices and Trainees..105
    Juniors..106
    Apprentices and trainees..106
  Transitional Provisions for Wages, Penalties and Loadings 109

Chapter 6: Calculating the Real Cost of Employment 111
  So Much Leave, They May Never Be At Work............................112
    Parental leave..112
    Annual leave 113
    Personal/carer's and compassionate leave...................................114
    Community service leave 116
    Long service leave 117
  Workers Compensation Insurance and Payroll Tax 122
    Workers compensation 122
    Payroll tax..123
  Paying Fringe Benefits Tax..125
    Defining fringe benefits 125
    Car fringe benefits..126
    Recording and reporting obligations 127
    Calculating FBT 127
    Reducing your FBT liability 128
  Don't Forget Superannuation! 129
    How much and how often? 129
    Super choice: It's an employee's right 132
    Using a default fund..134
  Making Use of the Real Cost Ready Reckoner 134

Chapter 7: Hiring: The Importance of the Employment Contract 137
  Working with an Employment Contract.....................................138
    Express and implied terms of employment.............................139
    Impact of statutory laws 141
  Creating Your Own Employment Contracts 142
    Setting out the terms and conditions....................................142
    Creating templates..143

Filling out the template to create a new contract..........................143
Staying on top of important attachments.............................147
Knowing who should sign the employment contract 148
Confidentiality..148
Attending to Privacy 150
Using a Checklist to Stay Organised..151

Part III: Putting the Employment Relationship to Work 153

Chapter 8: Making a Good Impression: Orientation Programs 155

Setting the Tone for the Future with Orientation 156
Preparing and providing a welcome pack 156
Reading, acknowledging and signing..................................157
Talking about and facilitating performance 158
Following an orientation checklist 159
Evaluating orientation: Don't be scared of constructive
    criticism!...161
The Staff Handbook: Setting the Rules of Engagement.................163
Values, philosophy, goals...163
Behaviour standards 163
Dress codes 165
General housekeeping...165
Employment Policies..166
Acceptable use of internet and social media policies.................167
Protecting intellectual property rights 168

Chapter 9: Performance Expectations: The Wage–Work Bargain ..171

Defining, Facilitating and Encouraging Performance...........................172
Defining performance standards 173
Removing the barriers to performance 174
Encouraging performance 175
The Art of Measuring the Right Stuff 176
Providing Feedback..178
Handling appraisal interviews 179
Learning from the experience 180
Reviewing the First Six Months...180
Applying a formal qualifying period....................................180
If any of you has reasons why . . . speak now or forever hold
    your peace..181
Addressing Poor Performance...182
Warnings, warnings and more warnings!............................182
Running through a simple checklist and procedure 182

Chapter 10: Pay Increase? You Must Be Joking! 185
  Adjusting Base Rates of Pay 186
    Recognising skills and experience......................................186
    Paying above minimum wages 187
  Rewarding Good Performance 188
    A job well done is its own reward . . . sometimes................189
    Providing fringe benefits and other rewards.....................189
    Paying bonuses and incentives...191
  Keeping Pace with Market Rates 194
    Getting the base wage right...194
    Competing in the market for wages 194
    Negotiating with unhappy staff...196

Part IV: The Non-Discriminating Employer . . . . _199_

Chapter 11: Managing Workplace Conflict 201
  Understanding the Causes of Conflict at Work.........................202
    Sources of conflict 202
    Don't ignore the signs of conflict (they won't go away) 205
  The Heavy Hand of the Law 205
  Resolving Conflict: Simple Methods that Just Might Work 207
    Examining the issues 207
    Understanding the legal constraints 208
    Pre-conditions for resolution 208
  Selecting the Right Method 210
    Working through conflicts with your employees...............210
    Considering alternative approaches 211
    Offering facilitation..213
    'A fair go all round' 214
  Third-Party Interventions and the Role of Government Tribunals.....215
    Mediation 215
    Conciliation and arbitration 216

**Chapter 12: A Journey through Australian Workplace
Rights and EEO** 219
  Understanding Unlawful Discrimination 220
    Direct discrimination of staff...221
    Indirect discrimination of staff..222
    Discrimination against prospective staff...........................223
  Adverse Action and Workplace Rights 224
    Understanding adverse action 225
    Understanding workplace rights 226
    Navigating the minefield of workplace rights...................227

Get Proactive: Develop a Strategy 229
    Making reasonable adjustments for disability 229
    Educating staff 230
Disclosing Personal Information Isn't Against the Law 231
Focusing on Suitability Not Disability 233
    Genuine occupational qualification 233
    Performing the inherent requirements of the job 233

Chapter 13: Harassment and Bullying — Gee, Can't You Take a Joke? 237

It's Not Always What You Say, But How You Say It 238
    Defining harassment 238
    Defining bullying 239
    Reasonable versus unreasonable management practice 240
Underlying Causes of Bullying and Harassment 241
    Identifying the risk factors 241
    Reducing the risks 242
Preventing Harassment and Bullying 243
    Educating your staff 244
    Using the policy as an education tool 244

Part V: A Healthy Workplace Is a Happy Workplace 247

Chapter 14: Safety at Work Is Everyone's Responsibility 249

Fulfilling Your Duty of Care 250
    Victoria and Western Australia 250
    Other states and territories 251
    Acting on health and safety 251
Health and Safety Duties of Staff and Others 253
    Staff duty of care 254
    Duties of other persons in the workplace 254
Prevention Is Better than the Cure 254
Risk Management Is the Key to a Healthy Workplace 256
    Identifying risk 256
    Evaluating risk 257
    Treating risk 259
    Monitoring and reviewing 260
Consulting with Employees and Others 261
    Consulting with staff at the right time 262
    Duty holders consulting with each other 262
Applying Standards, Codes and Regulations 263

Chapter 15: Workers Compensation and Rehabilitation 265

    Knowing Your Responsibilities 266

        Defining workers 267

        Understanding deemed workers...268

        Defining workplace injuries 270

        Injuries must occur in the workplace..271

        Excluding reckless and wilful behaviour 272

        Mental stress, anxiety and other psychological injuries 272

    Planning the Return to Work...273

        Rehabilitation starts right away..273

        Implementing a return to work policy..274

        Designing an individualised return to work plan 274

    Dealing with Doctors (and Not Getting a Headache).............................275

        Communicating well with doctors..276

        Confirming incapacity and suitable duties 277

    Disputing Claims of Workplace Injury...277

    Managing Permanently Incapacitated Staff..278

Part VI: The End of the Employment Relationship **283**

Chapter 16: Resignation of Employment. 285

    Understanding Notice of Resignation Requirements 286

        Providing notice under a modern award 286

        Including resignation notice in employment contracts 287

        When notice isn't needed from employees 288

    Working or Not Working the Notice Period..288

        Ending employment by agreement..289

        Payment in lieu of notice 289

    Termination Payments 290

        Annual and long service leave 290

        Tax and superannuation 291

        Withholding monies owed 294

    Exit Interviews: Finding Out the Reasons for Leaving 295

        Listening and learning..295

        Preparing exit questions 296

        Conducting the exit interview 297

Chapter 17: Employee Dismissal: A Matter of Fairness 299

    Working Out Who's Protected from Unfair Dismissal............................300

        Employees who are protected 300

        Employees who aren't protected..301

    Defining Unfair Dismissal..301

        Dismissal comes first..302

        Harsh, unjust or unreasonable dismissal 303

        Genuine redundancy 305

Getting to Know the Small Business Fair Dismissal Code 305
Understanding the code..306
Serious misconduct 307
Resolving Unfair Dismissal Disputes...309
Settling during conciliation 310
Putting your fate in someone else's hands with arbitration 313
Western Australia Is a Different System...315
Fair and reasonable dismissal..316
Remedies for Western Australians 316
Unlawful Dismissal Is Something Altogether Different 317
Workplace rights 317
When unlawful discrimination doesn't apply 317
Unlawful termination of employment...318

Chapter 18: Termination, Change and Redundancy 319
Introducing Change into Your Business 320
Working Out Genuine Redundancy 321
It's the job that is redundant not the person! 321
Consultation 322
Redundancy Pay Exemptions for Small Business...............................324
Redundancy pay 325
Redundancy pay and employment contracts 326
The Selection Dilemma 326
Looking at past performance 327
Spill and fill 327
Voluntary redundancy...327
Watch out for hazards 328
Working through a Checklist of Action 329
Contemplating Business to Business Transfers 330
Defining a transfer of business...330
Enterprise agreements transfer with staff.................................332
Recognising prior service of transferring employee....................334
Transferring employees and qualifying periods 335

Part VII: The Part of Tens 337

**Chapter 19: Ten Ways to Build a Successful Employment
Relationship 339**
Do Your Homework before Employing..339
Welcome People into Your Business 340
Explain Your Expectations..340
Be Consistent 341
Give Your Employees a Fair Go..342
Celebrate Success..343

Be Decisive 344
Get to Know the Person Not Just the Employee.....................344
Model Good Behaviour 345
Always Encourage and Reward Good Performance................347

Chapter 20: Ten Things You Should Never Do At Work...........349

Bring Family Problems to Work...349
Blame Others for Your Mistakes..350
Play Favourites 350
Sleep with Staff (Not a Good Look) 351
Pay Yourself before Others...351
Act Inconsistently 351
Avoid Saying Good Morning 352
Jump to Conclusions (and Over the Cliff).............................352
Put Off Important Decisions to another Day..........................353
Forget Honesty Is Truly the Best Policy 353

Index 355

Introduction

· ·

*I*n Australia, in excess of two million small businesses employ around 4.8 million people and contribute 20 per cent of the gross domestic product (GDP). Small-business owners take pride in the fact that their businesses contribute to the livelihood of Australian people and their families.

Unique to small business is the personal relationships that can develop between owner and the people they work alongside with to build the business. With that relationship comes great responsibility. My aim in writing this book is to share my knowledge and experience with small-business owners coming to grips with the difficult tasks of managing people — that is, *human resource management*, otherwise known as *HR*.

HR has often been seen as a 'tick the boxes' kind of activity. My view is that it's really about building a healthy and productive working environment in which everyone prospers. The strategies that I cover in the book can enable you to encourage your staff to create that prosperous future with you and for your small business. Along that path, as with any relationship, challenges and personal difficulties will need to be overcome. I provide you with the knowledge and the tools to apply effective solutions.

About This Book

This book doesn't offer a psychological analysis of the characteristics of a successful employment relationship. Instead, *HR for Small Business For Dummies* offers you, the small-business owner and employer, a simple and honest explanation of the rules and regulations that attach themselves to each and every phase of the employment relationship.

Thinking about the employment relationship as you would any other relationship in your life can open your mind to the possibilities and free you from the dread of learning boring and complex legal jargon and suffocating regulations. Most individuals understand that taking a risk on personal relationships and falling short is better than not trying at all. Small-business owners understand this principle better than most people.

Entering into an employment relationship is a risk but it offers the potential for wonderful results. Learning, understanding and meeting the challenges proffered by the rules that regulate every phase of the life of employment relationships will ultimately enable you to succeed. That is the aim of this book.

Throughout the chapters, I provide an overview of the Australian laws regulating how people must be employed, rewarded, nurtured and sometimes removed from small businesses. I explain the key elements of this regulatory framework at each and every phase of the employment relationship, and provide case studies, checklists and plenty of tips on how best to meet the challenges of satisfying the regulators, the employee and, importantly, you.

Foolish Assumptions

I know that small businesses operate in all sorts of industries and cover many occupations, trades and professions. I can't address every trait, nuance or idiosyncrasy peculiar to every Australian small business. However, I have assumed for purposes of brevity, certainty and simplicity that small business share particular characteristics and, therefore, tailored the topics and advice to suit those shared characteristics. For example, the employment relationships are personal, the future sometimes uncertain, cash flow critical, and government regulation a burden — but our ambitions are always exciting and success is always within our grasp.

This book isn't a substitute for specific legal advice that may be useful or necessary in particular circumstances. Therefore, I've also assumed that everyone who reads this book is smart enough to understand that they can only rely on its wisdom to guide rather than advise.

Icons Used in This Book

Throughout this book, you can find friendly and useful icons that help you note specific types of information. Here's what each icon means.

This icon highlights free resources, templates and sample work procedures and policies you can find online for free download at www.dummies.com/go/hrsmallbusinessau.

This icon flags concepts and facts that you should keep in mind as you hire, work with and (perhaps) dismiss staff.

Included with this icon are more complex examples and interesting technical stuff that you may want to read to become even more familiar with the topic.

This icon points out something that can save you time, headaches, money or all of the above!

Here I'm directing you away from blunders and errors that could land you in trouble with employee or government bodies, or both.

Beyond the Book

In addition to the material in the print or ebook you're reading right now, *HR for Small Business For Dummies* also comes with some access-anywhere resources on the internet. Check out the free Cheat Sheet at www.dummies.com/cheatsheet/hrsmallbusinessau for some quick, helpful tips. For free extra companion material, such as articles, visit www.dummies.com/extras/hrsmallbusinessau. Also check out www.dummies.com/go/hrsmallbusinessau for free online resources and templates.

Where to Go from Here

You don't have to read *HR for Small Business For Dummies* from cover to cover before you start organising your human resource management systems, policies and procedures. This book (like all *For Dummies* books) is written in modular fashion, with each chapter pretty much standing on its own.

Feel free to look over the table of contents so you can skip around to the topics that interest you most. I often direct you to other sections of the book that expand on a given subject or that give you more tips or information about the topic at hand.

For starters, I suggest that you read through Chapter 1 to get a quick overview of the major topics contained in this book — it's short, but it gives you an outline of everything so you can figure out what you want to read about next.

Part I of the book gives you every hint and suggestion on how to approach the question of whether to employ staff and, if so, how to go about it. Focus on this part first if you need some help with the reasons you may wish to employ as well as the rules that impinge on your 'right' to employ.

Need some help with the elements of the employment contract, the decisions on forms of employment, the national minimum standards of employment, the hidden costs of employing a person and how to invest early in the person you employ to provide the best chance of success? Head straight to Part II.

Don't know what comes next after employing a person? Flick to Part III, where I explain the importance of setting, measuring and rewarding the right performance standards; how you should apply well-structured probationary employment to see if the relationship is going to last; and set in place procedures to ride the inevitable highs and lows that occur in employment relationships including those between employees. I also show how to work out how much to pay staff and how best to reward them so that you get a really good return for your small business.

Head to Part IV for information on the complex world of anti-discrimination laws and bullying complaints, how they can impact on your business and how best to address the challenges wrought by the operation of the law. If you need help with health and safety, and return to work plans, I provide everything you need to know in Part V. And Part VI is where you should head if you need information on ending the employment relationship.

Whatever you choose to read first, enjoy it — and, more importantly, implement it!

Part I

Getting Started: So, You Need to Staff Your Small Business

getting started

with

HR

in small business

In this part . . .

✔ You have to start somewhere and there is no better place than looking at the big picture. Learn how to analyse whether you need to employ staff, the value they're likely to add and the array of regulations affecting the relationship with staff.

✔ Building your recruitment strategy requires homework and organisation. Discover how to design the job, calculate the cost of employment and describe the new role in a position description to attract the right candidates.

✔ Find out how to sort the good from the bad with job applicants, and use an objective eye to apply reliable selection criteria to suit the job you want filled.

Chapter 1

Looking at the Big Picture — Before You Employ

In This Chapter

▶ Working out what staff you really need

▶ Finetuning your recruitment strategy and process

▶ Understanding the importance of an employment contract and other rules

▶ Getting the best from staff

▶ Remunerating staff appropriately

▶ Avoiding discrimination, bullying and workers compensation in your business

▶ Ending the employment relationship properly

This business would be perfect if I didn't have to manage staff.

Anonymous small-business owner

Deciding to introduce an employee into the business is a really important move for small-business owners. The commitment is similar to the other financial investments made toward the success of your business but with one important difference: You're employing a person, not buying a piece of equipment.

I often use the analogy of a personal relationship to explain to small-business owners the nature of the relationship that you enter into when you employ staff. You start with the search for the ideal person, and then experience the initial joy at having found someone who seems to satisfy all of your desires. Next, you get to know each other and (hopefully) develop a rapport and solid foundation to your relationship. Then you settle into the long (sometimes short) journey towards what, in a working relationship, is the inevitable end of that relationship. During this employment relationship, you'll experience highs and lows, learning experiences, personal growth, exciting events, great achievements and regrettable mistakes. The lifecycle of employment has myriad rules and regulations that must be followed and every phase of the employment relationship creates unique challenges. Hopefully when you look back over the life of the employment relationships that you have with staff, you'll have only (or at least mostly) good memories.

In this chapter, I briefly take you through the employment relationship, from the initial search to the (hopefully) amicable end.

Understanding Your Reasons to Employ Staff

Some employers incorrectly assume that because a job has been performed in a particular manner in the past, that is the way it should be performed in the future. Nothing could be further from the truth. When a vacancy arises in your business or when you experience a moment of inspiration linking more staff to more business and profit, take the opportunity to test your thinking before you go ahead and employ someone.

Analysing what you really need

Deciding to employ staff for a job should arise naturally from a rational analysis of the operational needs of the business. If the analysis shows you don't need to employ, don't do it. However, if the analysis suggests that employing someone would be a good idea, go ahead with a clear understanding of the reason you have for doing so.

Job analysis is a basic tool to determine what type of job is needed for your small business. This means applying a simple procedure known as *workflow design* combined with an understanding of the chain of command (*organisational relationships*) to identify how tasks and decisions should be grouped to create a job. These concepts are covered in greater detail in Chapter 2.

Perhaps you're wondering what phrases like 'job analysis' and 'workflow design' have to do with you. *'I'm just a simple small-business owner who can't be bothered with this techno babble!'* I hear you scream. While these terms may seem rather remote and daunting, analysing the flow of work within the context of a thorough understanding of who does what and when, and who decides what should be done and when, enables you to understand the reasons to employ people and the responsibilities that they must perform when employed to provide the best return on your investment.

Putting workflow design to work

In Chapter 2, I show how to conduct a simple job analysis using workflow design. Here, Figure 1-1 shows how the process works just to whet your appetite. The skills, knowledge, personal attributes and abilities of the people that you employ are applied in an organised operational system combining raw materials and business infrastructure to produce goods and services. The areas that you concentrate on for the job analysis are shown in the shaded boxes in Figure 1-1.

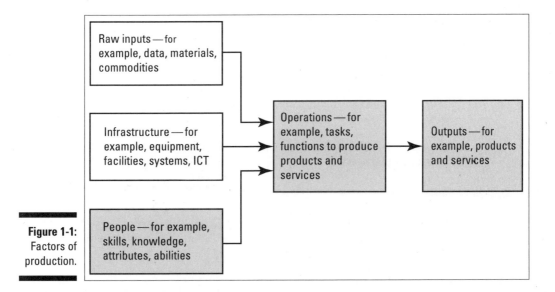

Figure 1-1: Factors of production.

Figure 1-2 shows how you can outline your business organisation structure. Doing so allows you to visualise:

- Accountability of people in the business to each other
- The efficient allocation of tasks and responsibilities
- The lines of communication necessary to keep the business coordinated and production moving
- Who has authority in making the key decisions

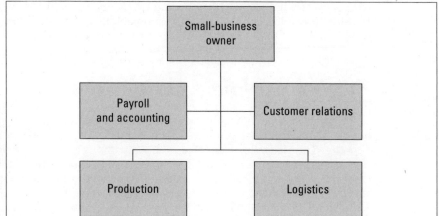

Figure 1-2:
Example
organisa-
tional
structure.

Of course, the information highlighted in the preceding list isn't all written down on your organisational chart. But to these building blocks you can add your analysis when deciding to recruit new staff and designing the job to best suit your business. Very large businesses tend to apply very complex methods to this task. Your small business has the advantage of being able to perform this task simply and more swiftly, thus enabling you to move quickly to adopt a competitive advantage.

See Chapter 2 for more on job analysis and designing a job that best suits your business needs.

Your Recruitment Strategy: The Key to Successful Employment

You must complete three fundamental tasks to help you select the best person for the job. The first task is *describing* the nature of the job including its purpose, range of tasks, and organisational context in which the person will work.

The second task is creating *selection criteria* that explain the skills, attributes, knowledge, experience and ability required to successfully perform the job. This criterion provides a template against which every candidate may be assessed.

The third task is to objectively rate the candidates to decide which one is most suitable for the job — that is, use a *scorecard*. These three tasks must be completed before you interview prospective employees.

Describing your ideal employee

You want to attract the best person to perform the job, so you need to describe the job and promote it in a way that attracts the right type of person. In Chapter 2, I explain how to build a job description, dividing it into sections that reflect the important elements of the job such as:

✔ Accountability

✔ Authority

✔ Business context

✔ Conditions

✔ Job title

✔ Purpose

✔ Responsibilities

Describing the elements of the job using these headings (drawn from the work that you do analysing the workflow and organisational relationships — refer to preceding section and see Chapter 2) makes the task much easier for you and ensures consistency in the way that you engage employees in your business.

Separate the selection criteria from the job description because each has a different purpose. This may sound unusual but think about the two in this way. The job description states what the person must *do*. The selection criteria states what the person must *be*.

When outlining your selection criteria, you should decide on your *mandatory* selection criteria and *desirable* selection criteria. Your mandatory criteria may include a relevant tertiary qualification, trade or certificate or driver's licence. You then need to clearly state these mandatory requirements in the selection criteria. Sifting through applicants who can't satisfy a fundamental criterion is pointless. The desirable criteria should include a mix of personal attributes (such as leadership, team player, good communicator, honesty and diligence), experience and competency (that is, how proficient the person is in performing the required skills, such as machinery operations, plumbing or haircuts).

The selection criteria should be drawn from the job analysis conducted before you decided to create and advertise the job. See Chapter 3 for a more thorough commentary on how you complete this task.

Investment in staff can be profitable

The employment relationship is fundamentally an economic relationship. But don't be fooled into thinking you can treat it purely as such. Employing someone is both an investment in the financial success of your business and an investment in the growth and well being of another person.

The reason I like to view the employment relationship as at least in part an economic investment is because this invokes the useful (and, as experience has shown, accurate) analogy of how most people like to invest their money. Chances are, you only invest your money after rigorous research and then subsequently monitor and nurture the investment to ensure the best possible yield.

The actual calculation of working out whether a new employee is worth the investment depends on the nature of the job and the person you employ. For example, a person employed to build furniture in a small factory could be expected to contribute a sufficient increase in the production of furniture supplied to the market to cover the costs of employment, inputs and a margin for profit based on the expected price that such a good would be expected to be purchased.

The return from a professional employee such as an optometrist, medical practitioner or physiotherapist will be measured in the volume of patients seen and the revenue generated from treatment. Lawyers fit a similar model to that of the health professionals insofar as the volume of clients is a convenient measurement of productivity and expected return on investment in people. The faster the product and service is supplied to the market, the greater propensity to generate the revenue that provides the return on the investment in employment. I provide information in Chapter 2 about how to decide whether the investment is worth the money.

Checking Before You Buy Saves Heartburn Later

The actual selection procedure isn't rocket science (despite what recruitment agencies may tell you). However, the process isn't entirely a lucky dip either.

When looking for potential employees, do your homework and, if necessary, get assistance from people you trust before you employ. Organisation is everything when you've decided to recruit a person to your small business. You should search intelligently for the candidates who will suit your business.

Three areas are worth exploring when looking for new staff:

- ✔ Advertised applicants
- ✔ Family and social networks
- ✔ Unsolicited interest

Although problems are inherent when employing people close to you such as family and friends you at least know what you're 'buying' when employing them. Some people may approach you for work — this shows initiative, which is a good thing. Even though you may not have work readily available keep a record of their details. When a job does emerge you can consider their suitability along with other candidates. Advertised applicants include the obvious list of people who respond to your advertisement of the job. In Chapter 3, I provide tips on how to manage the advertising, short-listing and selection procedures.

You need to be aware of several traps in employment. For example, pre-existing illness or injury, unlawful discrimination, criminal records and privacy all bear upon the recruitment and appointment of employees. Although these issues are complex in nature, you can take some simple measures to avoid the traps, including knowing how and when to ask questions. How and when to record information provided by potential employees, and what you can practically do to accommodate the individual circumstances of people who express an interest in working in your business are covered in Chapter 3.

Getting the Paperwork Right

I can't emphasise this point enough. If you fail to establish the necessary employment policies, procedures, contracts, payroll and employment records, and to provide required information to new staff such as superannuation choice forms, the fair work information statement and staff handbooks, you risk heavy fines and expose your business to claims of underpayment and other breaches of the law. In Chapters 4 to 7, I provide you with every bit of information that you need to document the employment relationship so that you are well organised, and compliant with the statutory and other regulatory requirements laid down by the law.

The importance of an employment contract

The employment contract is the fundamental record of employment from which everything else flows. You need to be able to draft an effective employment contract, and understand the National Employment Standards (NES) that underpin all employment conditions and the relationship to modern awards and superannuation. I cover the NES in Chapter 4 and employment contracts in Chapter 7.

You can't separate the cost of employing staff from the agreement that you make with an employee to work for you. Calculating the real cost of employing staff, including the hidden costs, is important — see Chapter 6 for more on this. Equally important is investing early in the person that you employ to provide the best chance of success — see Chapter 8 for more on how to structure a really effective orientation program for new staff.

Without rules, there's chaos

The National Employment Standards, modern awards, minimum wages, workplace health and safety, workplace rights and discrimination... so many rules. Where to start? You must comply with the rules of the game — otherwise, you risk incurring substantial penalties and potentially losing your business. These minimum standards of employment are the non-negotiable underpinnings of every employment relationship that you commence. Ignore them at your peril.

I explain these minimum standards of employment in Chapters 4 and 5, and in Chapter 7 provide a plan of action of where and how they should be applied in employment contracts and employment policies.

Managing the Employment Relationship through the Highs and Lows

Once you've employed someone, the fun really begins... or should I say misery begins? The answer depends on how well you manage the initial orientation and performance expectations for new employees.

Start with a thorough orientation program. The three key benefits you can expect from your employees after a successful orientation are

✔ Commitment to the business

✔ Greater productivity over shorter time frame

✔ Less reliance on supervision

Three drawbacks from ineffective orientation programs are

✔ High turnover of staff

✔ Low return on investment

✔ Supervision time greater than it should be

In Chapter 8 I cover how you can implement a structured orientation program over six weeks that will gradually enable your new employees to reach the standards of work performance that you want them to achieve. Of course, training and encouragement doesn't stop there — you want your employees to continue to work to a high standard. The best way to see this occur is to define, facilitate, encourage, measure, review and learn from past individual work performance. This cycle is summarised in Figure 1-3.

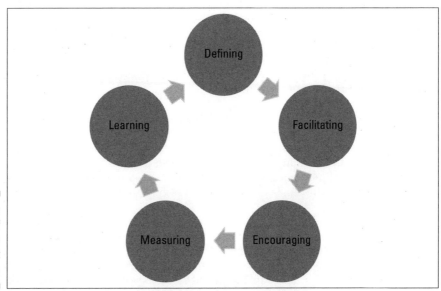

Figure 1-3:
Staff
performance
management
cycle.

You must be disciplined and persistent in your approach, and track your outcomes. This approach requires some record keeping; however, the extra time spent on this is worthwhile for two fundamental reasons:

- ✔ Employees want to do well and be rewarded for a job well done. A structured system that defines, facilitates, encourages, measures and rewards performance aligned to your business goals gives you a better chance of achieving your business goals.

- ✔ When you apply this system and record employee performance results, you can hold them accountable for their work performance. This provides a platform for even better performance and, in the event that the employment relationship ends badly, you can defend your business against accusations of unfair dismissal.

I explain how to design and implement this system in Chapter 9.

Pay, Pay and Pay Again: Remunerating Staff

As I mention earlier in this chapter, the employment relationship is fundamentally an economic relationship (refer to the section 'Investment in staff can be profitable' for more). Therefore, you must get the remuneration right for staff and right for you. Paying wages, allowances, bonuses, superannuation and fringe benefits may all form part of the remuneration mix you provide to employees in consideration for the work that they perform for your business.

Australia is awash with laws regulating the way you pay employees and you must be on top of all of them, and keep up to date. You need to be aware of your obligations to pay ever-changing minimum rates of pay, allowances, penalties, loadings and everything else provided in modern awards and national minimum wage orders. I cover staying on top of changes in Chapter 10.

Another aspect to be aware of is getting the best value from the 'wage–work bargain' made between you and your employees. For example, you may pay employees more than the minimum rates prescribed by the law. These higher wages or salaries can be linked to achievement of performance standards or additional hours of work, as well as that extra effort that you need from staff to keep a competitive edge over larger businesses.

I provide tips in this area in Chapter 10, going through the various forms of remuneration and what to do with them, including

✔ Deciding on the right level of remuneration compared to your competitors

✔ Implementing tax-effective salary sacrifice arrangements

✔ Negotiating with unhappy staff

✔ Paying bonuses and incentives

✔ Offering fringe benefits and non-monetary rewards

Making Sure Everyone Behaves Themselves

Before you put a group of people in the same place and force them to work together for up to 8 hours a day, 5 days a week, 52 weeks each year, you first need to set some ground rules. These ground rules should cover everything from dress codes, use of the internet, intellectual property, confidentiality and honesty, to respecting each of your fellow employees. Some of the areas that are most likely to get you in trouble if you don't manage them correctly are anti-discrimination, workplace bullying, and health and safety.

Employment policies and procedures are really effective tools that you should use to inform and educate your staff and guide you when you need to intervene when things go wrong. In Chapter 11, I explain how you can resolve conflicts that arise in your business between employees and with yourself, using a simple step-by-step approach.

Anti-discrimination in the workplace

You perceive and act on *differences* around you every day to chart the course of your life. This is a simple fact of life — without the ability to distinguish the differences between competing choices available to you, you wouldn't survive more than one day of adulthood, let alone operate a successful small business. Sometimes the choices people make are good ones and sometimes they unfairly affect others. However, not all unfair choices are unlawful — but some are.

Discrimination in employment is *unlawful* where an employee is disadvantaged or treated less favourably by an employer in some aspect of their employment because of a particular personal characteristic or attribute. In Chapter 12, I explain the numerous grounds upon which an employee can claim to have been unlawfully discriminated against at work. Importantly, I describe how you can stay out of trouble by implementing good education programs at work and modelling good behaviour.

Bullying makes for an unhappy workplace

Most people used to think of bullying as something that kids did to other kids at school. In recent years, people are recognising that such behaviour also occurs in Australian workplaces, and laws are now in place prohibiting workplace bullying and harassment. People now know about the personal impact on people subjected to bullying, and the size of the financial penalties imposed on employers who don't prevent it occurring in their businesses.

The term *bullying* is used to describe behaviour that may intimidate, humiliate or otherwise injure a person physically or mentally. The *Fair Work Act 2009* states that an employee will have been bullied at work if you, an employee or group of employees at work:

> *. . .repeatedly behaves unreasonably towards the employee, and that behaviour creates a risk to the health and safety of that person.*

On the other hand, the Act states that:

> *Bullying does not include reasonable management practices including performance management conducted in a reasonable manner.*

So the work that you need to do to properly address your obligation to ensure bullying doesn't occur comes down to what's considered 'reasonable' in the circumstances. This can be a tricky concept to get right, particularly in such an emotionally charged issue. In Chapter 13, I explain what's reasonable and not reasonable, identify the factors that are most likely to indicate a high risk of bullying behaviour, and some tips on how to prevent and resolve bullying complaints. I even provide you with a model employment policy to use in your own small business.

Health, safety and workers compensation

You can't ignore the often onerous obligations to ensure the health, safety and welfare of employees and others who are affected by your small business. What you can do is establish policies and procedures to minimise risk to health and safety commensurate with the nature of the work performed in your small business. Prevention through education is a primary method of addressing the general duty of care, but risk management is the key to ensuring people are safe at work. In Chapter 14, I explain the regulations operating across Australian states and territories, your duty of care and the various obligations that flow from this general duty.

Risk management underpins each and every state and territory workplace health and safety regulatory system. Risk management is a systematic examination of any activity, premises or operational system to

- ✔ Identify risks
- ✔ Evaluate the likelihood and potential consequences of the risks
- ✔ Act to eliminate or control the risk
- ✔ Review and monitor health and safety outcomes

In Chapter 14, I provide a step-by-step procedure to help you implement your own risk analysis and management system to address workplace health and safety.

In Chapter 15, I concentrate on what happens when an individual employee suffers a work-related injury or illness, and discuss your obligations and options on returning them to work. I know that dealing with treating doctors can be a difficult procedure and so I provide you with tips on what to ask and how to ask it. I also guide you through some of the traps — an injured employee may not always be capable of returning to their pre-injury duties. I cover your options in what is undoubtedly one of the more difficult aspects of managing the relationship.

Ending the Employment Relationship

All Things Must Pass was ex-Beatle George Harrison's triple album, released shortly after the band had split in the early 1970s. The album's title says it all. All things — good and bad — must eventually pass. And so it is for employment relationships. Sometimes, the passing is amicable and sometimes it's beyond your control. Other times, the employment relationship ends in acrimony. In any of these circumstances, you have obligations and entitlements that you must observe, particularly in three main areas:

- ✔ Dismissal
- ✔ Redundancy
- ✔ Resignation

Each area has certain obligations relating to how much notice must be provided, paying out accrued leave, superannuation, taxing any payments, and withholding payments. I cover these obligations in Chapters 16 to 18.

When you dismiss an employee for unsatisfactory work performance or misconduct, this single act can trigger a massive system of rights, obligations and institutional interventions into your small business, unless you're able to manage it correctly. I explain the rules governing dismissal in Chapter 17, and provide a checklist of action to ensure that you comply with the rules.

Nothing stands still and so change is inevitable with your small business. Introducing changes can affect your staff's jobs. In Chapter 18, I cover these affects and provide you with a roadmap for how to navigate your way through the hazards along the path of changing to a better business while looking after your staff — whether they're staying on or passing through to another working relationship.

Chapter 2

Building a Recruitment Strategy for Finding the Right Person

In This Chapter

▶ Working out whether a new employee is worth the investment

▶ Considering job analysis and the form of employment when designing a job

▶ Outlining your position description and key selection criteria

A horse! a horse! My kingdom for a horse!

William Shakespeare, *Richard III*

Shakespeare's King Richard III must have been pretty desperate to offer his entire kingdom for a horse when he finally met his fate in the Battle of Bosworth Field in 1485. Of course, it was pretty clear by that stage of the play that his business (England), was on the verge of a hostile takeover! (Richard III was the last king of the House of York and his defeat ended the War of the Roses and began the Tudor Dynasty, with the ascension of Henry Tudor to be Henry VII.)

Small-business owners are resourceful, adventurous and up for a challenge. But please don't go all Richard III and start offering big dollars to find someone to work like a horse in your business. In this chapter I guide you through the steps to developing your own recruitment strategy, including the initial planning, and job analysis and design.

As a part of your business strategy, your recruitment strategy should be founded on sensible business planning — your decision to employ staff should be an investment in your business. In this chapter, I provide an analytical approach you can use to justify the investment to yourself before you proceed, including some simple measures to help you calculate the return that you can expect from your investment.

I then provide simple steps to help you analyse what sort of employment position you need, and cover designing a job that has a clear purpose but that also incorporates some flexibility. The proposed position must be flexible enough to allow your employee to work successfully both today and the next 500 days. Finally, I explain how to use all your analysis to write a position description that's really useful to your business.

Calculating the Investment in Your Staff

Congratulations if you already understand the concepts of marginal revenue and marginal cost — you're probably an economist and not a small-business owner. Please stop reading this book immediately and go back to your university! Thank you.

Are you still with me? Good, please keep reading.

Comparing costs with revenue

Many different ways of estimating the financial return to expect from an employee exist, but I'm going to give you the easiest: Comparing costs with revenue.

When looking at costs versus revenue, the following terms are important to understand:

- **Marginal cost** means the cost of producing one additional unit of whatever it is you sell. A *unit of production* can be a good or service. For example, a unit could be an hour of work or a consultation with a client or patient, a haircut, or a meal served to a customer. It could also be a cake produced by a bakery.

- **Marginal revenue** means the revenue that you receive for producing one additional unit of whatever it is that you sell. Once again, the concept can readily be applied to services as well as goods.

Your objective when investing in staff is to increase the return to the business in the form of profits. Employing additional staff means you can provide additional products and services. If the marginal revenue received from the additional products and services is greater than the marginal cost of producing these products and services, the investment is a profitable one. You're making more money. If not, the new employee is costing you money.

When looking at the bigger picture and considering costs, you need to calculate all of your costs — both fixed and variable costs, as follows:

✔ **Fixed costs** are the costs of running a business that remain the same even if you don't produce one item for sale. These costs may include plant, equipment, property, rent, insurance and marketing costs.

✔ **Variable costs** are the additional costs that you incur in order to produce each unit of whatever it is that you produce. These costs include the wages that you pay employees in the business, service charges on utilities where usage depends on production levels (including lighting, water, heating and telephone calls), and raw materials.

So to calculate your total costs, you can use the following formula:

Total Cost (TC) = Fixed costs (FC) + (Variable costs (VC) × Quantity (Q))

For example, a physiotherapist may spend a total of $20,000 per year on the property lease, equipment, communications, utilities installation, layout of premises, marketing, insurance and professional license fees before she consults her first client. She may also want to extract a set profit from the business — say, $60,000 per year. These are her fixed costs. You can divide this amount ($80,000) by the amount of working days that the business is open (approximately 260 per year) to get the fixed cost per day — approximately $300.

Variable costs now need to be added to these fixed costs. In this example, the variable costs could be $30 per client consultation (these variable costs could come from use of diagnostic equipment, heat treatments and non-reusable materials), meaning the total costs per day are

$300 + ($30 × Q)

If the physiotherapist sees ten clients per day (Q = 10), her total costs would equal $600 per day.

Your *total revenue* (TR) (what you derive from the sale of the goods and services) should exceed your *total cost* (TC). In the example, if the physiotherapist charges a fee of $65 per consultation, TR will be $650 each day if she sees ten clients per day. (The fee of $65 equals marginal revenue. This is greater than marginal costs and average total costs are only $60 per consultation.) The return for the business is $50 per day or $5 per consultation ($13,000 per year).

Increasing revenue through adding staff

Perhaps business is going well for the physiotherapist in the preceding section, and she's thinking of hiring another physiotherapist so she can look after more clients. Employing another qualified physiotherapist to work in the business with her makes sense if the expected added revenue from doing so exceeds the expected added costs.

Say the physiotherapist business owner decided to employ a qualified physiotherapist to work full-time in her business, paying $60,000 per year inclusive of superannuation and salary. Variable costs may increase to $50, but fixed costs would still be $300 per day (the salary paid to the new physiotherapist is part of variable costs because the employment occurs only to treat new patients). With two physiotherapists working in the business they could consult up to 25 clients per day, because they could coordinate work over lunch breaks and perhaps extend business hours per day.

This would mean TC are

$300 + ($50 × 25) = $1,550 per day

Dividing these total costs over the 25 clients means average total costs per client increase to $62 with the employment of a physiotherapist; however, these costs are still less than marginal revenue ($65 per client). Total revenue each day increases from $650 to $1,625. The return to the business increases from $50 per day to $75 per day (or $19,500 per year).

Employing more doesn't necessarily mean more profit

Most businesses will experience a reduction in at least average costs as they increase the amount of business. But this doesn't last forever and, at some point, employing more staff will lead to diminishing returns to the business — unless further investment is made in the infrastructure or capacity of the business.

Continuing the example from the preceding sections, say the physiotherapist business owner was considering employing another physiotherapist, meaning variable costs would increase to $70. The increased variable costs are in wages, and the costs associated with actually treating clients such as the use of diagnostic equipment and non-reusable materials. But what if the building space didn't allow for additional consulting rooms, meaning the number of client consultations per day was limited to 32?

This would mean TC are

$300 + ($70 × 32) = $2,540 per day

Dividing these total costs over the 32 clients means average total costs per client increase to $79, where marginal revenue remains at $65 per client. In this scenario, the marginal and average costs would exceed the marginal revenue, eating away the profit of the business.

The business owner would have the following options to ensure her business remained profitable. She could

✔ Not employ a second physiotherapist

✔ Employ a second physiotherapist who will accept less remuneration, such as a new graduate

✔ Employ a part-time physiotherapist

✔ Reduce the time period of consultations (but not the fee charged)

✔ Increase fees charged to clients

When considering whether a new position is required in your business, the first thing you should do is calculate all the expected added costs from that position. You can then work out whether the expected added revenue covers these added costs and makes the new position worthwhile. If your production or service is limited by factors such as building space or capacity, you will reach a point where the costs of adding a new position outweigh the potential profits from that position.

Designing a Job that Suits Your Business

You don't need to be an economic genius to identify the reason that you should (or shouldn't) employ staff (refer to the preceding section for more on comparing the expected costs with the expected revenue of a new position). You must, however, have a good understanding of the tasks that need to be performed and how decisions are made in your business. This knowledge is fundamental to designing a job to suit your business.

Analysing the job

Job analysis is a really boring technical phrase used by human resources professionals to describe the process of discovering what people do all day at work. (And I don't mean surfing the internet or checking their Facebook page — although I'm sure some of that is going on in workplaces throughout this big wide brown land of ours!)

For your small business, job analysis simply means deciding how you will structure a job to ensure whoever performs it works efficiently and effectively. Performing a thorough job analysis at the start of the recruitment process helps you design a job that's right for your small business.

The process of job analysis means marrying the following two concepts in a simple analytical procedure:

- ✔ **Workflow design** is analysing the tasks necessary for the making of a product or service, including the knowledge and skills required to perform the tasks prior to allocating and assigning them to a particular job or person. In basic terms, a job is the sum of the tasks that are performed within the chain of command of an operational system. So mapping the flow of tasks from beginning to end provides a clear picture of how to structure a job.

- ✔ **Organisational structure** refers to the formal network of vertical and horizontal relationships that exist between the small-business owner and staff. This network outlines the chain of command to make decisions in the business. You need to think about where the job fits in the overall organisational structure.

Terms such as *workflow design* and *organisational structure* may seem rather technical, and remote and daunting. However, understanding the flow of work within the organisational chain of command provides a solid foundation for deciding to employ a person and the responsibilities that person must perform to provide the best return on your investment.

Workflow design

Workflow design starts with describing the raw materials, equipment and human resources (knowledge) required for producing the required goods and services, as follows:

- ✔ **Raw inputs:** List the information, materials, data and supplies that are needed to produce your goods or services.

✔ **Equipment:** Take note of the work systems and equipment or tools needed to transform your raw inputs into your goods and services. For example, many aspects of businesses can now be automated or at least tracked via computer software programs — from purchasing supplies through to registering retail sales. You need to include these systems and programs in your workflow outlines. Trades-related businesses need equipment such as trucks, power tools, ovens, knives, electrical equipment and business premises.

✔ **Human resources:** List the knowledge, skills and abilities required to take the raw inputs, apply the systems and use the equipment to produce the goods and services. This could include, for example, technical knowledge, proficiency in sewing fabrics into garments or good organisational skills.

Using a whiteboard, spreadsheet, or even pen and paper, now list the individual tasks that must be performed in the job — that is, applying the raw inputs, using the equipment, and employing the required knowledge, skills and abilities to produce your goods and services. Group the tasks (including the use of equipment and the human resources required) into discrete functions or activities that can be performed by one or more persons. Estimate how long it takes to perform these tasks to produce the goods and services.

This simple exercise provides the building blocks for deciding what type of new staff to recruit, and for designing the job that best suits your business.

Organisational structure

An *organisational structure* highlights lines of communication, authority and accountability, and so adds the dynamic elements to complete your job design.

Imagine the situation when you use the drive-through of a fast-food restaurant. When you place your order, you know that by the time you reach the window to collect and pay for your hamburger and fries, various tasks will have been performed to take the raw food stuffs, prepare them, cook them, package and deliver them to you. The people inside the fast-food restaurant will have applied knowledge, skills and abilities using equipment in established work systems to do all of this work. However, the process doesn't happen spontaneously and without a clear chain of command and communication between staff. This chain of command and communication is established through the organisational structure.

You can map your organisational structure using a similar approach. Ask yourself: Who leads and who then follows? And what must be communicated and to whom?

Combining your organisational structure with your workflow design (refer to preceding section) gives you the basic building blocks required to design jobs that suit your business.

Considering the form of employment

An employee isn't just an employee. You have various forms of employment from which to choose when employing staff — including full-time, part-time, casual or independent contractor.

The form of employment is important because it affects your obligations to employees — for example, whether or not they get holidays and sick leave, and the circumstances in which you can end the employment. Selecting the most appropriate form of employment flows on from having a clear idea of how you intend to use employees in the business. In other words, decide what you need and then choose the form of employment that matches that need.

In the following sections, I outline the characteristics of full-time, part-time and casual employment, and cover the use of independent contractors and temporary (instead of permanent) employment.

Full-time employment

If you need an employee working most business days, full-time employment may be the form that best suits your needs. *Full-time employment* means 38 ordinary hours of work per week. This is the traditional standard working week for the majority of employees in Australia, and the form that suits most small businesses that are open for business for between five and seven days per week. Full-time employees usually attend work during times of the day and on days of the week that follow a reasonably predictable pattern over the full year. Although some variation exists on the theme of full-time employment — for example, averaging of ordinary hours over two or four weeks and using rostered days off work — the typical pattern is 7.6 hours per day, five days per week.

Full-time employees are entitled to *paid annual leave* (to go on a holiday), *personal leave* (when they are ill and unable to attend work or are caring for an immediate family member who is ill) and *parental leave*. They're also entitled to contingent entitlements such as redundancy pay and notice of termination of employment.

Although the maximum ordinary hours of work per week is 38, a full-time employee may work reasonable additional hours where that suits the business. However, rules exist to limit the circumstances when that can occur, and overtime payments may apply under a modern award. See Chapter 4 for more on the rules regulating maximum hours of work.

Part-time employment

Part-time employment means employment for fewer than 38 ordinary hours of work per week. A characteristic of part-time employment, and something that distinguishes it from casual employment, is the pattern of employment — that is, the employment is *regular* and the hours of work *predictable* over the full year.

In most other respects, part-time employment is the same as full-time employment. The employee is entitled to the same entitlements as full-time staff, such as paid annual leave and personal leave (refer to the preceding section for more). Although a part-time employee works fewer hours, the employment is continuous in the same manner as full-time employment.

Casual employment

Casual employment is *intermittent* or irregular employment where the hours of employment aren't predictable. As the employer, you're not obliged to offer continuing employment beyond the period in which the casual employee has accepted work — for example, one day or one week.

Casual employees don't receive the entitlements that full-time and part-time employees receive, such as paid annual leave, personal leave, parental leave and contingent entitlements such as redundancy pay and notice of termination of employment. Instead, casual employees are paid a loading on their ordinary hourly wage to cover these entitlements.

Independent contracting alternative

Independent contractors are people engaged under a contract for service as opposed to employees (whether full-time, part-time or casual) who are employed under a contract of service.

An emerging trend in new businesses is to collaborate with independent contractors to perform specific tasks — for example, project work or manage logistics, provide additional expertise, or a multitude of other business functions that in the past may have been performed by employees in a traditional business structure. When using a contractor, you engage a person to perform work for your small business, determine terms for the completion of the task and, once the task is complete, pay the person the agreed fee. The person usually has an Australian Business Number (ABN) and provides an invoice for payment for the work performed. This is a contract for service.

Because you're only engaging the contractor to perform a specific task, this modern business model enables small businesses to grow and adapt in highly flexible and efficient forms to meet market demands. However, you need to be careful your use of contractors doesn't cross over to a more employment-like relationship, because this affects your obligations to:

✔ Apply the minimum national standards for annual, personal, parental, long service leave and public holidays

✔ Insure the person for accident compensation

✔ Pay modern award rates of pay and conditions

✔ Pay the superannuation guarantee

Engaging a person as an independent contractor when he's really an employee may mean penalties from the Tax Office and Fair Work Ombudsman and repayment of award wages, penalties, overtime, annual leave and superannuation — see the sidebar 'Independent contractor versus employee' for more information.

Independent contractor versus employee

Australian law makers and enforcers have been notoriously suspicious of businesses that use independent contractors where once they used an employee. They think these businesses could be either attempting to evade tax or underpaying the contractor, or both! Therefore, although independent contracting is a really good alternative to employment, you should proceed with caution and clearly understand the difference between an independent contractor and an employee.

The tests to determine whether a person is a genuine contractor are complex and imprecise. Therefore, I recommend the following simple method to determine the matter: *If it walks like a duck, quacks like a duck and duck dives into the pond to obtain its fish dinner, it's probably a duck!* If the person you intend to engage as an independent contractor relies upon you for work and is treated the same as an employee in all of the normal respects, chances are that person is an employee.

The following example helps to illustrate the difference between an employee and an independent contractor. Trekkies ICT Contractors is a business that provides computing and communications equipment and maintenance services to other businesses. Norbert Poindexter is an ICT student who performs occasional work for Trekkies under a contract for service. He is paid an agreed fee for the work that he performs, has registered a business (Poindexter Enterprises), uses an ABN and provides Trekkies with an invoice for the work that he completes for the business. However, Norbert works exclusively for Trekkies and wears a Trekkies uniform when he performs work at its clients' offices. The fee that he charges Trekkies is set by the Trekkies managing director. Norbert also uses business equipment owned by Trekkies when performing the work.

Chances are Norbert isn't an independent contractor but an employee, based on the following tests used by Australian courts, tribunals and government regulatory authorities to distinguish an employee from an independent contractor:

- **Control test:** This test refers to the degree of control exercised by the employer over the person. For example, do you as the employer decide when and where the work is to be performed? Is the person required to follow your directions on how to perform the work? Do you control the manner in which the work is performed? Must the person perform the work herself (without using another contractor)? If the answer is 'Yes' to these questions, the person is likely an employee and not an independent contractor.

- **Integration test:** This test examines the extent to which the person is *integrated* into the business that he is working in. For example, is the person working for other businesses? Is the person supplying his own equipment and facilities? Does the person complete and provide invoices? Does he work through a corporate entity? Does he display his own business name rather than the name of the employer on

equipment and marketing material? If the answer is 'No' to these questions and the person relies upon or is treated the same as an employee, the person is likely an employee.

- **Results test:** This test considers whether the person is employed to achieve a specific result rather than employed generally to perform work under the direction of an employer. Performance of the tasks required of a particular job will normally be at the discretion of the independent contractor. Payment of an agreed fee is dependent upon the satisfactory completion of the task or delivery of a result. The independent contractor bears the risk of losing a payment, and rectifying faults, for failure to satisfactorily complete the job or deliver the result agreed between the parties.

Even the existence of these tests doesn't make it completely black and white — the tests aren't precise and are often applied in differing combinations and emphasis. That's why I like my 'Walk, Quack and Swim Like a Duck' test best.

Temporary versus permanent employment

Many small-business owners refer to their regular full-time and part-time staff as *permanent* employees; however permanent employment doesn't exist as a form of employment.

You can have employees who are regularly employed and whose employment may be terminated with written notice — for example, notice of between one and five weeks. The vast majority of full-time and part-time employees in Australia are in this group. On the other hand, you can employ people for *a specified task or period* and this employment may be terminated only if a serious breach of the terms of employment occurs, or when the period expires or the task is completed. This form of employment is referred to as *fixed-term employment*.

Fixed-term employment is often incorrectly applied to the more common practice of employing a person for a specified period or task but where that employment may be terminated by providing written notice before the expiry of the specified period or completion of the task. This latter form of employment is more accurately described as *temporary* employment. As a small-business owner you're less likely to employ a person on a truly fixed-term employment, because to do so would require the full payment of salary owing on the balance of the fixed-term if the employment arrangement isn't working out to your expectations and you terminate the contract before it expires.

The following example illustrates the difference between fixed-term and temporary employment. Say a person is engaged for 12 months to replace an employee on parental leave. If the person doesn't perform to your satisfaction during the first few months of employment, you would normally be able to dismiss the person with one week's notice (or payment in lieu of notice) and then find someone else to do the job. This is temporary employment. Under a fixed-term employment arrangement, however, you have no capacity to dismiss the employee with notice. You dismiss the employee immediately only if that employee has seriously breached the fundamental terms of employment — otherwise, you need to pay the balance of the 12 months' salary.

Get into the habit of describing your employees correctly, according to the form of employment that best fits the nature of how they are employed. The consequences of misapplying the form of employment are real. For example, a common mistake of business owners is employing staff on a rolling series of short-term contracts, because they assume this means they can avoid the scrutiny of an unfair dismissal application by not renewing the employment beyond the expiry date of the latest contract of employment. If you do this, you may be in for a nasty surprise. The tribunal entrusted with responsibility for dealing with unfair dismissal applications only excludes employees who have been engaged under genuine fixed-term employment. Temporary full-time and part-time employees will have their day in court. See the sidebar 'Some casuals are more equal than others — exceptions to the rules' for more information, and Chapter 17 for coverage of who may, or may not, apply for a remedy if unfairly dismissed.

Table 2-1 provides a checklist of the different forms of employment and the situations each form is best suited to.

Table 2-1	Choosing Forms of Employment Checklist
When is the Employee Needed?	*Form of Employment*
Most or all business operating days throughout the year	Full-time or part-time
Regular peak trading times during the week or hours of the day	Part-time
Covering absences of regular employees on annual leave or absent due to illness	Casual
Pre-Christmas trading peak for no more than three months	Casual or temporary full-time or part-time
Fewer than ten hours every week to assist in administration	Part-time
Temporary replacement of employee absent on parental leave	Temporary full-time or part-time
Temporary work to manage or assist in a project	Temporary full-time or part-time
Seasonal work	Casual

Deciding when you want staff to work and for how long

The number of 38 hours of work each week isn't a magical one conjured up by the great wizard of human resource management or the result of some major mathematical formula designed to calculate optimal working arrangements. This is an arbitrary number of hours per week resulting from the combination of political and social forces following the days of the industrial revolution. You can deviate from the norm of 38 hours per week. Going over 38 hours per week just might cost you more than it's worth, but deciding to employ for fewer than 38 hours may work out to be more efficient for your business.

Follow these steps to calculate when you want staff to work and for how long:

1. **Estimate the optimal number of hours each day or week in which you can usefully employ staff.**

   That is, how long does it take a person working at a reasonable pace to complete the tasks in the manner required by you?

2. **Work out the hours of the day and days of the week in which the work would be most usefully performed.**

3. **Map the hours and the days of the week you would prefer the work to be completed in a simple weekly calendar.**

You can use this map of hours and days to determine the form of employment you require — full-time, part-time or casual.

Some casuals are more equal than others — exceptions to the rules

Although casual employment is intermittent and irregular, and generally excluded from the benefits applicable to full-time and part-time employees, Australian employment law makers have made exceptions to the rules for some entitlements. For example, casual employees who are employed on a regular and systematic basis may lodge a claim for unfair dismissal if their employment is terminated. Or they may qualify for an entitlement in a modern award, legislation or other regulatory instrument if they fit particular criteria — usually relating to their length of service. These exceptions can be confusing but, no matter how complex, the risk of fines and penalties for failing to comply is sufficient incentive to familiarise yourself with the rules. The following table shows how the exceptions apply in some common situations.

Entitlement	*Casual Included YES/NO*	*Exception to the Rule*
Annual leave	NO	None
Carer's leave (paid)	NO	Casual employees are entitled to two days unpaid leave for each occasion when a member of the employee's immediate family, or a member of the employee's household, requires care or support because of either
		A personal illness, or personal injury, affecting the member
		An unexpected emergency affecting the member
Compassionate leave (paid)	NO	Casual employees are entitled to two days of unpaid compassionate leave for each occasion when a member of the employee's immediate family, or a member of the employee's household:
		– Contracts or develops a personal illness that poses a serious threat to his or her life
		– Sustains a personal injury that poses a serious threat to his or her life
		– Dies

Community service leave	YES	Employees must be provided with unpaid time off work to attend approved community service activities such as emergency services
Long service leave	YES	Casual employees are generally entitled to long service leave on the same basis as full-time and part-time employees. The period of service in order to qualify will be continuous where no more than three months break has occurred between periods of casual employment with the one employer
Notice of termination of employment	NO	Casuals may be dismissed without notice
Paid Parental Leave (PPL) (18 weeks payment from the Australian Government linked to the national minimum wage*)	YES	Casual employees are entitled to PPL if they are eligible mothers or primary carers and satisfy the PPL Work Test — that is, they have both Been in paid work continuously for at least ten of the 13 months prior to the birth or adoption of the child Worked for at least 330 hours in that ten-month period (just over one day a week) with no more than an eight-week gap between two consecutive working days
Parental leave (unpaid)	YES	Long-term casuals, where they have a total of 12 months continuous service immediately before the expected date of birth or adoption of a child, *and* have a reasonable expectation of continuing employment by the one employer on a regular and systematic basis, are entitled to 12 months unpaid parental leave
Personal leave	NO	Casual loadings are paid partly to compensate for the loss of paid personal leave
Public holidays	YES	Casual employees have the right to refuse to work on a public holiday but are not entitled to payment where they don't work on a public holiday
Redundancy pay	NO	Casuals aren't entitled to redundancy pay because the employment isn't continuous and the casual loading partly compensates for the insecure nature of casual employment
Unfair dismissal	NO	Casual employees who have been employed on a regular and systematic basis and who would have had a reasonable expectation of continuing employment if the dismissal had not occurred, may apply for compensation or reinstatement

At the time of writing, the Australian Government plans to introduce a scheme of 6 months paid parental leave (PPL) on the employee's full wage plus superannuation.

Describing the Job: Creating a Position Description

I'm not sure who invented the position description, but whoever it was did the world a great disservice. Over the years, I've seen hundreds of position descriptions and 99 per cent are useless. They may be great for consultants but they're useless because they don't reflect the inherently dynamic nature of the employment relationship.

In this section, I explain how to create a really useful position description that fits in with the other 1 per cent, a description that gives you a tool to outline the role correctly, find the right person for that role, and so drive efficiency and productivity from your staff.

Setting out useful headings and information

In this section, I outline how to create a position description using specific headings that cover a theme relevant to the job, which makes the task much easier. Each heading is a succinct theme directly relating to the information you can discern after completing a thorough job analysis (refer to the section 'Designing a Job that Suits Your Business' for more on this). All you need to do is translate the relevant details under each heading and ensure the terminology and descriptions are consistent.

Adding the job title

Inserting the job title is a pretty obvious beginning to any job description. But how you name the job is important because the title is the key phrase that prospective employees will use to search for the job. If you don't describe it accurately, you have less chance of attracting the right candidates. Try to work out what these recently advertised jobs are:

- Front Office Agent
- Strategic Sourcing Specialist
- Customer Service Champions

I hope you worked them out because I have no idea. Something to do with hospitality, perhaps? I am intrigued (especially the about the champion job) but you can't bank on intrigue being enough to inspire an enquiry. Make sure your job title clearly captures the position you're creating.

Check online to find out what job titles are used for similar positions to yours. You may be able to spot certain key words that prospective employees are also likely to use when job searching online.

Describing the business context

Your position description should also describe what your business does and what you're in business to achieve. This also allows you to describe the characteristics that make your business unique. For example, a coffee shop isn't just a place where coffee is served. It could be

> *A vibrant and energetic hub in the heart of the city's legal district, making great coffee and producing fresh and delicious food served in our relaxed cafe, or delivered to our customers at work within the CBD. The City Larder is a unique experience in food service combining casual ambience with an uncompromising approach to quality in service and produce. Our fair trade–certified coffee is selected from the finest plantations and treated with love and affection all the way from the highlands of New Guinea to the cup that we pour for our customers.*

Good description — I'm hungry already!

The description is clearly over the top but no doubt you understand the message I'm trying to convey. If you want to attract suitable candidates, you need to sell your philosophy and your style — the candidates you wish to attract will need to fit your business, not the other way around.

Primary purpose

Under this heading, describe in no more than 100 words the primary purpose of the job — that is, what the employee is there to achieve. For example, for a medical practice manager job you might describe the primary purpose as follows:

> *The Practice Manager works with the practice partners, leading our team of committed medical, allied health and support service professionals in the delivery of high-quality medical care to our patients. The Practice Manager will coordinate the daily clinical schedule, manage accreditation and quality standards, implement our business plan, manage the business accounts and oversee compliance with all legal, financial, employment and health and safety regulatory standards.*

The primary purpose of the job should clearly summarise the fundamental nature of the role and what it's supposed to achieve for the business.

Responsibilities

Under this heading, list the duties of the job. Try to be as succinct as possible and don't go overboard describing every little task. Divide the duties into groups or themes for clarity. Continuing the example of the medical practice manager (refer to the preceding section) you could list the responsibilities as shown in Figure 2-1.

1. Lead the Practice's medical, allied health and support services team including:

   a. Recruit suitably qualified staff to work in the Practice

   b. Ensure all staff are employed in accordance with regulatory standards and have current employment contracts

   c. Coordinate the weekly roster of hours of work

   d. Mentor and encourage staff to work to our high standards of care to patients

   e. Manage the professional development and performance review program

2. Manage quality standards and accreditation including:

   a. Implement the approved quality standards program for the Practice

   b. Maintain all documentation on quality standards

   c. Conduct sample audits to ensure ongoing compliance

   d. Manage response to patient grievances

   e. Liaise with quality standards auditors and regulatory authorities such as the Health Insurance Commission

   f. Coordinate activities to prepare the Practice for accreditation

3. Develop and implement with the Practice partners the Practice business plan including:

   a. Project patient demand and trends

   b. Conduct workforce needs analysis

   c. Analyse risks to the business

   d. Forecast expenditure and revenue

   e. Assess ICT capability

4. Manage the Practice business accounts including:

   a. Establish a yearly budget

   b. Manage accounts payable and receivable

   c. Monitor cash flow

   d. Ensure revenue targets are being met

   e. Provide monthly reports to Practice partners

   f. Liaise with accountants and auditors

Figure 2-1:
Example responsibilities for a medical practice manager.

Conditions

Under this heading, state whether:

- ✔ The position is full-time, part-time, casual or temporary
- ✔ The employee is required to work shifts, be on-call or work overtime
- ✔ Allowances are paid and/or fringe benefits are included
- ✔ An industrial instrument such as an award or enterprise agreement applies

Listing the fundamentals of the job is really important because you must comply with applicable modern awards and the National Employment Standards (NES). If unsure of the applicable modern award, seek advice from the relevant government authority. (See Chapter 4 for more information on NES.)

Authority

In the employment context, *authority* means the power to make a decision for, or on behalf of, your business — such as expenditure of petty cash, advertising, pricing or engaging suppliers and negotiating agreements.

Say you have a small retail business and you want to engage a manager for this business. You may delegate authority to this manager to manage the petty cash, negotiate the telephone, internet and utilities supplies, and organise stock orders. The manager may also have the authority to resolve customer disputes and respond to enquiries from suppliers.

Include in your position description what sort of authority the role involves.

Accountability

Everyone has to be accountable to someone else in the business. In your position description, outline the level of supervision or direction that the employee is subject to in the performance of the job. This means the extent to which you allow the employee to make decisions on how the job is performed and how closely you or others supervise the performance of the job. For example:

- ✔ **Close supervision** means employees receive detailed instruction on job requirements, methods to be adopted and unusual or difficult features. Employees' work is subject to progress checking.

- ✔ **Limited direction** means employees receive limited instructions but with clearly stated objectives. Employees have a significant degree of competence and experience and are able to achieve their objectives by conforming to instructions but with minimal guidance.

Where a line of accountability exists through an intermediary supervisor, you should be clear about the nature of that supervision. Many businesses fail to make this line of accountability clear and this can lead to issues down the track. For example, at any one time during a busy period at a restaurant or bar the food and beverage attendants (or wait staff) may be told to clear and clean tables by the service manager, attend to a dissatisfied customer by the owner and pour drinks by the bar manager. The poor wait staff may not know what to do and may end up pleasing no-one. Avoid a situation such as this by clarifying who may direct who and in what circumstances.

Go to dummies.com for a sample job description template, which includes a glossary of useful employment terms you can use within your description.

Outlining your key selection criteria

Separating the description of the job from the criteria that you will use to select successful candidates for the job is useful. I discuss key selection criteria, and how you can use them within the interviewing process, in more detail in Chapter 3, but you should also include a summary list of the criteria that a person who is to perform the job should possess with your job description. This enables those interested in applying for the job to understand the type of skills, knowledge, ability and experience that must be demonstrated to be offered the job.

Having in place key selection criteria also enables you, as the employer, to measure the performance of employees objectively during the course of their employment, particularly when assessing how well they're performing during the first 12 months of employment.

List your key selection criteria in order of priority, starting with the most important skills, experience, knowledge and/or qualifications required to perform the position. You can also divide the criteria between mandatory and desirable skills.

Chapter 3

Sorting the Good from the Not So Good

In This Chapter

▶ Understanding how selection criteria can guide your decision

▶ Opening up the field of suitable candidates before narrowing your choices

▶ Applying strong interview techniques to uncover the applicant's better qualities

▶ Considering delicate subjects when choosing an employee

But, soft! what light through yonder window breaks? It is the east, and Juliet is the sun.

William Shakespeare, *Romeo and Juliet*

With sincere apologies to William Shakespeare, imagine if each time you decided to employ a person, the ideal employee appeared upon a nearby balcony, to light up your life like a brilliant dawn sun. A slightly less fanciful, far less romantic but certainly more practical strategy is to use more than one means to promote your job and then create a short list of potential candidates from which to select your best employee. The task is not difficult but it does require a bit of organisation — and in this chapter I take you through the full process.

A short list of candidates is of little use unless you have a clear idea of the qualities you desire in your ideal employee and can assess the capability of potential employees. Establishing selection criteria based on a person's skill, knowledge, attitude, experience and qualifications enables you to sort through the short list, guides your selection procedure and, ultimately, helps determine who you employ. This chapter also covers a multi-pronged approach to interview technique and assessment methods, providing the best way to find the right person for the job.

Being Prepared with Key Selection Criteria

The decision to employ your ideal employee is a big one. So don't make the choice on a whim, a feeling, a hunch ... okay, you get the picture. Two fundamental tasks can help you select the best person for the job. The first task is outlining *selection criteria* that describe the skills, qualities, knowledge, experience and ability required to successfully perform the job — these criteria provide a template against which you may assess every candidate.

The second task is preparing a system, or *scorecard*, to objectively rate the candidates and so decide which one is most suitable for the job.

These two tasks are fundamental to a successful recruitment procedure and must be completed before you interview prospective employees. If you apply these two recruitment tools, you can quickly work out who to interview and, ultimately, who to employ.

Selection criteria versus the job description

A common mistake with employers is confusing the job description with the criteria used to select employees. Both are necessary but serve different purposes.

The *job description* lists the primary objectives, duties, responsibilities, authority and accountability of the role within the business's organisational structure. (Refer to Chapter 2 for more information on job descriptions.)

The job description is all about *what* the employee will be doing. The selection criteria are all about *capability* to do the job.

When selecting people to interview, and therefore potential employees, decide which key criteria to use, listing each measure under the following five key themes:

- ✔ **Ability:** The enduring capability of a person.
- ✔ **Experience:** The cumulative body of personal knowledge, understanding, connection, empathy, behaviours and learned skills.
- ✔ **Knowledge:** The factual or procedural information that the person must have to perform the job.
- ✔ **Qualities:** The personal traits, characteristics and attributes that a person brings to the performance of a job such as honesty, determination, friendliness and integrity.

> ✔ **Skill:** A person's proficiency at performing a task; often referred to as *competency*.

These themes are important to the development not only of the selection criteria but also your job advertisement. A multi-dimensional approach to the selection of your ideal candidate is more likely to lead to a better fit and an enduring employment relationship.

Figure 3-1 provides a simple form that works through each of the five selection criteria themes for a motor mechanic position. Figure 3-2 shows you the related job advertisement.

Theme	*Description*	*Selection Criteria*
Ability	Sound understanding of motor vehicle mechanical engineering, and ability to diagnose issues and perform appropriate servicing and repair to ensure vehicles are working in good order	Proficient in all areas of mechanical diagnostics, servicing and repair work
Experience	Experience of *x* years working as a motor mechanic	Experience working in a similar motor mechanical shop environment
Knowledge	Trades level knowledge and understanding of all aspects of motor mechanical engineering maintenance and repair of Australian and imported passenger vehicles	Trades qualified motor mechanic or mechanical engineer Roadworthy certificate assessment licence
Qualities	Reliable with good communication skills and work ethic who has a keen passion for automotive care	Reliability Good communication Good work ethic Passionate about automotive care Friendly manner Able to work with a team
Skills	Conduct diagnostic testing on engine efficiency, brake and fuel systems, steering, electrical and suspension systems Competent in rebuilding, replacing, testing and repairing of all mechanical parts and components in new and old passenger vehicles Able to work under pressure and meet daily work schedules	Must know how to service and repair mechanical components and engines of most Australian and imported passenger vehicles using modern mechanical technology Must be able to complete tasks in a timely manner
Other	Must work in a safe manner	Understand and adhere to health and safety procedures

Figure 3-1: A form to help create selection criteria.

Fred's Motor Repairs is seeking a qualified motor mechanic with a RWC License to join our friendly team.

We need a reliable person with good communication skills and strong work ethic who has a keen passion for automotive care.

Please provide your resume and reference by either post or email to:

Fred's Motor Repair

Attn: Fred Ferrari

Lot 7, 227 Autoland Rd

Chelsea Heights VIC 3196

fredsmotor@bigpond.com

Figure 3-2: Job advertisement for Fred's Motor Repairs.

The information in the second column of Figure 3-1 describes the particular nature or type of knowledge, skills, qualities, ability and experience that Fred is searching for in an employee. This in turn informs the particular criteria he will use to select the best motor mechanic for the job. You can create a similar form to that shown in Figure 3-1 for your own job position, using the descriptions you add to Column 3 for your selection criteria.

Using a scorecard

A *scorecard* is a useful tool you can use to assess candidates when deciding who to employ. Used together with selection criteria, this scorecard will help you rank potential employees on your short list (see the section 'Creating a short list of suitable candidates' later in this chapter).

Rating systems

The scorecard should be simple and relevant. It must reliably measure the level of the candidates' capability, knowledge, experience, skills and qualities.

The selection criteria usually give you clues as to what is appropriate to include in the scorecard. For example, you could take the following approach:

Knowledge, or mandatory qualifications:

☐ YES

☐ NO

☐ Not yet completed

Qualities:

☐ Evident

☐ Not evident

Skills:

On a scale of 1 to 5 with 5 indicating highly proficient and 1 being not proficient, rate the candidate: _____.

Experience:

On a scale of 1 to 5 whereby 1 equals insufficient experience and 5 equals very experienced, rate the applicant: _____.

Ability:

Using a scale of 1 to 5, with 5 being the best, measure according to how highly you rate the person's known enduring capability: _____.

Weightings

You should weight each criterion on your scorecard according to relative importance in the performance of the job. For example, proficiency in the skills required to perform the job may be four times more important than experience. The qualities of a person may be half as important as the formal knowledge and the person's general ability in the applicable field. Thus the final selection criteria scorecard may look something like the one filled out in Figure 3-3.

Motor Mechanic	Candidate #1		
Selection Criteria	Rating	Weighting	Score
Trades qualified motor mechanic and RWC licence	Yes=1 No=0	25% (weighted average)	2.5
Must know how to service and repair mechanical components and engines of most Australian and imported passenger vehicles using modern mechanical technology	4	40% (weighted average)	14
Must be able to complete tasks in a timely manner	3		
Reliability	4	10% (weighted average)	3.6
Good communication	2		
Good work ethic	4		
Passionate	4		
Friendly manner	2		
Able to work with a team	2		
Experience working in a similar motor mechanical shop environment	3	10%	3
Proficient in all areas of mechanical diagnostics, servicing and repair work.	3	10%	3
Understand and adhere to health and safety procedures	3	5%	1.5
Total		100%	27.6

Figure 3-3:
An example
of a score-
card for
weighting
selection
criteria.

Finding and Selecting Applications

The job advertisement is online and in the newspaper. The note is in the shop window. You have told everyone you know that you're looking for a person to work in your business, and the recruitment agent has circulated the job description. Now you can just sit back and watch the job applications pour in ... right? Unfortunately, wrong.

Thinking that you can attract an extensive list of suitable candidates from which to select your ideal employee just by relying on advertisements and word of mouth is a nice idea. However, that rarely happens in real life. Don't be discouraged if very few people express interest. However, you can improve your chances of attracting a good list of candidates from which to select your ideal employee with the strategies outlined in the following sections.

Opening up the field of candidates

You have three avenues for attracting interest in your job:

✔ **People who you already know.** This includes family, friends and people already employed in the business who may want to perform another role, as well as people who have been referred to you by family and friends.

✔ **Unsolicited applicants.** People who have expressed an interest in working in your business quite independently from a job advertisement. It doesn't matter how long ago such people approached you — they may still be interested.

✔ **Candidates who provide written applications.** This is the group who respond to the advertisement. Consider applicants who provide a current resume and address the job selection criteria. Disregard those applicants who don't do this. If people haven't taken the time to update their employment history or address the actual job, they aren't worth employing in your business.

Employing friends, family members and even friends of family and friends can be fraught with the kinds of difficulties that you wouldn't normally encounter with people you're not connected to. You also face the risk of fracturing personal relationships that you value highly. (Keep in mind the old joke where a man has recently broken up with a girlfriend who is the sister of his best mate. His other mate consoles him as he reflects with sadness on the end of the great times. 'Yeah,' he concludes 'I'll really miss my best mate'!)

However, benefits also exist that aren't necessarily evident where employees don't have a personal interest in the success of the business and their part in it. Small business is personal business and so keeping it that way through the people you employ can be worthwhile. Make a few enquiries about the friends or family members and, if you like what you hear, invite them to provide you with a written resume.

Your group of unsolicited applicants can be a really interesting category, and can include people you might mistakenly ignore unless a job is immediately available when the person enquires. People may have written to you, telephoned or visited your business over the past six months. If they have made the effort to learn about your business and have shown the initiative to approach you for work, don't ignore them. They may possess the sort of qualities that you are looking for in an employee.

If you like people when you meet them, or when they're making an unsolicited application, make a note of their names and phone numbers, and ask them to send you a resume for future reference.

The third category of people, those who make a written application, may include some gems but be wary. They may be motivated solely by

✔ A desire to get away from their current employer

✔ The job's location

✔ The need to find a job (any job)

✔ Finding working hours that suit their lifestyle

And then you have the people who are genuinely interested in the job and your business. You can call them all *potential employees*.

Creating a short list of suitable candidates

You wouldn't date every person who asked you out to dinner, would you? (Please say no!) So it's not sensible to seriously consider every person who expresses interest in a job you're advertising. The same principle applies to finding and deciding on a suitable employee.

From your groups of potential employees (refer to the preceding section) eliminate those people who don't satisfy the essential selection criteria. *Essential criteria* are the qualities that the successful candidate must possess. For example, if you need a hairdresser, you wouldn't consider a beautician or unqualified shop assistant. Likewise a delivery driver without a driver's licence or a food and beverage attendant without a certificate of competency in responsible serving of alcohol isn't worth considering unless you're prepared to pay for training.

Once you've eliminated those who don't meet the essential criteria, re-order the remaining candidates according to those who best address the selection criteria. For example, you may value people who are able to work to deadlines or are self-motivated. The resumes provided will include some hints about people's prior experience and education, which should give you an idea about whether or not they are likely to possess the qualities you seek.

If you're assessing the list of applicants who responded to the job advertisement (that is, the ones you don't know), you could telephone them and ask a series of questions to get a better feel for their capability (see the sidebar 'Short list filtering questions' for more).

Try to identify those people who want to work with you because they're a good fit for your business — not because it simply suits them. Ideally, consider seriously no more than five candidates.

If you use a professional recruiter, this person will filter the applicants according to your criteria and ask particular questions similar to those listed in the sidebar 'Short list filtering questions'.

Short list filtering questions

Once you have filtered the promising candidates from the rest, you can reduce the list further by contacting applicants and conducting a quick phone interview, making sure you ask the right questions of your potential employees. Of course, asking the right questions is one thing; knowing which answers will get you closer to your ideal employee is another. Take a look at these example conversations as a guide.

Thanks for your application. Now tell me:

Q: *What aspect of the job motivated you to express an interest?*
A: *It looked like a really good opportunity.*
Q: *What kind of opportunity are you looking for?*
A: *I only want to work in Balwyn.*

Wrong answer. Don't add people who respond in this way to your short list because they're only interested in the location of the job.

Q: *Why do you believe the job would be a good fit for you?*
A: *I believe I can contribute to world peace and reduce global warming by working in your book store.*

That's nice, but this person isn't likely to sell a book while thinking about world peace. Don't put people who answer in this way on your short list.

Q: *Why would you want to leave your current job for this one?*
A: *I enjoy the work I do but I feel I would be able to make a more valuable contribution to your business.*

Nice flattery and it could be true. People who respond in this way should be on your short list — not because of the flattery but because they may actually take pride in their work.

Q: *What do you know or have found out about my business?*
A: *I had a look at your website and asked a few people what they thought of your business. I really like your mission statement and your reputation for producing quality products is excellent.* Good answer. Put people who respond in this way on your short list too, because they've taken the time to learn something about your business.

Providing feedback

Even if they didn't quite make the cut, recognising the people who made the effort to express interest in your business is important, and is good business practice. Create a simple template that both acknowledges that you have received a person's application and thanks them for the effort. Unsuccessful applicants will appreciate the gesture and will be more likely to accept your decision graciously and pass on the goodwill to others who may be interested in your business.

Go to www.dummies.com/go/hrsmallbusinessau for a sample acknowledgement letter template for unsuccessful job applicants.

Interviewing Techniques 101

Most small-business employers prefer to interview prospective employees using the traditional technique of face-to-face question and answer. However, university researchers have consistently found that this method (on its own) is the least reliable indicator of how suitable the person will be once employed. When you interview your shortlist of candidates, you should make sure this isn't the only method that you use to decide who gets the job. Instead, learn something about your candidates by engaging them in a conversation and asking the right questions. The following sections show you how.

The engaging interviewer

A useful interview technique is to engage the person in a conversation whereby you learn something about your candidate and he learns something about you and your business. This technique stands in contrast to the traditional question and answer session that most job interviews tend to follow.

Nothing is wrong with asking people about themselves. You can and should ask applicants to talk about their lives. What interests them? What do they do outside of work? What movies and TV shows do they like? Do they play sport or read books? How about bungee jumping? The objective is to relax the interviewees and converse so that they reveal a little bit of themselves to you. This won't happen if the interview is conducted like a quiz.

When talking with your candidates, highlight items, key words and phrases from their resumes. Candidates will have included them on purpose so you may as well ask about them. Words and phrases in the resume can then act as prompts for conversation starters. For example, young people usually list their school and some of the activities they engaged in during that part of their life. Asking them to talk about the school, and the associated teachers, friends and activities may reveal aspects such as their level of maturity, how well socialised they are, and attitudes to authority.

Although engaging candidates in conversations about their lives is acceptable, you must be careful not to overstep the boundaries of good manners and socially acceptable topics of conversation. The general rule is to let them do the talking. If the person talks in a sexually suggestive manner or tells an obscene joke, don't join in!

Where the person has listed an interest in politics or religious groups, asking them about those activities is acceptable insofar as they bear upon the selection criteria and nature of the job. However, this isn't an open invitation to promote your own personal political views and attitude to religion.

Stay away from conversations about personal appearance unless a direct relevance exists to the job. Telling someone she looks really great in that short skirt isn't acceptable. An explanation of the dress code of your business is acceptable.

A bit like speed dating: Asking the right questions

You and the candidate have one opportunity to impress each other. Yes, that's correct: You need to impress the applicant as well. The best candidate is one who's quietly assessing you and your business as the interview unfolds. Don't ask those same old boring and predictable questions most people have been asked many times before, such as

- Where do you see yourself in five years time?
- What are your good and bad qualities?
- How would you handle a difficult customer?

Applicants simply give you the answers they think you want to hear, so you don't learn anything true about the person. Also, the good applicants are probably quietly crossing you off their list of preferred employers at this point and mentally moving on to the next interview they have lined up with one of your competitors.

You haven't got all day to interview people and you can find out answers to the preceding questions using other selection methods. So use the time that you do have usefully.

Try these steps when interviewing:

1. **Thank the interviewee for taking the time to express an interest in your business.**

2. **Talk about your business, your mission, your values and why this business is so important to you.**

3. **Explain how and where this job fits within your grand plan for a successful business.**

4. **Invite the interviewee to talk about herself. This should occupy most of the interview.**

5. **Move on to the key selection criteria only when you have taken the time to get to know your candidate.**

6. **Ask for referees to attest to the resume.**

7. **Offer the candidate an opportunity to ask questions of you.**

A job interview should last no more than 30 to 45 minutes. If you're well organised, you should be able to learn enough about potential employees in that time to decide whether they're suitable for your business.

Really useful assessment tools

A person's skill, knowledge and experience in the fields applicable to the job are generally a matter of fact. You don't need to spend time asking questions about stuff that you can more reliably verify through other means.

For example, your potential employee can either make a double decaf latte with skinny milk and a hint of nutmeg or not. Ask candidates to demonstrate their skills to you. Likewise with cutting hair, serving tables, pouring drinks, cleaning cars, driving vans, answering phones and greeting customers or any other activity that requires the proficient application of a set of skills or application of knowledge. Professional, managerial and trades-qualified competence can usually be verified by providing you with current registration, accreditation and proof of qualifications.

You can also ask previous employers, referees and even do your own research on candidates' history using the internet. You can learn a lot about the person by searching social media but make sure you understand the context of every bit of information. A personally embarrassing picture on the internet is not necessarily an indicator of conduct during employment.

Table 3-1 shows areas of competency, knowledge and experience and the assessment tools that you can apply to obtain the most valid and reliable results that will inform your recruitment decision.

Table 3-1	Areas of Competency, Knowledge and Experience	
Criteria	*Assessment Technique*	*Usefulness Meter*
Attitude	Behavioural-based interview where candidate is invited to recount real life situations such as responding to difficult customers and problem solving.	Is a more reliable predictor of future behaviour than hypothetical scenario style questioning.
	Social media such as Facebook can provide a useful window into the general attitudes and lifestyle of the person.	Social media is not always accessible and should not be viewed by stealth. Ask permission to view it. Don't be offended if politely refused.
Qualifications	Certificate, diploma, degree, masters, doctorate, trades certificate (as relevant)	Mandatory for some jobs and easily verifiable by checking with the institution that issued the qualification.
Experience	Public records, previous employer, referees	The past is not necessarily an indicator of the future but is probably as good an indicator as you have available.
Capability	Referees can attest to candidates' capability but the best test is to have them demonstrate their proficiency in one or more tasks relevant to the job.	Very useful; complements the interview procedure to provide a well-rounded assessment.
Cognitive ability	Numeracy, literacy, comprehension and abstract reasoning tests.	Very old-fashioned but nevertheless provide valid results where such ability is an important criteria to successfully perform the job.
Personality	Psychological tests such as Myer Briggs Type Indicator can reveal personality traits such as whether the person is an extravert, emotionally stable, agreeable, conscientious and inquisitive.	The jury is out on whether such testing provides valid and reliable indications of how a person will behave on the job. May not be worth the expenditure.

Don't go there! Topics to avoid

In this age of politically correct behaviour, you may feel hesitant to ask potential employees some very personal questions, even where they may be relevant to the performance of the job. Certainly many topics exist that you must not probe, and those matters are more thoroughly discussed in Chapter 12. However, you may venture into many personal topics — and probably *should* enquire about these topics — before you select the right person for the job.

Asking a personal question of a potential employee during the course of an interview or assessment is generally okay if the question is relevant to the performance of the job and the environment in which the job is performed. It's what you do with the answer that may get you into trouble — that is, not offering a job because of the personal attributes may be contrary to the law if you don't pay proper attention to the inherent requirements of the job and the practicality of making adjustments to the work environment.

Personal attributes

A person mustn't be discriminated against in the offering of employment where the reason is based on personal attributes or traits such as age, race, colour, sex, religion, nationality, pregnancy, marital status, physical or mental disability, national extraction, political opinion or social origin. In some circumstances, discriminating on the basis of the person's criminal record is also unlawful.

Therefore, you should avoid any questioning and assessment of a potential employee on these traits unless you have a *genuine occupational requirement* for a person to have a particular attribute to perform the work or where a person's attribute would prevent them from performing the *inherent requirements* of the job.

Exceptions to the rule

The *genuine occupational requirement* exemption is generally limited to personal traits such as sex, race and disability and applies in specific circumstances — where you have a need, for example, to ensure authenticity in a theatrical performance and in relation to public decency. Jobs in public toilets or changing room attendants in public baths or pools are further examples.

Anti-discrimination laws recognise that it may sometimes be difficult to accommodate a person in a business where the person's disability means that he can't perform the inherent requirements of the job, or requires services or facilities in order to perform the fundamental requirements of the job that impose an unreasonable burden or hardship on the employer.

The *inherent requirements of the job* are the fundamental aspects of a job that the person must be able to perform in order to satisfy the essential objective of the job. For example, a delivery driver must be capable of acquiring a driver's licence and be physically able to see and perform all of the functions necessary to drive a vehicle. A person whose job is to answer the telephone, converse with customers and greet and direct visitors to the business in English must be sufficiently capable of communicating in this language.

Although the definition of *inherent requirements* isn't necessarily associated with the operational requirements of the business, the exemption would usually apply in circumstances consistent with the operational requirements of a business. For instance, a person who has young children or a dependent grandparent who requires daily care may not be able to meet the inherent requirements of a commercial sales job. Frequent travel may be both an operational imperative and fundamental requirement for the performance of the role, and this would entitle you as an employer to refuse that person the job because of the inability to meet the requirements.

Be aware that the inherent requirements of the job exemption only apply where the required facilities, adjustments or services that would enable the person to perform the job would impose an unreasonable burden or hardship on the business. Each particular circumstance must be considered on its merits. General exemptions don't apply.

Reasonable adjustments to the workplace

Some disabilities may be obvious so don't be shy to ask about them — you're obliged to consider whether the person could be employed (all other things being equal) were you to make reasonable adjustments to the workplace to accommodate the disability.

Make sure you enquire in a manner that's sensitive and raised in the context of the work environment and job expectations. The question itself isn't discriminatory. What you do with the information — that is, your decision regarding the employment of this person — is what's important. Therefore, before you make a decision to either employ or not employ a person who has disclosed personal health information that will affect her capacity to perform the job, ask yourself: '*Am I able to make any reasonable adjustments to the job or the workplace that would enable the person to perform the role?*'

What constitutes a *reasonable adjustment* has no fixed rules, but may include the installation of a wheelchair ramp, adjustment of the hours of work, or purchase of specialised equipment. What's required will depend upon the circumstances of the individual person who has applied for a job in your business.

You're expected to have made a reasonable effort to inform yourself of measures that can be taken to adjust the workplace to accommodate employees with disabilities.

A Fit and Proper Person

When you employee a person, you take on the whole package. In this modern working world you can't reasonably require employees to leave their family life and other problems at home. Therefore, you're entitled to know a bit more about candidates than just whether they can perform the selection criteria, before you decide to employ them.

Health issues

Finding a balance between the need to know about prospective employees' state of health and their right to privacy can be difficult. This information is both personal and sensitive and is subject to national privacy laws. Countered against this is the duty to ensure the health, safety and welfare of all the people who work in your business.

So how can you resolve this conundrum?

Genuine occupational requirements allow you to exclude people who don't possess attributes specific to the performance of the job or environment in which the job is located or performed (refer to the preceding section for more on this). Therefore, questions on candidates' state of health may be asked in some circumstances. For example, the fitness level of a personal trainer employed at a gym.

Secondly, you may invite prospective employees to disclose to you any illness, injuries or disability that may inhibit their capacity to perform the job. You can even place a section on an application form for the person to complete before they're interviewed. However, you must let them know before they fill out the form the purpose of acquiring the information and that it won't be disclosed to anyone for any other purpose.

Figure 3-4 shows a sample application form with space for answering the question.

Candidates don't have to disclose personal health information to you (that is, they can choose not to give you any information about their health at all). However, if they choose not to do so, you may take the failure to disclose into account in deciding upon the person that you select for the job.

Do you have a pre-existing injury or illness that may be affected by the nature of work involved in the position that you have applied for? ☐ Yes ☐ No

If the answer is YES, what is that pre-existing injury or illness?

_____

_____

_____

Please note that failing to notify or hiding a pre-existing injury that might be affected by the nature of the proposed employment could result in that injury not being eligible for future compensation claims and may result in your employment being terminated.

Figure 3-4:
Pre-existing injuries or illness question on a typical application form.

Criminal record checks

If you really want to know whether a potential employee has been convicted in the past of a criminal offence, you need to adhere to a few rules.

Firstly, denying employment to a person on the basis of her criminal record is acceptable as long as the criminal conviction is for an offence that's relevant to the nature of the job that you're advertising. Denying a person a job because he has a criminal record per se is not acceptable.

Discrimination on the grounds of an *irrelevant criminal record* is unlawful in the Northern Territory and Tasmania, while discrimination on the grounds of a *spent conviction* (that is, a reasonable period of time has elapsed without further conviction) is unlawful in Western Australia and the Australian Capital Territory.

Both the Northern Territory and Tasmanian anti-discrimination laws recognise that the offence for which the person was convicted may, in some circumstances, be directly relevant to the performance of the job and, therefore, the person may be denied the job for that reason. Each of these laws also includes a specific exemption with respect to discrimination in relation to the education, training or care of children.

In both Tasmania and the Northern Territory, a variety of legal remedies are available if a finding of discrimination is made, including issuing an order to not repeat the conduct, to pay compensation or to take specific action such as re-employing a person.

The states other than Tasmania and Western Australia distinguish between 'unlawful' discrimination and conduct that carries no real or practical sanction. Explaining what this distinction means would get me into the kind of legal jargon and obfuscation that is beyond the scope of this book.

Even if your business is outside Tasmania, Western Australia, the Australian Capital Territory and the Northern Territory, follow this general rule when deciding whether to investigate a person's criminal record: Check the record if the nature of the job necessitates hiring a person without a criminal record.

Examples of jobs where conducting a criminal history check is worthwhile (and, in some instances, mandatory) are bookkeepers, childcare workers, coaches for children's sporting teams, and personal care workers for older or disabled persons.

Criminal records are kept by police services in each state and territory in Australia, and you can request a criminal history check with the consent of the person being considered. The police can issue a National Police Certificate that will provide information searched on every database throughout Australia.

If you do receive information from a police check that shows a conviction, you still have an important issue to address before you reach any final conclusion as to the suitability of the person for your business. Is the criminal record relevant to the job that you're offering? For example, a person convicted of fraud or dishonestly isn't going to be a suitable bookkeeper for your business. However, a drunk and disorderly offence committed while on schoolies week when the person was 18 years old may not seriously exclude the person from becoming your office cleaner or food and beverage attendant. Every case depends upon the individual circumstances.

Part II

Getting the Ground Rules and Paperwork for Hiring Right

Total Employment Cost Calculation Sheet - Tasty Catering Pty Ltd

EMPLOYEE DETAILS

Employee Name	Jimmy Waitstaff
Address	1 Super Highway Hipsterville VIC Australia
Date of birth	1-Jul-95
Tax File Number	111 222 444
Superannuation Fund	Super Delicious Employees Industry Fund
Date of Commencement	1-Jul-14

Position and Award

Occupation	Food & Beverage Attendant
Award	Hospitality Industry (General) Award 2010
Classification	Level 2 (Food & Beverage Attendent Grade 2)
Status	Part-time

Wages, Loadings, Penalties Overtime	Award clause	Award Rate	Weekly Hours	Weekly Wages
Adult Minimum Hourly Wage	cl 20.1	$17.05		
% Adult Rate (Junior)	cl 20.5	70%		
Casual Loading	cl 13.1	0%		
Ordinary Hourly Wage		$11.94	0	$0.00
Penalties				
M-F 7pm - Midnight	cl 32.3	$13.13	5	$65.64
M-F Midnight - 7am	cl 32.3	$13.73		
Saturday	cl 32.1	$14.92	10	$149.19
Sunday	cl 32.1	$20.89	10	$208.86
Public holiday	cl 32.2	$29.84		$0.00
Sub-Total			25	$423.69

Allowances	Award clause	Award Rate	Frequency	Amount
Meal Allowance	cl 21.1 (a)	$11.45	overtime meal	
Clothing Equipment & Tools	cl 21.1 (b)	$1.55	day	
Uniform Laundry Allowance	cl 21.1 (c)	$2.05	item	
Vehicle Allowance	cl 21.1 (e)	$0.75	kilometre	
Sub-total				$0.00

Accrued Leave	NES and Award	Rate %		Amount
Annual leave	NES	7.7%		$22.97
Personal/Carer's leave	NES	3.8%		$11.34
Long Service leave	NES	1.7%		$4.98
Annual leave loading	cl 34.2	1.3%		$3.88
Sub-total				$43.17

Taxes, Levies, Charges & Other	Rate %			Amount
Workers Compensation	3.0%			$12.71
Superannuation	9.0%			$38.13
Payroll Tax	0.0%			$0.00
Uniform	1.0%			$4.24
FBT	0.0%			$0.00
Other	0.0%			$0.00
Sub-total	13.0%			$55.08

Total Employment Cost				$521.95

Check out www.dummies.com/extras/hrsmallbusinessau to find out more (free!) tips on getting the ground rules right.

In this part ...

✔ Understand the basic minimum conditions of employment —
the National Employment Standards — applicable to every
employee, from hours of work, public holidays, personal leave,
annual leave and long service. If you operate in Western
Australia, you can take note of the rules and regulations that
apply there.

✔ Learn how to identify the modern awards applicable to your
small business and the minimum wages and range of
conditions that must be observed. Understand how wages are
set and who they apply to, including penalties, casual loadings,
overtime, juniors and apprenticeships.

✔ Learn how to calculate the real cost of employing staff,
including everything from the cost of paid leave and taxes, to
superannuation and workers compensation.

✔ Use an employment contract template (found online at
www.dummies.com/go/hrsmallbusinessau) and
understand why you include particular information in it to truly
reflect the way you want the employment relationship to work
in practice.

Chapter 4

The National Employment Standards

In This Chapter

▶ Getting to know the national minimum standards of employment

▶ Understanding entitlements in Western Australia

'Hey, a rule is a rule. And . . . without rules, there's chaos.'

Cosmo Kramer, *Seinfeld*

Y ou may believe that you look after each and every one of your staff in many wonderful, thoughtful and generous ways, and I have no doubt this is true. Unfortunately, your pleadings count for zero if you don't comply with Australia's comprehensive framework of minimum wages and conditions of employment.

In this chapter, I summarise the ten National Employment Standards (NES), which help set the safety net of minimum standards of employment. These standards are essential, non-negotiable minimum employment standards to which you are duty bound to adhere. No ifs, buts or maybes! Along the way, I also provide you with some useful tips on how to apply the NES to suit both your employees and your small business.

If you operate an unincorporated small business in Western Australia, you aren't a national system employer and the NES, national minimum wage and modern awards don't apply. Instead, Western Australian state awards and minimum conditions apply to your business and your employees. I explain how to work out whether the national or the WA state system applies to your specific business and I summarise the key features of the Western Australian system of employee relations at the end of this chapter.

Understanding the Basics of National Minimum Standards

The National Employment Standards are minimum standards prescribed by Australian law in the *Fair Work Act 2009*. Colloquially known as the NES, these standards apply to national system employees and employers. National system employers include businesses that are constitutional corporations, operate in the Australian Capital or Northern territories, or Australian states that have referred their powers to make employment laws to the Australian Government, which includes Victoria, Queensland, New South Wales, South Australia and Tasmania.

The NES apply whether or not the employer and employee is covered by a modern award. They are the minimum standards that need to be met, regardless of any other awards or contracts.

Maximum hours of work

Here's how the NES apply to the maximum hours of work you can ask your employees to perform: You must not request or require an employee to work more than 38 hours in a week, unless the additional hours are reasonable. Employees may refuse to work additional hours if they are unreasonable.

Working reasonable additional hours

Additional hours are the hours of work that you would normally associate with overtime. They're normally worked in exceptional circumstances where additional work is required to complete work tasks — for example, dispatching orders for your products and services. In some circumstances, the additional hours could be worked on a more regular basis, such as where the needs of the business normally require some or all of the staff to work extra hours to manage the business. For example, a manager of a small retail or franchise business may be paid a yearly salary and expected to work during the usual business or trading hours (and in excess of the maximum weekly hours prescribed in the NES) to get the job done.

The NES allows these additional hours to be worked as long as they're *reasonable*. All of the following points are taken into account in determining whether the additional hours are reasonable:

✔ Risks to health and safety

✔ The employee's personal circumstances including family responsibilities

✔ The needs of the workplace

✔ Whether the employee is entitled to receive overtime payment, penalty rates or other compensation for the additional hours of work

✔ The notice given by the employer to work the additional hours

✔ The notice given by the employee if refusing to work the additional hours

✔ The usual pattern of work in the industry

✔ The nature of the employee's role and level of responsibility

✔ Whether the additional hours are in accordance with averaging terms under an award or agreement with the employee (see the following section for more on this)

✔ Any other relevant matters

The preceding list of considerations is quite broad, especially the last one ... *'Any other relevant matters'*. Classic legalise! In reality, complying isn't too difficult. When you want an employee to work more than 38 hours, organise it by agreement and compensate the employee by means of overtime payment, time off work or an annualised salary in excess of the minimum award or national minimum wage.

A few additional hours per week may be more common in some industries than others. Therefore, the expectation to work additional hours each week or occasionally to satisfy the operational needs of your business can be agreed up-front with little fuss when you employ staff. See Chapter 7 on the formulation of the employment contract to learn how to make these arrangements.

Averaging weekly hours of work

Averaging the normal hours of work over several weeks can smooth out the peaks and troughs in the business cycle, allowing you to engage employees in excess of 38 hours in some weeks and for fewer than 38 in the remainder. For example, I have a client who operates a small sprinkler and fire hose equipment testing business. The owner and staff conduct regular equipment and systems maintenance checks to ensure the fire fighting equipment is compliant with applicable building regulations. Because the work needs to be completed on-site over extended hours and often at various locations throughout the state, employees may work up to 44 hours in a week. This pattern of work could mean the business incurring extensive additional costs and the business owner experiencing uncertainty in the availability of staff to work those hours. In order to properly manage the additional hours, employees are provided with a combination of overtime payments and scheduled time off work to ensure that they work no more than 152 ordinary hours over 20 days every four weeks. Employees can also 'bank' some of the additional hours of work to be taken in conjunction with annual leave.

The maximum weekly hours worked may be averaged only in accordance with the terms of an applicable modern award or, if the employee isn't covered by a modern award, over a maximum period of 26 weeks. Where employee terms and conditions are regulated by a modern award, the 38 hours may be averaged over a maximum of four weeks.

Request for flexible work arrangements

Many aspects of the employment relationship can be adjusted to allow employees to work in a manner that accommodates their personal circumstances. You may happily agree to these adjustments if they also suit your business. These arrangements are described as *flexible* and may apply to any and every employee employed in your small business. The arrangements may be as novel or diverse as the circumstances affecting people's lives. However, the *flexible work arrangement* prescribed in the NES is limited to particular employees. The NES also outlines how to respond to requests for flexible work arrangements.

Applying flexible work arrangements

The NES flexible work arrangement entitlements apply to employees who

- ✔ Are parents or have responsibility for the care of a child of school age or younger (including an employee returning from parental leave)
- ✔ Have a disability
- ✔ Are carers
- ✔ Are 55 years or older
- ✔ Are experiencing domestic violence or caring for immediate family who are experiencing domestic violence

Employees returning from parental leave are the ones most likely to request flexible work arrangements under the NES. For example, employees who previously worked full-time hours may wish to return to work on part-time hours after completing their parental leave, so that they can share the caring responsibility for the new child with their partner and extended family while fulfilling the desire to continue work.

Not all employees are entitled to make a request for flexible work arrangements under the NES. Employees must have been employed for at least 12 months. If employed on a casual basis, only long-term casuals with a reasonable expectation of continuing employment may make a request.

Responding to requests for flexible work

Small-business owners have always been very good at accommodating the personal circumstances of staff in the life of their businesses. Small business pretty much wrote the manual when it comes to flexibility — it's the hallmark of this kind of business. However, arrangements have tended to be informal in nature, with little documentation (such as a formal agreement). Unfortunately, the rules of the game have changed and everything has to be in writing.

Since the NES commenced on 1 January 2010, eligible employees have been required to put requests for flexible work arrangements in writing. When an eligible employee makes the request, you have the following obligations:

- ✔ You must give the employee a written response within 21 days of the request
- ✔ You may only refuse the request on 'reasonable business grounds'
- ✔ Your reasons if you refuse the request must be provided to the employee in writing

Reasonable business grounds isn't defined within the NES, but common sense suggests this phrase means the effect the request (if agreed to) would have on the business in areas important to its success. Areas of the business to consider could include the following:

- ✔ Financial impact and the impact on efficiency, productivity and customer service
- ✔ Practicability (or impracticability) of organising work among existing staff
- ✔ Ability (or inability) to recruit a replacement employee
- ✔ Practicality (or impracticality) of the arrangements that may need to be put in place to accommodate the employee's request

The NES provide an entitlement to *request* flexible work arrangements. They don't provide a *right* to flexible work arrangements. Although employees can't appeal or challenge an employer's decision to refuse a request for flexible work arrangements, please be careful that your reasons are genuinely business related, because both Australian and state-based anti-discrimination laws may also regulate employer conduct in this area. The written reasons for refusal are part of the employment record and so may be drawn into evidence in a dispute finding its way into Australian or state anti-discrimination tribunals. See Chapter 12 for more on how Australian workplace rights and anti-discrimination laws affect small-business employment relationships and decision-making.

Parental leave

The NES provides for the following on parental leave: An employee (including a long-term casual employee) is entitled to 12 months unpaid leave in relation to the birth of a child of the employee or their spouse, or the placement of a child with the employee for adoption, as long as the employee has responsibility for care of the child. The person's partner may take 8 weeks unpaid leave concurrently with them from the date of birth or adoption of the child.

Paid Parental Leave provided by the Australian Government is a benefit entirely separate from the NES; however, it may be taken in conjunction with unpaid parental leave provided under the NES. People eligible under the Australian Government scheme are able to access up to 18 weeks of government-funded Paid Parental Leave or two weeks Dad and Partner Pay when they take time off work to care for a new child. This leave and payment is in addition to any other paid or unpaid leave, such as annual and long service leave, provided by you within 12 months of the birth or adoption of a child. Full-time, part-time, casual, seasonal, contract and self-employed workers are eligible for the Australian Government Paid Parental Leave scheme. ***Note:*** At the time of writing, the Australian Government plans to introduce a scheme of 6 months paid parental leave on the employee's full wage plus superannuation.

Details on the Australian Government Paid Parental Leave scheme can be viewed on www.humanservices.gov.au/customer/services/centrelink/parental-leave-pay.

Pregnancy is not an illness. Don't treat it as one. Nevertheless, employees who are expecting to give birth may suffer illness or other health issues that are related to the pregnancy and, therefore, you should familiarise yourself with the 'do's and don'ts' in managing pregnant employees. It likely goes without saying but I'll say it anyway . . . Refusing to employ, treating unfavourably while employed or dismissing employees for reasons that include the fact that they are pregnant is illegal. Here are some further points directly relating to discrimination and pregnancy:

✔ Employees expecting to give birth are entitled to continue working uninterrupted until at least six weeks prior to the expected date of birth.

✔ Employees expecting to give birth may work within six weeks of the expected date of birth where a medical practitioner provides a statement that the employee is fit for work.

✔ Female employees may take unpaid *special maternity leave* if they're not fit for work due to either:

• Pregnancy-related illness

• Pregnancy ending within 28 weeks of the expected date of birth otherwise than by the birth of a living child

Female employees may access paid personal/carer's leave rather than taking unpaid special maternity leave.

The period of special maternity leave is limited to the period the employee would have taken parental leave for, or a lesser amount notified to you by the employee.

✔ Female employees must be transferred to a *safe* job (if one exists) if they provide a medical certificate indicating they are fit for work but that continuing to work in the current job is inadvisable because of illness or risks arising out of the pregnancy, or hazards connected with the job. An appropriate safe job is one that has the same ordinary hours or a different number agreed by the employee.

Where no *safe job* to transfer female employees to exists, they are entitled to take paid *no safe job leave* for the period of the risk to the employee stated in the medical certificate. Employees must be paid the base rate of pay for the ordinary hours of work they would have worked if a safe job was available to be transferred into for the risk period. The risk period continues as long as the medical evidence indicates the employee is fit to work, but in these situations continuing to work in the job while pregnant is usually inadvisable. If employees haven't had at least 12 months continuous service, they may be sent on unpaid *no safe job leave*.

For further details on your and your employees' parental leave obligations, see the sidebar 'Notices, evidence and obligations while your employee is on parental leave'.

Notices, evidence and obligations while your employee is on parental leave

Here's a quick list of the parental leave obligations that apply to you and your employees:

✔ Eligible employees must give you at least ten weeks written notice of an intention to take parental leave, including the intended commencement and finishing dates.

✔ Employees must confirm the dates for the leave at least four weeks before the intended commencement date stated in the notice of intention.

✔ You may request a medical certificate confirming the expected date of birth.

✔ Pregnant employees may be required to commence leave six weeks prior to the expected date of birth.

✔ Parental leave may be extended to a maximum of 24 months by agreement. If you refuse the request for an extension, you must provide a written response detailing the reasons (although the refusal may only be due to 'reasonable business grounds').

✔ You and your employee may agree to reduce the period of leave once it has commenced.

✔ You must consult with employees while they're on parental leave when reorganising the business in a way that is going to have a significant impact on the employees' status, pay or location of work.

✔ When returning to work after a period of parental leave, employees are entitled to the job that they performed prior to the leave or, if that no longer exists, an available job that the employee is qualified and suitable for nearest in status and pay.

✔ Employees aren't generally entitled to personal/carer's leave, or compassionate leave during unpaid parental leave, with the exception of female employees that would otherwise have to take unpaid special maternity leave due to personal illness or injury.

✔ Employees' continuity of service isn't broken by unpaid parental leave, but the period isn't taken into account when calculating the total period of continuous service for annual, personal/carer's and long service leave.

Annual leave

The NES provide the following with regards to annual leave: Full- and part-time employees are entitled to four weeks annual leave per year, and regular shift workers are entitled to five weeks leave.

Accruing annual leave

Annual leave accrues progressively during a year of service according to the employee's ordinary hours of work. A simple formula to work out the period of annual leave that has been accrued by full- or part-time workers is to divide the employee's ordinary hours of work by 13.035714. For example, if employees work 38 hours in a week, they accrue 2.91 hours annual leave in that week. For regular shift workers, divide the employee's ordinary hours of work by 10.428571.

Regular shift workers are defined as such in applicable modern awards. Where employees aren't covered by a modern award, they can be defined as regular shift workers if they meet all of the following:

✔ Are employed in a business in which shifts are continuously rostered 24 hours per day and 7 days each week

✔ Are regularly rostered to work those shifts

✔ Regularly work on Sundays and public holidays

Taking annual leave

Annual leave may be taken at times agreed between you and your staff. However, you may direct staff to take annual leave if the requirement is reasonable. For example, you may close the business over Christmas and New Year and so taking leave over this period is clearly reasonable. Other periods of the year may be low trading periods and, therefore, are opportune moments to direct staff to take annual leave.

Make clear in the contract of employment the periods of the year in which annual leave must be taken. If such requirements are in writing, you shouldn't have any arguments when the time arises. See Chapter 7 for an explanation on how to include such requirements in the employment contract.

Cashing out annual leave

Sometimes, employees would rather be paid their annual leave and continue working (known as *cashing out* annual leave). Although this is a relatively recent phenomenon, possibly reflecting the modern financial pressures that people place themselves under, cashing out some annual leave may be beneficial to you as well. Doing so is an opportunity to clear part of a liability from your balance sheet.

However, annual leave may only be cashed-out in accordance with the terms provided in a modern award or enterprise agreement. In the case of employees who aren't covered by a modern award, annual leave may only be cashed out where the balance of annual leave remaining after a portion of leave has been cashed out is at least four weeks of accrued leave.

At the time of writing, modern awards don't include terms that allow cashing out of annual leave while an employee continues their employment. Therefore cashing out may only be done where an enterprise agreement is in place or where your employee isn't covered by a modern award.

You may not direct employees to cash out annual leave, and agreements to cash out annual leave must be in writing on each occasion that you and eligible employees agree to cash out a portion of annual leave. When you agree to cash out annual leave, employees must be paid at least the full amount of money they would have been paid if they had taken the leave. *Discounting* (paying less than the full amount) isn't allowed.

Personal/carer's and compassionate leave

Full-time and part-time employees are entitled to take time off work when they're ill, or when they have to care for and support immediate family members who may be ill or injured. They're also entitled to take time off where immediate family members suffer serious illness resulting in death.

The phrase *sick leave* has traditionally been used by small-business owners to describe the periods in which employees are absent due to illness or injury. The phrase *bereavement leave* has sometimes been used interchangeably with compassionate leave when referring to the time taken off work to grieve for a close companion or family member who has died. The entitlements and obligations prescribed under the title *personal/carer's and compassionate leave* incorporates all of these benefits within a standard of paid and unpaid leave that all employers must observe.

Personal/carer's leave

Personal/carer's leave accrues progressively during a year of service according to employees' ordinary hours of work. A simple formula to calculate the period of leave that has accrued is to divide full- and part-time employees' ordinary hours of work by 26.071428. For example, if employees work 38 hours in a week, they accrue 1.457 hours paid personal/carer's leave in that week.

Full-time employees are entitled to ten days paid personal/carer's leave, and can claim this entitlement in the event of any of the following:

- ✔ They are ill and unfit for work
- ✔ They are required to care and support an immediate family member who is ill or injured
- ✔ An unexpected emergency is affecting an immediate family member

Where employees don't have sufficient paid personal/carer's leave, they're entitled to take up to two days of unpaid leave on each occasion an immediate member of their family or household requires their care and support due to illness or injury or unexpected emergency.

The following are defined by the NES as *immediate* family members:

- ✔ A spouse, de facto partner, child, parent, grandparent, grandchild or sibling of the employee
- ✔ A child, parent, grandparent, grandchild or sibling of a spouse or de facto partner of the employee

Under the NES, the term *child* has the same meaning as that applied under the *Family Law Act 1975* and includes a child who has been adopted, a stepchild and adult children.

A *member of a household* isn't defined in the NES but you can surmise that it's intended to include people other than those listed as immediate family members. Importantly, a member of the household would be expected to be a close personal companion akin to an immediate family member, such as a same sex partner. In the case of carer's leave entitlements, employees must be responsible for household members' care to access the leave.

Compassionate leave

According to the NES, two days paid compassionate leave is available to full- or part-time employees when an immediate family member or a member of their household does any of the following:

- ✔ Contracts or develops a personal illness that poses a serious threat to life
- ✔ Sustains a personal injury that poses a serious threat to life
- ✔ Dies

Casual employees are entitled to two days unpaid leave.

Providing notices and evidence for personal/carer's leave

When taking personal/carer's leave (including compassionate leave), employees must notify you that they're unable to work as soon as possible. They must also inform you of the period of leave, or expected period of leave. You're entitled to request evidence that substantiates the reason for leave, such as a medical certificate from a registered medical practitioner.

The evidence that you're entitled to receive from employees notifying you of their intention to take personal/carer's leave must satisfy a reasonable person that the reasons provided for the absence are permissible. That is, the evidence genuinely indicates that employees are unable to attend work because of personal illness, caring responsibilities or the serious illness or death of an immediate member of their family or household. This normally means one of the following:

- A medical certificate from a registered medical practitioner
- A statutory declaration from the employee
- A copy of the death notice published in a metropolitan or local newspaper (online notices are acceptable)

A reasonable person wouldn't accept a note from the employee's mother (unless, of course, the employee is under the age of 18 years).

Community service leave

According to the NES, community service leave is an unspecified period of absence to perform:

- Jury service
- A voluntary emergency management activity such as volunteer fire fighting
- An activity prescribed in regulations

An employer must pay full-time or part-time employees absent on jury service their ordinary rate of pay for a maximum of ten days absence. Casual employees are not entitled to payment.

State and territory laws also apply to community service leave where they provide more beneficial entitlements than the NES in relation to eligible activities. For example, Western Australian and Victorian state laws provide for greater than ten days of paid leave while on jury service. Check with the applicable state government department for the specific period that you must continue to pay your employee.

Voluntary emergency management activity

Employees engage in a voluntary emergency management activity only if they

- Engage in an activity that involves dealing with an emergency or natural disaster.
- Engage in the activity on a voluntary basis.

✔ Are a member of, or have a member-like association with, a 'recognised emergency management body' and were requested by or on behalf of the body to engage in the activity. If no such request was made, it must be reasonable to expect that, if the circumstances had permitted the making of such a request, such a request would likely have been made.

A recognised emergency management body is

✔ A body or part of a body that has a role or function under a plan that

  • Is for coping with emergencies and/or disasters

  • Is prepared by the Commonwealth, a state or a territory

✔ A fire-fighting, civil defence or rescue body, or part of such a body

✔ Any other body, or part of a body, which substantially involves

  • Securing the safety of persons or animals in an emergency or natural disaster

  • Protecting property in an emergency or natural disaster

  • Otherwise responding to an emergency or natural disaster

Recognised emergency management bodies include the State Emergency Service (SES), Country Fire Authority (CFA) and the Royal Society for the Preventions of Cruelty to Animals (RSPCA).

Too much community service leave is never enough!

No limits exist on the amount of community service leave an employee is entitled to take. Employees may be absent from their employment

✔ For the time they're engaged in the eligible community service activity, including reasonable travelling time associated with the activity, and reasonable rest time immediately following the activity

✔ If the absence is reasonable in all the circumstances (jury service is taken to always be reasonable)

Providing notice of absence on community service leave

You don't have to approve employees' absence from employment on community service leave if employees don't provide you with notice of the absence as soon as practicable, including the period or expected period of absence. What is 'practicable' depends upon the circumstances of each case. For example, it may be practicable for employees to provide notice at the commencement of summer that they could be called to service on any day of high fire danger, but clearly impracticable to provide notice ahead of service to fight a fire that ignited in a particular district.

You may require an employee who has given notice of taking community service leave to provide evidence that would satisfy a reasonable person that the employee is entitled to the leave. (Humph ... that word again, *reasonable* — refer to the section 'Providing notices and evidence for personal/carer's leave'.)

Evidence that would satisfy a reasonable person includes a letter from a person in authority at the recognised emergency management body explaining the activities that employees would be engaged in. This would include any training activities that they would be expected to attend and the circumstances where they may be called up to participate in actual emergencies.

Long service leave

The NES doesn't actually establish a uniform national standard of long service leave. The standards do cover long service leave indirectly, by saying that employees are entitled to long service leave in accordance with the terms of applicable pre-modern awards, agreements or state legislation.

The NES vagueness makes working out the exact standard of long service applicable to your employees difficult, but don't stress — identifying the correct standard is possible.

Every state and territory in Australia has enacted laws (some dating back to the 1950s) regulating long service leave for employees working in that particular jurisdiction. Each of those laws applies to all Australian employees who don't have their terms and conditions of employment covered by a modern award.

Where your small business and employees are covered by a modern award, a pre-modern award likely would have applied to your business and it either:

- ✔ Prescribes the entitlement to long service leave
- ✔ Refers to the relevant state or territory long service leave laws

Very few pre-modern awards applicable to small business prescribe the entitlement to long service leave, and, of those that do, most provide entitlements that are consistent with the state and territory entitlements. Even fewer small businesses have enterprise agreements in place covering long service. This means, in all likelihood, the employees in your small business are covered by the relevant state and territory entitlements. Check with your state or territory long service leave scheme agency for more information.

First check whether your business is covered by a pre-modern award and whether this prescribes your employees' entitlement to long service leave before referring to the relevant laws in your state or territory (see Figure 4-1).

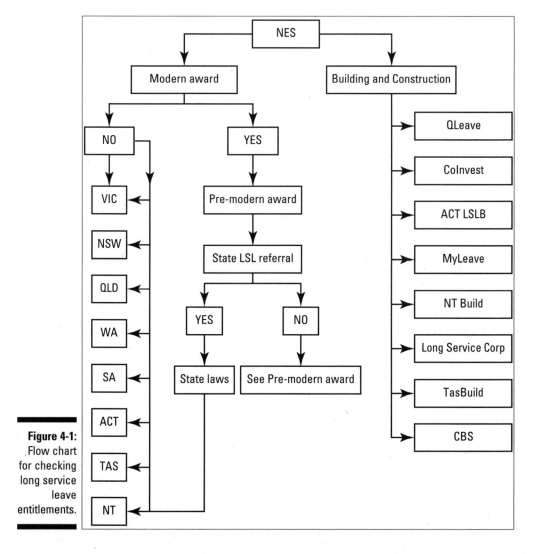

Figure 4-1:
Flow chart for checking long service leave entitlements.

Building and construction businesses have specific long service leave entitlements that need a closer look to ensure your small business complies with the law. Check with your state or territory long service leave scheme agency for more information if this applies to you. The names of the agencies are listed in Figure 4-1

See Chapter 6 for more on long service leave entitlements by state and territory.

Public holidays

Australians seem to enjoy their public holidays like no other nation on Earth. Whether it be the long weekend created by cleverly moving a holiday falling on Saturday or Sunday to the following Monday, or celebrating a horse race by giving people a paid holiday, Australians definitely embrace a day off work — especially if it's paid.

The dilemma for small business owners is that the seven-day-a-week trading cycle doesn't necessarily stop for public holidays. Restaurants, cafes, hotels, convenience stores, retail and tourist businesses are usually open for business and may actually experience their highest levels of business on these days. Ensuring that you have sufficient staff at work and covering the additional costs is the challenge faced by your small business.

Understanding the public holidays your employees are entitled to

According to the NES, your employees are entitled to be absent from work on the following days or part-days that are public holidays in the state or territory where they're employed:

- ✔ 1 January (New Year's Day)
- ✔ 26 January (Australia Day)
- ✔ Good Friday
- ✔ Easter Monday
- ✔ 25 April (ANZAC Day)
- ✔ Queen's Birthday
- ✔ 25 December (Christmas Day)
- ✔ 26 December (Boxing Day)
- ✔ Any other day, or part-day, declared or prescribed by or under a law of a state or territory to be observed generally within the state or territory, or a region of the state or territory, as a public holiday

Taking into account the additional public holidays

Each state and territory publishes the other days of the year that have been declared public holidays in addition to those national holidays listed in the preceding section, and that are observed in that state or territory. For example, in Victoria Melbourne Cup (the first Tuesday in November) is a public holiday applicable to the Melbourne metropolitan area. In Tasmania, the additional holidays are divided between the north (which gets Recreation Day) and south of the island (Hobart Regatta Day). Each state and territory celebrates Eight Hour Day or Labour Day, although the dates for this public holiday vary. Western Australia declares the first Monday in June of each year a public holiday known as Western Australia Day. Many local holidays are also observed throughout Australian rural and regional areas.

The easiest way to find out which additional public holidays apply in the place that you operate your small business is to look up the relevant state or territory government website, or go to www.fairwork.gov.au/leave/ public-holidays/pages/default.aspx, where you can access lists of them all.

Substituting public holidays

In order to satisfy our insatiable appetite for the long weekend, Australia has a unique system whereby public holidays may be substituted to another day, usually a Monday or Tuesday, in one of three ways:

- ✔ State or territory government laws allow substituting another day on which a public holiday is to be observed, such as Christmas and Boxing days. Under these laws, public holidays are observed on the substituted day unless an applicable modern award or enterprise agreement substitutes another day. Normally, state and territory laws substitute the following Monday and Tuesday for public holidays that fall on a weekend.

- ✔ Modern awards or enterprise agreements may include terms providing for an employer and employee to agree to observe a public holiday on another day. For example, the Clerks — Private Sector Award 2010 allows employers and clerical employees to agree to substitute another day for any of the public holidays listed in the NES. Other modern awards such as the Restaurant Industry Award allow the employer and the majority of employees to agree to observe the holiday on another day.

  For many small businesses that trade on public holidays these terms provide the opportunity to have employees working on the days when they're needed most. On other occasions, you may simply find substituting one or more of the public holidays to another day more convenient — for example, in conjunction with annual leave.

- ✔ An employer and employees whose employment isn't regulated by an award or enterprise agreement may agree to observe a public holiday on another day.

In recent years, some Australian state governments have declared the Monday and/or Tuesday following public holidays that fall on a weekend, such as Christmas, Boxing and New Year's days, to be *additional* public holidays rather than *substituted* days. This means that some public holidays may be observed on more than one day per year. Strange but true! For example, in 2010 when Christmas Day was observed on Saturday 25 December, the following Tuesday (28 December) was declared an additional public holiday. This also occurred when New Year's Day was observed on both Saturday 1 January and Monday 3 January 2011. Rather than substituting the public holiday, an additional day provides employees with more paid days off work than was previously the case prior to the NES, particularly if they're employed on seven-day rotating rosters. Employers who operate businesses over six or seven days must pay penalty rates for work on more days than was previously the case.

Payment for not working on public holiday

Only employees who would otherwise have worked on the public holiday are entitled to payment for the day. This means that full-time employees receive their ordinary wage for the public holiday, and part-time employees only receive an ordinary wage for the public holiday if they would have normally worked on that day. Casual employees would not normally be paid if they don't work on public holidays.

When working out whether employees are entitled to public holiday pay, look at whether they're entitled to the day off work *without loss of pay* rather than additional payment. For example, a part-time employee who works on Monday, Tuesday and Wednesday isn't entitled to additional payment for the Good Friday holiday.

Working on public holidays

You may ask an employee to work on the public holiday but the employee may refuse if the request isn't *reasonable*. The factors that may be taken into account in deciding whether a request isn't reasonable include

- ✔ The nature of the workplace (including its operational requirements) and the nature of the work performed by the employee

- ✔ The employee's personal circumstances, including family responsibilities

- ✔ Whether the employee could reasonably expect that the employer might request work on the public holiday

- ✔ Whether the employee is entitled to overtime, penalty rates or other compensation for, or a level of remuneration that reflects an expectation of, work on the public holiday

✔ The type of employment of the employee (for example, full-time, part-time, casual or shift work)

✔ The amount of notice in advance of the public holiday given by the employer when making the request

When looking at whether a refusal of a request is reasonable, the amount of notice in advance of the public holiday given by the employee when refusing the request may be taken into account, along with any other relevant matter.

When employees work on a public holiday, they're usually entitled to additional wages in the form of a penalty rate provided by an applicable modern award.

The NES prescribes the nationally recognised public holidays and the right of employees to the day off work without loss of pay. You should read the NES in conjunction with applicable modern awards and the relevant state laws to understand what other days are declared public holidays, as well as the penalty rates applicable for work performed on those public holidays.

Notice of termination of employment and redundancy

In addition to the obligations affecting termination of employment in redundancy and unfair dismissals, according to the NES, you can't terminate an employee's employment without providing the specified period of written notice or making a payment in lieu of the notice period.

Understanding notice periods required when terminating employment

Table 4-1 outlines the required notice periods, based on the employee's period of continuous service.

Table 4-1 Notice Periods Required for Termination of Employment

Employee's Period of Continuous Service*	Notice Period
Not more than 1 year	1 week
More than 1 year but fewer than 3 years	2 weeks
More than 3 years but fewer than 5 years	3 weeks
More than 5 years	4 weeks

*With the employer as at the end of the day the notice is given.

An additional one week notice is required where the employee is over 45 and has completed at least two years of continuous service with your small business at the end of the day the notice is given.

Working out when notice periods don't apply

The requirement to give notice before terminating employment doesn't apply to

- A casual employee
- An employee engaged for a specified period, task or season
- A person dismissed for serious misconduct
- A trainee

Casual employment means intermittent or irregular employment where the hours of employment aren't predictable. You don't normally have an obligation to offer continuing employment beyond the period of employment in which the casual employee has accepted work.

An employee engaged for a *specified period or task* means an employee employed under a fixed-term that can't be terminated unless a serious breach of a term of employment has occurred. Under these forms of employment, you don't need to provide notice of the end of employment because it's already specified by the nature of the arrangement. *Seasonal* employment is the same — when the season ends, the employment ends.

Serious misconduct very broadly means behaviour that's inconsistent with the continuation of the employment relationship. This includes circumstances where an employee causes serious and imminent risk to the health and safety of another person, or to the reputation or profits of your business. Examples of misconduct include:

- Assault
- Being intoxicated by alcohol or illicit drugs at work
- Fraud
- Refusing to carry out a lawful and reasonable instruction that's consistent with the nature of the employment
- Theft

Trainees are employees who have been employed to undertake work in conjunction with a formal training arrangement approved by a registered training provider. Trainees' employment is usually limited to the period of the training arrangement. For example, a person may be employed in a restaurant for the period that it takes to obtain a vocational qualification in hospitality.

Traditional apprenticeships such as electricians, plumbers, hairdressers and carpenters aren't considered training arrangements for the purpose of the exclusion from the obligation to provide notice of termination.

Making a payment in lieu of notice

If you're making a payment in lieu of notice of employment termination, your employees must be paid the full rate of pay they would have received had they worked over the period of notice. The payment must include the following:

- ✔ Allowances
- ✔ Incentive-based payments and bonuses
- ✔ Overtime and penalty rates
- ✔ Shift and annual leave loadings
- ✔ Any other separately identifiable amounts they would normally be paid

Redundancy pay

The good news is, under the NES, small business employers aren't obliged to make redundancy payments. The bad news is small business is defined quite narrowly.

Firstly, a *small business employer* means an employer who employs fewer than 15 employees excluding casual employees (unless they have been employed on a regular and systematic basis). So if you stand everyone you employ in a nice neat line and get to 14 (or fewer), congratulations — you're a small business. (Small-business concessions relating to termination of employment are covered in more detail in Chapter 17.)

Where employees aren't employed by a small-business employer, they're entitled to be paid redundancy pay by the employer if their employment is terminated in the following situations:

- ✔ At the employer's initiative because the employer no longer wants the job done by the employee to be performed by anyone, except where this is due to the ordinary and customary turnover of labour
- ✔ Because of the insolvency or bankruptcy of the employer

You're not obliged to pay redundancy pay where the employee's employment is transferred to another employer and the new employer recognises the employee's service for the purpose of redundancy.

The following employees aren't entitled to redundancy pay:

✔ Apprentices and trainees

✔ Casual employees

✔ A daily hire employee in the building and construction industry and the meat industry

✔ An employee engaged for a specified period, task or season

✔ A person dismissed for serious misconduct

✔ A weekly hire employee in the meat industry dismissed for seasonal reasons

The amount of the redundancy payment you must make equals the total amount payable to the employee for the redundancy pay period (see Table 4-2), at the employee's base rate of pay for ordinary hours of work.

Table 4-2	Redundancy Pay Period
Employee's Period of Continuous Service*	*Redundancy Pay*
At least 1 year but not more than 2 years	4 weeks
At least 2 years but not more than 3 years	6 weeks
At least 3 years but not more than 4 years	7 weeks
At least 4 years but not more than 5 years	8 weeks
At least 5 years but not more than 6 years	10 weeks
At least 6 years but not more than 7 years	11 weeks
At least 7 years but not more than 8 years	13 weeks
At least 8 years but not more than 9 years	14 weeks
At least 9 years but not more than 10 years	16 weeks
More than 10 years	12 weeks

With the employer on termination.

The amount of redundancy pay may be reduced by order of the Fair Work Commission if the employer obtains acceptable alternative employment for the employee or can't pay the amount.

Providing the Fair Work Information Statement

The Fair Work Ombudsman publishes the Fair Work Information Statement, and this must be provided to all new employees as soon as practical after they commence employment. The statement contains information on the NES, modern awards, making agreements, termination of employment, individual flexibility arrangements, the right to freedom of association and the role of the Fair Work Ombudsman.

The Fair Work Information Statement can be downloaded from the website of the Fair Work Ombudsman — www.fairwork.gov.au.

Recognising the Special Case of Western Australia

The national system of workplace relations under the *Fair Work Act 2009*, including the NES and modern awards, applies to the employees of employers that are either *constitutional corporations* or who work in a state that has *referred* its powers to make laws in respect of employee relations to the Australian federal government.

Western Australia is geographically the largest state in Australia, and its capital city of Perth is the most distant major city from the national capital of Canberra. The state prides itself on its self-reliance and independence. So it being the only Australian state that hasn't referred its powers to make employment laws is perhaps not surprising. Western Australian small businesses may be covered by either the national system or the Western Australian system of workplace relations, depending upon their legal structure.

Working out constitutional corporations

The term *constitutional corporation* is defined in the Fair Work Act as being a corporation to which paragraph 51(xx) of the Constitution applies. Section 51(xx) of the Australian Constitution allows the Australian

Parliament to make laws regulating foreign corporations, and trading and financial corporations formed within the limits of the Commonwealth of Australia.

Great, that makes it all clear ... not!

As with so many laws regulating employment arrangements in Australia, no one absolute rule determines whether a particular corporation is covered by the national workplace relations system. However, as a small-business owner trying to work within the law of the land, you can take a little comfort from the following, where I attempt to make the situation a bit clearer for you.

Your small business is either a

✔ **National system employer:** A constitutional corporation must be incorporated. (I know, pretty obvious.) Therefore, if your small business is based in Western Australia but is a Proprietary Limited (Pty Ltd) or Limited (Ltd) company, welcome to the National system of workplace relations. The *Fair Work Act 2009* regulates the employment arrangements for your small business (refer to the earlier sections in this chapter).

✔ **Western Australian system employer:** The Western Australian state system covers employers who aren't constitutional corporations and their employees. In general terms, this includes employers who are *sole traders*, and some *partnership* and *trust* arrangements. (However, if the partnership operates in conjunction with an incorporated entity, it may be covered by the national system — check with your lawyer if you think this may apply to you.) Trusts can't be employers but the beneficiaries may be employers.

Understanding the Western Australian features

The Western Australian state system is regulated by the *Industrial Relations Act 1979* and *Minimum Conditions of Employment Act 1993*. In the Western Australian state system, employees are covered by one of the following employment arrangements:

✔ 'Common-law' contracts of employment where no state award or agreement applies

✔ Registered employer–employee agreements applying to individual employees

✔ Registered industrial agreements applying to specific businesses

✔ State awards applying to certain industries and occupations

The Minimum Conditions of Employment Act provides a minimum standard of pay and conditions that underpins all of these employment arrangements.

Just like the national system, the Western Australian system of employee relations seems frequently to be under review or in transition to something else. The Western Australian Government introduced the *Labour Relations Legislation Amendment and Repeal Bill 2012* into the Western Australian Parliament in 2012 and, at the time of writing, was undertaking consultations with the Western Australian public on it. The proposed amendments to the law regulating employment arrangements in the Western Australian System that may impact on small business employers include the following:

✔ Modernising of all state private sector awards. The WA Industrial Relations Commission (the Commission) will also be required to review all state awards every four years to ensure they remain relevant.

✔ Providing that industrial agreements can only be terminated by the Commission, and extending the maximum nominal expiry date of industrial agreements to four years and enterprise orders to three years.

✔ Harmonising the unfair dismissal provisions with the *Fair Work Act 2009*.

✔ Requiring union officials to meet a 'fit and proper person' test before being issued with a right of entry permit. Unions will generally be required to give at least 24 hours written notice before entering premises, unless the entry relates to a suspected contravention of occupational safety and health laws.

✔ Streamlining the process for determining state minimum wages by removing the requirement that the Commission hold a formal hearing. When making its state minimum wage order, the Commission will be required to consider, among other things, the national minimum wage order and the capacity of employers to whom the order extends to bear the wage increase (rather than all employers in Western Australia, as is currently the case).

✔ Increasing the maximum penalties for contravention of an industrial instrument, order of the Commission or statutory minimum condition of employment.

✔ Repealing the *Minimum Conditions of Employment Act 1993* and incorporating statutory minimum conditions of employment in the state Industrial Relations Act.

✔ Prohibiting the engagement of children on unpaid trial work under the *Children and Community Services Act 2004*.

The reality of the Western Australian system is that it's not dramatically different to the national system except in relation to individual employment arrangements, which aren't allowed in the national system. As a small-business owner you need to find out whether an award applies to your business by looking to the industry coverage provisions of the state awards and the job classifications contained within the award, as you would in the national system (described in Chapter 5).

For further information on the Western Australian system, go to www.commerce.wa.gov.au/labourrelations/content/Employers/ About_IR_in_WA/index.htm.

Chapter 5

Modern Awards and Pay

. . . .

In This Chapter

▶ Understanding and applying modern awards

▶ Recognising that minimum wages are not negotiable

▶ Managing juniors, apprentices and trainees

▶ Avoiding being tripped up by transitional provisions for penalties, loadings and overtime

. . . .

*A*ustralia is unique in the world of employment regulation in that it has applied a system of state and national awards since federation in the early 1900s — but these awards are nothing like the Academy Awards. Minimum wages and conditions of employment were *awarded* to classes of employees based on either their occupation, profession or industry, and usually following protracted industrial disputes between employees and employers in industries such as manufacturing, mining, transport, shearing and meat works. The awards were given legal effect by tribunals established by governments of the day with similar status to statutory regulations or ordinances. Over time these awards evolved into comprehensive codes regulating minimum terms and conditions of employment for over half of the Australian working population. In 2010, hundreds of state and national awards were collapsed into 123 national modern awards based on uniquely defined industries and occupations.

In this chapter, I explain how to determine whether a modern award applies to some or all of your employees. I describe each element of the modern award, and how you can arrange your employment relationship with staff in a way that complies with the requirements but also suits your business. I explain the system of minimum award wages and the national minimum wage for those employees not covered by a modern award, and address the special arrangements for apprentices, trainees, juniors and people with disabilities. If that's not enough for you, I finish with coverage of the somewhat challenging transitional provisions applicable to minimum award wages, penalties and loadings.

Modern Awards and You

Okay, time to work out whether your business is covered by one or more of the employment instruments otherwise known as *modern awards*. Your task is to find out which awards may apply and get to know them, because the national minimum wage (NMW), modern awards and the National Employment Standards (NES) form the safety net of national minimum standards for your employees.

Finding out which award applies to your business

A common misconception among small-business owners is that they can choose an award to apply to their employees. I have no idea who spread this rumour but it's not true. When you employ people only two possibilities exist: A modern award applies to their terms and conditions of employment or they are *award-free*. If they're award-free, the NMW and the NES provide the minimum safety net of terms and conditions.

Here is how you find out whether a modern award covers your business and applies to your employee:

1. **Go to www.fairwork.gov.au and download a list of the modern awards from the Fair Work Ombudsman.**

2. **Identify the industry that your small business operates in (not the occupation of employees).**

   For example, if you own a retail pharmacy and you're employing a pharmacist, look for a modern award that covers pharmacies, not the professional occupation of a pharmacist.

3. **Read the Coverage clause of modern awards (not just the title of the modern award) to determine the award that covers your business.**

   This clause defines the industry and provides a clearer indication than the title of the award of whether it may cover employees. Look for this clause in the contents list of the modern award that you suspect may cover your business. Following the example of the pharmacy business, you could readily and confidently conclude from its Coverage clause that the Pharmacy Industry Award is the modern award that covers a pharmacy business.

4. **Go to the Schedule B: Classification Definitions section of the award that covers your business.**

   If a classification is listed here that accurately describes the occupation, profession or job that the employee will perform for you, this is the modern award that applies to that employee. For example, *Pharmacist, Experienced Pharmacist, Pharmacist in Charge, Pharmacy Manager, Pharmacy Student* and *Pharmacy Intern* are described in the Classification Definitions of the Pharmacy Industry Award.

5. Look up the section of the relevant modern award that provides the Minimum Weekly Wages for the classification that matches your employee's job.

Don't be surprised if the occupation, profession or job you require isn't accurately described in the modern award that covers your business. This is not a precise science and some jobs aren't adequately described.

If you can't find your required occupation, profession or job, search the coverage and classification descriptions in one or more of the occupational-based modern awards. For example, the Clerks — Private Sector Award applies only where no other industry award covers the employer, or where an industry award that covers an employer doesn't contain a clerical occupation that reflects the job of the employee. Once again using the example of the pharmacy business, the Pharmacy Industry Award doesn't describe jobs that are primarily clerical or administrative in nature within this area. For instance, a large pharmacy may employ a person to administer the payroll, process accounts and other office-based functions for the business. The Clerks — Private Sector Award covers work of that nature.

Getting to know your award

Finding the modern award applicable to your staff is one thing (see the preceding section). Understanding the terms and conditions contained within it is another thing altogether. But understanding these terms and conditions is well worth your while — so perhaps prepare yourself for a bit of late-night reading!

Modern awards impose the minimum obligations on you in relation to:

- ✔ Forms of employment
- ✔ Individual flexibility arrangements
- ✔ Minimum wages and allowances
- ✔ Overtime and penalty rates
- ✔ Procedures for consultation and dispute settlement
- ✔ Public holidays, leave and leave loadings
- ✔ Superannuation
- ✔ When work is performed

Forms of employment

In Chapter 2, I discuss the choices available when employing staff. In particular, I explain the differences between the various forms of employment such as full-time, part-time and casual employment. Modern awards add another dimension to the way in which staff may be employed and the entitlements attached to each of the forms. Although the arrangements are generally consistent across all modern awards some differences do occur due to the particular circumstances prevailing in an industry, so it is best to check the applicable modern award.

Full-time employment

Full-time employment is relatively simple — that is, an employee is engaged to work an average of 38 hours of work each week. This is the traditional standard working week for many employees in Australia and will suit most small businesses that are open for business for between five and seven days per week.

Full-time employees usually attend work on times of the day and days of the week that follow a reasonably predictable pattern over the full year. Although some variations on the theme of full-time employment are expressed in modern awards — for example, averaging of ordinary hours over two or four weeks and rostered days off work — the typical pattern is 7.6 hours per day, five days per week.

Although full-time employment is defined as an average of 38 hours per week, modern awards limit how you may allocate those full-time hours on each day and throughout the working week. Therefore, you must read the Hours of Work provisions of the applicable modern award to properly understand how full-time employment may be applied in your business.

Part-time employment

Part-time employees are engaged for fewer than full-time hours. The employment is regular and the hours of work generally predictable over the full year. Although a part-time employee works fewer hours, the employment is continuous in the same manner as full-time employment. Nevertheless, modern awards may impose limitations on the arrangement of hours of employment of part-time employees, and the circumstances of how they may be altered. For example, the Fast Food Industry Award is typical of the modern award arrangements for part-time employees — see the sidebar 'Fast Food Industry Award' for more information.

Casual employment

Casual employment isn't defined precisely or uniformly in modern awards but is commonly understood as being employment of an *intermittent* or *irregular* nature. In this form of employment, you're not normally obliged to offer continuing employment beyond the period of employment in which the casual employee has accepted work.

Fast Food Industry Award

Here's how the Fast Food Industry Award covers part-time employees:

12.1 A part-time employee is an employee who:

> *(a) works less than 38 hours per week; and*

> *(b) has reasonably predictable hours of work.*

12.2 At the time of first being employed, the employer and the part-time employee will agree, in writing, on a regular pattern of work, specifying at least:

> *the number of hours worked each day;*

> *which days of the week the employee will work;*

> *the actual starting and finishing times of each day;*

> *that any variation will be in writing;*

> *that the minimum daily engagement is three hours; and*

> *the times of taking and the duration of meal breaks.*

12.3 Any agreement to vary the regular pattern of work will be made in writing before the variation occurs.

12.4 The agreement and any variation to it will be retained by the employer and a copy given by the employer to the employee.

12.5 An employer is required to roster a part-time employee for a minimum of three consecutive hours on any shift.

12.6 An employee who does not meet the definition of a part-time employee and who is not a full-time employee will be paid as a casual employee in accordance with clause 13 — Casual employment.

12.7 A part-time employee employed under the provisions of this clause will be paid for ordinary hours worked at the rate of 1/38th of the weekly rate prescribed for the class of work performed. All time worked in excess of the hours as agreed under clause 12.2 or varied under clause 12.3 will be overtime and paid for at the rates prescribed in clause 26.2 — Overtime and penalty rates.

The inflexibility of the Fast Food Industry Award can trap unsuspecting small-business owners but with some foresight and planning you can build in the flexibility that you need for your business without compromising your legal obligations.

For example, you may initially want your part-time employee to work no more than 15 hours per week, but with improvements in business and where occasional gaps in staffing need to be filled due to absences of other staff, you may want to offer the employee more hours of employment. The problem is the modern award imposes the additional cost of overtime payments and cumbersome administrative requirements to vary the agreed hours. You may think you may as well offer the additional hours to a casual employee. However, you can build into the employment contract a contingency allowing variations to the hours of employment, as and when the needs of the business change. In other words, you and your employee agree in advance that the part-time hours of work may be varied to suit the mutual interests of your business and the employee, thus satisfying the requirements of clauses 12.2 and 12.3 of the Fast Food Industry Award and not creating the requirement to pay overtime rates. See Chapter 7 for more on how you can build contingencies such as these into the employment contract.

Modern awards prescribe a loading of 25 per cent on the ordinary hourly wage in lieu of entitlements that full-time and part-time employees receive, such as annual leave, personal leave, long service leave, parental leave and contingent entitlements such as redundancy pay and notice of termination of employment.

Most modern awards provide a minimum period that a casual employee must be offered to work. For example:

✔ The Fast Food Industry Award requires three hours per day

✔ The Restaurant Industry Award requires two hours minimum engagement

✔ The General Retail Industry Award requires a minimum of three hours engaged, except for school-aged employees who work between 3 pm and 6.30 pm and where working the three hours isn't possible, either because of the operational requirements of the employer or the unavailability of the young employee.

This isn't the case of all modern awards, however — the Hair and Beauty Industry Award doesn't impose any minimum period of engagement of a casual employee.

This lack of uniformity or logical differentiation suggests checking the applicable modern award before you employ a casual employee is prudent, to ensure you understand what you're required to pay as a casual wage, and for how long.

Fixed-term and temporary employment

Many small-business owners refer to their regular full-time and part-time staff as *permanent* employees and employees engaged for a limited period of time as *fixed-term* or *temporary*. Modern awards don't refer to permanent employment, fixed-term or temporary employment. Nevertheless, you may employ people for temporary periods and those employees are entitled to the same benefits and obligations as full-time and part-time employees for the duration of their employment.

Refer to Chapter 2 for more on the differences between fixed-term employment and the more common practice of employing a person for a specified period or task, and the requirements each may impose on you.

Individual flexibility arrangements

All modern awards include a provision entitled Award Flexibility, which allows you and your employee to agree to vary the application of certain terms of the award to '... meet the genuine individual needs of the employer and individual employee'.

The objective of this provision is to allow some measure of flexibility in the employment relationship that may not otherwise be accommodated by the terms of the modern award. Where such an arrangement is made, it overrides the modern award in respect of that matter for the individual employee.

Sounds promising, but you must be careful to ensure that your employee is better off overall in comparison to the award. Failing to adhere to the requirements for making an individual flexibility agreement may render you liable for short-falls in wages or other modern award benefits. (See the sidebar 'Understanding the Award Flexibility provisions' for a full example of the arrangements.)

Understanding the Award Flexibility provisions

The following is the Award Flexibility provisions from the Clerks — Private Sector Award.

7 Award flexibility

7.1 Notwithstanding any other provision of this award, an employer and an individual employee may agree to vary the application of certain terms of this award to meet the genuine individual needs of the employer and the individual employee. The terms the employer and the individual employee may agree to vary the application of are those concerning:

    (a) arrangements for when work is performed;

    (b) overtime rates;

    (c) penalty rates;

    (d) allowances; and

    (e) leave loading.

7.2 The employer and the individual employee must have genuinely made the agreement without coercion or duress. An agreement under this clause can only be entered into after the individual employee has commenced employment with the employer.

7.3 The agreement between the employer and the individual employee must:

    (a) be confined to a variation in the application of one or more of the terms listed in clause 7.1; and

    (b) result in the employee being better off overall at the time the agreement is made than the employee would have been if no individual flexibility agreement had been agreed to.

7.4 The agreement between the employer and the individual employee must also:

    (a) be in writing, name the parties to the agreement and be signed by the employer and the individual employee and, if the employee is under 18 years of age, the employee's parent or guardian;

    (b) state each term of this award that the employer and the individual employee have agreed to vary;

    (c) detail how the application of each term has been varied by agreement between the employer and the individual employee;

(continued)

(continued)

(d) detail how the agreement results in the individual employee being better off overall in relation to the individual employee's terms and conditions of employment; and

(e) state the date the agreement commences to operate.

7.5 The employer must give the individual employee a copy of the agreement and keep the agreement as a time and wages record.

7.6 Except as provided in clause (a) the agreement must not require the approval or consent of a person other than the employer and the individual employee.

7.7 An employer seeking to enter into an agreement must provide a written proposal to the employee. Where the employee's understanding of written English is limited the employer must take measures, including translation into an appropriate language, to ensure the employee understands the proposal.

7.8 The agreement may be terminated:

(a) by the employer or the individual employee giving 13 weeks' notice of termination, in writing, to the other party and the agreement ceasing to operate at the end of the notice period; or

(b) at any time, by written agreement between the employer and the individual employee.

Note: If any of the requirements of s.144(4), which are reflected in the requirements of this clause, are not met, then the agreement may be terminated by either the employee or the employer, giving written notice of not more than 28 days (see s.145 of the Fair Work Act 2009 (Cth))

7.9 The right to make an agreement pursuant to this clause is in addition to, and is not intended to otherwise affect, any provision for an agreement between an employer and an individual employee contained in any other term of this award.

The Award Flexibility provisions mean you can vary the application of the modern award in limited circumstances — but only where this arrangement means your employee is better off overall than if you applied the modern award provisions. (So the provisions are perhaps not as promising as they first seemed.) Your business interests are secondary to the employee. Nevertheless the two sets of interests don't have to be incompatible. Your challenge is to find a means to satisfy your business interests and also benefit the employee, if you wish to have an effective individual flexibility arrangement (IFA).

Here are a couple of ways that might suit your employee and your business:

- ✔ **Rolling up award allowances, overtime and leave loading benefits in the total salary paid to the employee to cover the periods such entitlements might accrue over the year.** In this scenario, the employee receives the benefit of the payments in advance of the event and you're able to spread the payments over the full year, benefiting your cash flow.

> ✔ **Allowing your employee to make up for time off work spent attending occasional family related activities.** This allows employees to attend activities such as school sports days, volunteering and the like, and means employees receive a really good family friendly benefit. They then make up the time that they're absent during other times of the day or days of the week, without payment of penalties or overtime.

If you make an IFA with your employee, you may agree to terminate it when it no longer suits you. Alternatively, you or your employee may provide notice to the other person that the arrangement will terminate. On the expiry of the notice period, the conditions of employment covered by the IFA will revert to the modern award provision.

Holidays, leave and leave loading

Public holidays, annual leave, personal carer's leave, compassionate leave, long service leave, community service leave and parental leave are generally covered by the NES (refer to Chapter 4), but modern awards may include provisions in relation to annual, personal/carer's, and community service leave that also apply to your employees. The modern award provisions are designed to complement the NES provisions and, as such, generally provide additional benefits or new obligations, or otherwise explain how and to whom the benefits are applied. For example, modern awards may provide details of the following:

> ✔ Allowances so employers can direct employees to take leave during shutdowns of the business
>
> ✔ Annual leave loading
>
> ✔ Definitions for shift workers eligible for additional annual leave
>
> ✔ Penalty payments for work performed on public holidays
>
> ✔ Reimbursement of annual leave where the employee is ill
>
> ✔ Substitution of public holidays to alternative days

Other types of leave may also be provided, such as Aboriginal and Torres Strait Islander cultural leave, that aren't covered in the NES.

When work is performed

While the NES prescribes the maximum number of ordinary hours of work that employees may be asked to work each week, modern awards prescribe the manner in which those hours may be worked. These arrangements vary across modern awards, depending upon the nature of the industry that is covered. (See the sidebar 'Understanding hours of work provisions' for an example from one modern award.)

Understanding hours of work provisions

Here's how the Clerks — Private Sector Award covers how hours may be worked for those doing office-based work:

25.1 Weekly hours of work — day workers

(a) The ordinary hours of work for day workers are to be an average of 38 per week but not exceeding 152 hours in 28 days, or an average of 38 over the period of an agreed roster cycle.

(b) The ordinary hours of work may be worked from 7.00 am to 7.00 pm Monday to Friday and from 7.00 am to 12.30 pm Saturday. Provided that where an employee works in association with other classes of employees who work ordinary hours outside the spread prescribed by this clause, the hours during which ordinary hours may be worked are as prescribed by the modern award applying to the majority of the employees in the workplace.

(c) Not more than 10 hours exclusive of meal breaks (except if paid for at over-time rates) are to be worked in any one day.

Whereas the Fast Food Industry Award recognises the seven-days-per-week trading typical of the industry, as follows:

25. Hours of work

25.1 This clause does not operate to limit or increase or in any way alter the trading hours of any employer as determined by the relevant State or Territory legislation.

25.2 Ordinary hours

(a) The ordinary hours of work are an average of 38 per week over a period of no more than four weeks.

(b) Hours of work on any day will be con-tinuous, except for rest pauses and meal breaks.

25.3 Maximum hours on a day

An employee may be rostered to work up to a maximum of 11 ordinary hours on any day.

25.4 38 hour week rosters

A full-time employee will be rostered for an average of 38 hours per week, worked in any of the following forms:

(a) 38 hours in one week;

(b) 76 hours in two consecutive weeks;

(c) 114 hours in three consecutive weeks; or

(d) 152 hours in four consecutive weeks.

The hours of work arrangements in modern awards provide a framework within which you can employ staff to meet the operational needs of your business. Staff can be employed outside the arrangement of ordinary hours; however, such work costs you more in the form of overtime payments and penalty rates.

Consulting with your staff about changes to the business

Generally, two types of changes can occur in a small business:

- ✔ Changes to improve the business
- ✔ Changes to save the business

No matter what the reason, all modern awards impose an obligation on employers to consult and share information with employees where a definite decision has been made to introduce changes in production, program, organisation, structure or technology that are likely to have a significant effect on employees.

In modern awards, changes that have *significant* effects include:

- ✔ Alteration of the hours of work
- ✔ Creation of the need for retraining
- ✔ Major changes in the composition, operation or size of your workforce, or in the skills required
- ✔ Reduction of job opportunities, promotions or job tenure
- ✔ Transfer of employees to another work location and the restructure of jobs
- ✔ Termination of employment

Just about every operational decision is covered by the duty to consult.

Changes to improve the business and changes to save the business always include changes of the nature of those outlined in the preceding list. Therefore, the consultation will sometimes include good news for your employees and sometimes not so good news. Although the duty to consult may seem like an annoying intrusion into the way in which you run your business, the impact is generally benign and, if handled well, positive for the business.

As a small-business owner, you're well placed to share information about upcoming changes with your employees by talking directly to them and in a manner that is sensitive to their interests as well as your business.

Focus on the reason for the introduction of the change to your business and, in particular, explain how the change is either necessary to ensure the survival of the business, or will benefit the business and improve employee opportunities. You don't have to divulge commercially sensitive or confidential information about the business. If the actual impact on employees is positive, celebrate the benefits of the change. If the impact is not positive, be honest and treat the employee or employees affected with respect and dignity. They will generally return the compliment.

Resolving employment disputes

No matter hard you try to keep all your staff happy, conflict can occur. One source of conflict is the terms and conditions of employment provided under a modern award and the NES.

The resolution of disputes between you and your employees about matters arising under a modern award or the NES — that is, their basic terms and conditions of employment — can be a highly emotional journey for you and your employees. Small business is by its very nature a very personal affair and where conflict occurs it takes a lot of patience, maturity and respect to resolve it satisfactorily.

Try to resolve grievances quickly and amicably. To help things along, encourage employees to bring any issues to you without fear or favour, and work to encourage trust and confidence that you will deal with problems objectively and honestly. The issues may seem trivial to you or even plain annoying, but you must treat every grievance seriously and act to resolve them objectively. If you made a mistake, admit it and rectify it. If you believe the employee is wrong, be honest but measured.

Every modern award includes a procedure where such a conflict, if not resolved at the workplace, may be escalated to the Fair Work Commission.

The Fair Work Commission can't impose a resolution on you (unless you agree in advance to allow it to arbitrate) but it normally attempts to mediate or conciliate a resolution acceptable to you and your employee.

The Fair Work Commission will notify you if it has received a complaint from an employee and will arrange for a conference between you, your employee and representatives, usually within a couple of weeks of the filing of the complaint. You must attend the conference and must not penalise or adversely treat the employee for having made a complaint.

Superannuation

Mandatory superannuation contributions are regulated by the *Superannuation Guarantee (Administration) Act 1992*, the *Superannuation Charge Act 1992*, the *Superannuation Industry (Supervision) Act 1993* and the *Superannuation (Resolution of Complaints) Act 1993*. Over 20 separate overriding laws regulate superannuation in Australia.

Notwithstanding the comprehensive coverage of the subject in legislation, modern awards also impose limitations on your choice of superannuation fund where employees fail to nominate their choice of fund to receive the mandatory contributions. Where employees haven't nominated a fund, modern awards generally provide that the contributions must be made into a fund listed in the modern award.

See Chapter 6 for more detail on your superannuation obligations and the cost to your small business.

Minimum Wages, Allowances, Penalties and Loadings

I'm sometimes asked to explain to employers how minimum wages in Australia are determined. Putting aside the yearly ritual determining a single national minimum wage (NMW) known as the annual wage review, minimum wages in modern awards have been established using a loosely interrelated hierarchical structure of pay rates based on an arbitrary and somewhat eclectic view of the value of work performed by employees who are covered by modern awards.

The aim of Australia's minimum wage system in the dim dark days of yore was to control wage-fuelled inflation through a system where award covered jobs were paid no more than another job of equivalent value, no matter what industry or occupation in which the work was performed. The system of Australian modern award minimum wages is the successor of that system, and has largely retained the same underlying objective and philosophy.

Modern award minimum wages

In Australia, 123 modern awards cover a broad range of industries and occupations. Each of these awards provides a minimum wage structure that matches jobs to a minimum weekly, hourly or yearly wage. If you can match the job performed by your employees to the correct modern award classification, you can find and apply the correct minimum wage to that employee.

You can always pay employees more than the minimum wage, but must not pay less than the wage prescribed for the job that matches the job performed by those employees.

Some modern awards prescribe multiple pay points within each wage classification, reflecting the acquisition and application of new or enhanced skills as employees continue their employment in that job. Where a wage classification in a modern award that applies to your employee has multiple pay points, your employees are eligible for progression to the higher pay points only where they have completed 12 months of continuous service in that classification level and have satisfactorily demonstrated their competence in the job.

How you can assess competence is covered in Chapter 9, when I examine the wage–work bargain, including how performance standards are established, applied and measured.

The key lesson for you as a small-business employer is not to waste your time trying to understand the full workings of the minimum wage system and why it was put in place in the way it was. The system is a product of a range of social, economic and political antecedents. Learning how to identify the modern award that covers your business and the classification description that applies to your employees is the skill that will help you comply with the law and save you money in the long term.

National minimum wage

The national minimum wage (NMW) applies to employees not covered by modern awards or enterprise agreements. A minimum wage is in place for adults, juniors, apprentices and trainees as well as employees with a disability. Minimum wages are set and reviewed by the Fair Work Commission and apply from the nearest pay period commencing on or immediately after 1 July each year. For example, the NMW applicable from 1 July 2013 is as shown in Table 5-1.

Table 5-1	National Minimum Wage by Category for 2013	
Category	*Subcategory*	*National Minimum Wage (per hour)*
Adults		$16.37
Juniors	Under 16 years of age	$6.03
	At 16 years of age	$7.74
	At 17 years of age	$9.46
	At 18 years of age	$11.18
	At 19 years of age	$13.51
	At 20 years of age	$16.00
Apprentices	Year 1 of apprenticeship	$10.49
	Year 2 of apprenticeship	$12.39
	Year 3 of apprenticeship	$15.25
	Year 4 of apprenticeship	$18.11

Source: Fair Work Ombudsman (www.fairwork.gov.au).

Employees with disabilities

People with physical, mental or intellectual disabilities may be in receipt of a disability pension but still may wish to participate in employment. In some cases, the disability limits their capacity to perform a job as competently as an employee without a disability. All modern awards provide a method for assessing the capacity of employees with a recognised disability and setting the minimum wage for these employees. This capacity is known as the supported wage system.

Two special national minimum wages are also applicable to employees with a disability whose terms and conditions of employment are not covered by an award or agreement, as follows:

- ✔ **Special national minimum wage 1** is for employees whose disability doesn't inhibit their capacity to perform their job. They must be paid at least the equivalent of the NMW applicable to a person without a disability.

- ✔ **Special national minimum wage 2** is for employees with a disability that does inhibit or limit their capacity to perform their job. Such employees are paid a percentage of the special national minimum wage 1 based on an assessment of their productive capacity. For example, someone with a capacity of 80 per cent would get 80 per cent of special national minimum wage 1 (that is, at least 80 per cent of $16.37 per hour for 2013).

Small businesses are great employers of people from all walks of life and most are ready to give people a go as long as they seem keen and willing. If you wish to employ a person who has a disability, even for a few hours each week, undertaking a *Job Capacity Assessment* before you agree to employ the person is a good way to accommodate the person's desire for work and your need for an employee. Job Capacity Assessments are undertaken by organisations accredited by the Australian Department of Education, Employment and Workplace Relations. Job Access has been established to assist people with disabilities to enter and stay in the workforce, and its website is a great place to start finding out more (jobaccess.gov.au/Home/Home.aspx).

Allowances

Monetary allowances in a modern award fall into three categories:

- ✔ Allowances paid to compensate areas of work considered difficult, dirty, noxious, or that otherwise cause employees some discomfort associated with the nature of the industry

- ✔ Recognition of specialist qualifications and application of valuable expertise
- ✔ Reimbursement of expense-related activities undertaken in the course of performing work, such as travel and meal allowances

All modern awards provide allowances that must be paid to employees where they incur expenses in the course of performing work for their employer. For example, where employees are asked by their employer to use their own private motor vehicle to deliver goods and services, they are entitled to reimbursement of the expense incurred by payment of an allowance linked to the distance in kilometres travelled.

The key to understanding when an employee is entitled to an allowance is that the expense must be incurred in the course of performing work on behalf of the employer. Travelling to and from work from home, for example, doesn't attract the entitlement to an allowance.

Allowances that are paid to compensate for an area of work considered difficult, dirty or noxious, or that otherwise causes some discomfort associated with the nature of the industry, normally appear in modern awards where the work covered is physical or performed outdoors, such as the building and construction industry, electrical and plumbing trades, mining, and in parts of the health industry. Allowances are paid for wet work, cold work, hot work, dirty work, work underground, above ground or in confined spaces, remote work, toxic substances handling, furnace work, work with bitumen, stonemasonry, bagging, plastering, slushing and many more.

Industry allowances paid as compensation for the nature of the required work are normally treated as income and are often applied for *all* purposes — such as annual leave payments. If an allowance applies to your employees, check the applicable modern award to find out whether the allowance is paid in addition to the ordinary weekly wage and whether it applies during periods of annual and personal leave.

Allowances recognising employees' qualifications or application of some special skill are also paid and treated as income for all purposes such as annual leave and personal leave. Check the applicable award to identify the specific qualifications and skills that are recognised and paid as allowances in addition to the ordinary minimum wage.

Recognition of qualifications or application of special skill allowances can take various forms in the modern awards. For example, the Hair and Beauty Industry Award provides an allowance for employees who perform a managerial role for one week or more during the course of their employment. An employee who is required to occasionally interpret for patients of a non-English speaking background in a health service is entitled to an allowance under the Health Professionals and Support Services Award. The Building and Construction On-site Award has multiple allowances recognising the application of specific skills and functions. Check the Allowances section of the applicable modern awards to determine the eligibility of your employees.

Shift loading, penalty rates, casual loadings and overtime

All employers struggle with the idea that they must pay loadings, penalties and overtime for work performed at different times of the day and week, especially if those times and days are the main trading periods. Small-business owners are no different. However, these sorts of payments must be paid — in this section, I explain when and how obligations arise.

You can absorb loadings, penalties and overtime in the actual wage or salary paid to your employees if this suits you and your employee. This can be done as long as the wage or salary sufficiently accounts for the amount the employee would have received in the form of minimum wage, allowances, penalties, loadings and overtime. This idea of *rolling-up* or *setting-off* award allowances, overtime and leave loading benefits in the total salary paid to the employee isn't a new concept, but does need careful attention in case you find yourself faced with a bill from the regulatory agency to make up short falls in award entitlements. See Chapter 7 for an explanation of how rolling up payments such as loadings and penalties in the total salary may be included in the employment contract.

Penalty rates and shift loadings

Any employee covered by a modern award who works outside of the traditional nine to five and Monday to Friday is more than likely entitled to a shift loading, penalty rate or overtime payment in addition to the ordinary wage. How much the employee is entitled to and the precise hours in which the additional payments occur depend upon the applicable modern award.

Penalty rates are usually expressed as a percentage of the ordinary hourly wage and are designed to compensate employees for working 'unsociable' hours of work, such as early mornings, evenings, weekends and public holidays.

Shift loadings are also paid to compensate for unsociable hours of work and are normally paid to employees who are engaged on fixed or rotating shifts over seven days per week. For example, nurses and other staff in public hospitals are paid shift loadings for working afternoon and night shifts. Shifts are also common in manufacturing businesses.

Sometimes the shift loading details appear in a modern award under another title such as 'Other penalty'. The Hospitality Industry Award is an example of this — in this award, the shift loading is normally paid (when required) during Monday to Friday and penalties are paid in substitution of the loading on weekends and public holidays.

Casual loadings

Casual employees are entitled to 25 per cent loading on the applicable minimum wage during ordinary hours, but this may vary where they are also eligible for shift or penalty rates depending on the applicable modern awards.

The casual loading is usually applied to the ordinary hourly rate and added to the penalty or shift loading that's also calculated on the ordinary hourly rate (not the loaded casual rate). This is because the loading is paid in lieu of leave entitlements, notice of termination and insecurity of employment.

So a casual working hours that required penalty rate payments would be paid as follows:

Ordinary rate + Casual loading + Penalty rate = Casual rate of pay

However, you need to check the modern award covering your business, because the arrangements aren't uniform across industries (refer to the section 'Finding out which award applies to your business', earlier in this chapter, to find your relevant award).

Overtime payments

You must pay your employees for all of the hours of work that they perform for your business, including the *reasonable additional hours* that they perform in excess of the maximum ordinary hours per week. The fundamental question for you as the employer is: How much do you need to pay?

Overtime is the period in which work is performed by an employee in addition to the ordinary daily or weekly hours of employment. The maximum ordinary hours of work that an employee may be required to attend work is an average of 38 hours per week, plus reasonable additional hours.

Overtime payments (for example, 150 per cent of the ordinary wage) only apply where the employee has worked overtime that has been approved by you and where a modern award applicable to the employee says you must pay overtime. Employees who are award-free aren't entitled to overtime payments and the ordinary wage would apply (unless overtime payment is provided in the employment contract).

Most modern awards require overtime payment of 150 per cent of the ordinary wage for the first two hours and double time thereafter. Each day stands alone and, therefore, two hours overtime on two days in a week are paid at 150 per cent of the ordinary rate and not double time on the second day.

Time off work in lieu of overtime payment (TOIL) is a common method used by businesses to minimise the cost of employing staff beyond their normal or ordinary hours of employment. Most modern awards allow you and your employee to agree to TOIL but make sure you check each particular modern award that relates to your business before making such an arrangement with staff.

Juniors, Apprentices and Trainees

Our national system of employment regulation recognises that some employees must be treated differently due to the nature of the employment and/or the vulnerability or special circumstances of that class of person. Young persons or juniors — that is, employees who are under the age of 21 years, employees undertaking a traditional apprenticeship or undergoing formal training to obtain a vocational qualification — are classes of employees who have terms and conditions that are fundamentally different to the adult workforce. The differences are marked in several important areas of the employment relationship:

- ✔ Employment and training agreements
- ✔ Superannuation
- ✔ Termination of employment
- ✔ Wages

One aspect that apprentices and trainees have in common with junior employees is that they tend to be younger people. Generally, the same laws that exist for adult employees apply to young people when entering into an employment relationship, whether they're undertaking an apprenticeship, traineeship or are simply paid junior wages. However, employees under 18 years of age require a parent or guardian to sign employment contracts, IFAs and training agreements on their behalf. Important thresholds must also be met before a young person under the age of 18 years is entitled to superannuation guarantee contributions from their employer. For example, employees who are younger than 18 must be paid at least $450 per month and work at least 30 hours per week to be entitled to the super guarantee.

The important differences and characteristics of each of these classes of employee are explained in the following sections.

Juniors

Employees who are under 21 years of age and aren't undertaking an apprenticeship or traineeship in a related vocational qualification must be paid at least the minimum wages expressed as a percentage of the adult wage under an applicable modern award, or the monetary amounts prescribed in the national minimum wage for juniors. These minimum wages are a sliding scale of wages matched to the age of the junior employee and are adjusted periodically in conjunction with decisions made in the annual wage review. As an example, Table 5-2 shows the General Retail Industry Award scale of junior rates of pay.

Table 5-2	General Retail Industry Award Junior Rates
Age	*% of Weekly Rate of Pay*
Under 16 years of age	45
16 years of age	50
17 years of age	60
18 years of age	70
19 years of age	80
20 years of age	90

Current minimum wages for juniors may be ascertained from government agency websites such as www.fairwork.gov.au and www.fwc.gov.au.

Unlike apprentices and trainees (see following section), junior employees aren't excluded from the making of an application for reinstatement or compensation for unfair dismissal.

Apprentices and trainees

In the beginning (back in the 'olden days') ... apprentices were employed by master tradesmen, and they learnt their trade on the job and became fully qualified after four years of work and formal training at an accredited trades school. These plumbers, carpenters, electricians, boiler makers,

chefs, hairdressers, gardeners, butchers and the like then went out
into the workforce, usually on their own to establish their own small
businesses. Otherwise, they were free to work in their chosen field as an
employee. Meanwhile the rest of us either worked full-time or extended our
adolescence through lazy days attempting to obtain our first degree. (Ah,
those were the days!)

Then some people got the bright idea to expand vocational education and
training to every conceivable occupation and would-be profession in this
big wide brown land. They opened the opportunity to undertake training
to anyone who was already employed, as well as people wanting to obtain
a qualification before they entered the workforce. Thus traineeships are
available for occupations in every industry and forevermore shall they
grow in number and complexity. (Don't ask me who the people who had the
bright idea are. They know who they are!) In this section, I cover the basic
provisions for apprentices and trainees.

Apprentice and training wages

Apprentice wages are either provided in an applicable modern award
or, where the apprentice is award-free, the national minimum wage for
apprentices.

On the other hand, wages of employees undertaking a traineeship are
provided in the schedules of most modern awards. Where an employee is
undertaking a traineeship but isn't covered by one or other of the industry-
based modern awards, the minimum training wages provided in the
Miscellaneous Award apply by default.

Where an award applies to the apprentices or trainees, it applies to them
(subject to any express exclusions) in all other respects as if they were full-
time or part-time employees.

Termination of employment

Training agreements provide the circumstance and procedures by which
the traineeship may be terminated by either party as well as the criteria
for successful completion of the qualification. The Fair Work Act provides
the requirements to properly terminate the employment of the trainee or
apprentice.

Table 5-3 outlines which provisions of the Fair Work Act related to
termination of employment apply to apprentices and trainees.

Table 5-3	Fair Work Act Employment Termination Provisions for Apprentices and Trainees	
Fair Work Act Provision	*Apprentice*	*Trainee*
Notice of termination of employment (NES)	Yes	No (as long as the period of employment is limited to the duration of the training)
Redundancy pay (NES)	No	No (as long as the period of employment is limited to the duration of the training)
Unfair dismissal	No (as long as the period of employment is limited to the duration of the training and termination occurs at the end of the training arrangement)	No (as long as the period of employment is limited to the duration of the training and termination occurs at the end of the training arrangement)
Unlawful dismissal and general protections	Yes	Yes

All employment termination provisions for apprentices and trainees are also subject to small-business employer exclusions and special considerations in the Fair Work Act. These aspects are discussed in detail in Chapter 17.

Training agreement and employment contract

All apprentices and trainees sign traineeship agreements with their employers through an accredited Australian Apprenticeship Centre. The training agreement is usually forwarded to the relevant state training authority that has overarching responsibility for the integrity and supervision of the training system. A registered training organisation is engaged to train and assess the competency of the apprentice and trainee and issue the qualifications.

The big mistake that many employers make is to rely entirely on the training agreement to control the entire terms and conditions of employment for that apprentice or trainee. The agreement isn't designed for that purpose and it doesn't cover the other terms and conditions of employment that all apprentices and trainees are entitled during the course of their traineeship. Therefore, you're a smart employer if you complement the training agreement with an employment agreement.

The employment contract can be quite simple insofar as it can expressly refer to the training agreement as well as the other terms and conditions that apply to their employment. See Chapter 7 for an explanation of the employment contract and the template that you can use for employees undertaking traineeships.

Don't be under the misconception that when the training agreement is completed or terminated before training has been completed the employment is also automatically terminated. You must separately terminate the employment of the apprentice or trainee. The risk of not terminating the employment properly is exposure to claims of unfair dismissal, unlawful dismissal and other breaches of the law.

Transitional Provisions for Wages, Penalties and Loadings

The modern awards commenced on 1 January 2010 and replaced federal awards and state awards made prior to the Fair Work Act (or the 'pre-modern awards').

However, not all of the provisions of the modern award commenced on 1 January 2010. Where a difference exists (either higher or lower) in minimum wages, casual and part-time loadings, evening, weekend and public holiday penalties, industry and shift allowances, the modern award provisions are phased in over five years ending 1 July 2014.

The transitional provisions are described in Schedule A of each modern award. The wording can get a little dense but, in summary, the transitional provisions require you to calculate the difference between the minimum wage provided in applicable pre-modern awards and the corresponding minimum wage in the modern awards (known as the *transitional amount*). Add or subtract (depending on whether the pre-modern award is lower or higher) 20 per cent of that transitional amount each year from the modern award minimum wage while incorporating any increases granted by the Fair Work Commission. Okay, that's still pretty complicated! The transitional provisions for penalties, loadings and shift allowances are even more complex.

The good news is by the time you read this book the modern awards will be (or will almost be) fully operational and chances are you will have no need to apply transitional provisions. The bad news is employees have seven years to reclaim monies owed if underpaid during the transitional period. Therefore, working out whether you were paying your employees correctly over this period is worthwhile. This might be a job for you and your accountant or bookkeeper when you have a quiet moment (yeah, sure!).

If you need to calculate minimum wages between 1 July 2010 and 30 June 2014 the government agency responsible for enforcing the minimum wages has completed the hard work for you in most of the minimum wages affected by the transitional provisions. The transitional minimum wages are published in Pay and Conditions Guides that can be downloaded from www.fairwork.gov.au.

Chapter 6

Calculating the Real Cost of Employment

In This Chapter

▶ Understanding the cost of paying leave entitlements

▶ Working with workers compensation insurance and payroll tax

▶ Factoring in fringe benefits tax

▶ Making sure you remember superannuation

▶ Getting a little help with the employment costs ready reckoner

*I*mmediate costs, contingent liabilities, taxes, levies and superannuation charges are involved whenever you employ staff. These costs are in addition to wages, are real, and should be understood from the perspective of your business balance sheet. You can't change them, but must work out how to manage them.

In this chapter, I explain where the cost of employment happens and how it impacts on the way you administer your business and manage the people within it. I cover how paid and unpaid leave affects the cost of employment and how you can manage those costs. I list the taxes, levies, fees and charges that governments like to impose on employers whenever a person is employed and provide some insight into the traps befalling unsuspecting small business employers who don't read the fine print, especially on fringe benefits.

I also look at the system of mandatory superannuation savings that you must contribute on behalf of your employees, covering the frequency of payments and the choice of superannuation funds in the latter part of the chapter.

To make your life a whole lot easier, I also provide a simple 'Ready Reckoner' at the end of this chapter to help you calculate the cost of employing a person.

So Much Leave, They May Never Be At Work

To some employers, their staff are entitled to so much leave it feels like they're never at work (although their staff may feel the opposite). In Chapter 4 I cover the amount of paid and unpaid leave employees are actually entitled to access under the National Employment Standards. In the following sections, I outline the direct costs of paying that leave and the hidden costs in administrating the leave.

Parental leave

Two separate entitlements arise from the birth or adoption of a child to an employee, as follows:

- ✓ 12 months of *unpaid leave* in relation to the birth of a child of the employee or their spouse, or the placement of a child with the employee for adoption, as long as the employee has responsibility for care of the child.

- ✓ *Paid Parental Leave* (PPL) of 18 weeks and *Paid Dad and Partner Leave* (PDPL) of 8 weeks provided by the Australian Government (equivalent to the national minimum wage). This is a benefit under a different law from the NES. ***Note:*** At the time of writing, the Australian Government plans to increase paid parental leave to 6 months on full wage plus superannuation.

The entitlement to take parental leave in both of the preceding cases occurs concurrently. Although PPL and PDPL is funded by the Australian Government, the leave nevertheless imposes administrative costs on you because you're required to pay the benefit to the eligible person through your business payroll. The payment to you for your time is nil, zero, zip, nothing. On the upside, at least you're not obliged to pay the employee until you've actually received the funds from the Australian Government.

Employer obligations to administer the PPL and PDPL are more generally described on the Department of Human Services website (check out www.humanservices.gov.au). Visit the website for more information and contact the government agency responsible if you have further questions (your taxes pay for it, so you may as well get your money's worth!).

Unless you offer employees paid leave when they or their partners give birth or adopt a child, parental leave doesn't create any direct costs to your business. As long as employees provide the required notice of when they intend to commence leave, the only immediate cost to you is in the recruitment and payment of employees to replace them while they're away on leave.

The most obvious hidden cost is in administration for the entire period of the PPL. Of course quantifying that cost is hard. Further, if you use a bookkeeping service, the provider should be capable of adjusting your payroll accounts to ensure the payments are completed in the manner required by law.

If you administer your business's payroll yourself, you also have to correctly administer any required parental leave payments. Get on the internet and download the Australian Government's Paid Parental Leave scheme Employer Toolkit — available at `www.humanservices.gov.au/business/publications/fpr081`.

Another, less obvious, hidden cost of parental leave is the loss of productivity that can occur while attempting to train the replacement employee. A simple way to minimise the cost from the loss of productivity is to have the replacement employee commence work before the leave commences, so a handover of the work can occur. Clearly, you incur the cost of paying two people for the one job during the handover but that cost needs to be weighed against the loss of productivity and potential disruption to the business that might occur were no handover to occur. Besides, you will have to do the handover if the employee has already departed.

Annual leave

Full- and part-time employees are entitled to four weeks annual leave per year and regular shift workers are entitled to five weeks leave. This entitlement is cumulative and represents a liability of approximately 7.7 and 9.6 per cent of salary respectively.

Annual leave accrues progressively during a year of service according to the employee's ordinary hours of work. For example, if employees work 38 hours in a week, they accrue 2.91 hours annual leave in that week.

Annual leave is designed to provide employees with a paid rest from work. Therefore, the primary method to manage the liability is to ensure leave is taken every year.

The NES states that leave may be taken at times agreed between the employer and the employee, and employers must not unreasonably refuse a request to take annual leave. However, you do have options to schedule leave with the employee at times that are suitable to your small business — refer to Chapter 4 for more details.

Sometimes, employees would rather be paid their annual leave and continue working, known as *cashing out*. Chapter 4 also covers the provisions that apply to cashing out annual leave, but keep in mind that, if you are allowed to pay out your employees' annual leave, you must pay at least the full amount of money they would have been paid if they had taken the leave. Discounting is not allowed.

If employees haven't taken or cashed out their entitlement to annual leave, it must be paid out when they resign or the employment otherwise terminates. Making provision for annual leave in your bank accounts, and not just on the balance sheet, is always useful because these payments represent real money and a real cost to the business.

Personal/carer's and compassionate leave

Although personal/carer's and compassionate leave entitlements are contingent on the employee satisfying the eligibility criteria (refer to Chapter 4 for more), you have an obligation to accrue the leave progressively according to the employee's ordinary hours of work. For example, if an employee works 38 hours in a week, they accrue 1.457 hours paid personal/carer's leave in that week. This entitlement is cumulative and represents a liability of approximately 3.8 per cent of salary.

Cashing out personal/carer's leave

You and your employee may agree to cash out some of the accrued paid personal/carer's leave if the employee is covered by a modern award or enterprise agreement that allows cashing out and as long as the employee maintains a balance of at least 15 days paid leave after cashing out the leave. Employees must be paid at least the full amount of money they would have been paid if they had taken the leave.

Several problems arise with cashing out leave as a strategy to manage the liability and reduce costs. Firstly, no modern award currently allows cashing out. So you'd need to negotiate an enterprise agreement just to allow cashing out of personal/carer's leave. Secondly, the liability to pay personal/carer's leave is contingent on the employee actually being unfit for work or having to care for ill or injured immediate family members. Thirdly, the accrued liability isn't paid out on termination of employment. So why pay out an entitlement that might never be accessed? Besides, the employees may still become ill and unable to attend work.

Back-filling employees on personal/carer's leave

The common term used when employing staff to cover a vacancy due to an employee's absence on personal/carer's leave is to *back-fill* the position. Back-filling means paying double wages (one for the employee on leave and one for the replacement employee) and so is a significant cost to the business.

The most common strategy to avoid the double wages back-fill is for you or your family members to perform the job while the employee is on leave. (Assuming you can convince a family member to do you a favour and work for nothing.) While this strategy avoids the cost of another wage you should ask yourself the question: Is this really the best use of your time? In some cases, paying someone else to do the back-fill so you can focus on other things is worthwhile. The following section looks at some other options.

Planning for emergencies relating to personal/carer's leave

Depending upon the nature of your small business, a cost-effective strategy to respond to staff absences on personal/carer's leave is to reorganise the work to be performed when they return from leave — so anything non-urgent is put on hold. However, in many small businesses that's not possible — for example, in retail, hospitality and professional small businesses that rely on a daily schedule of customers or clients. Therefore, you need a plan to ensure the work is performed when staff are unexpectedly absent due to personal or family illness.

Plan 9 from Outer Space was a movie released in 1959 and voted the worst movie ever made. Produced and directed by the infamous Ed Wood Jr, the plot involved aliens invading Earth and raising the dead to take over the world. I don't know what happened to the alien's Plan 1 through 8, but Plan 9 wasn't particularly successful. Unlike the aliens in that movie you should develop a simple contingency plan to ensure the work necessary to keep your business operating successfully continues during emergencies.

Here's how to develop a contingency plan for covering staff personal leave:

1. **Identify the hazard.**

   In this case, the hazard is illness and injuries that prevent staff from attending work, such as the yearly colds and flu epidemics.

2. **Rate the consequences for the business when staff are absent due to illness or injury.**

   For example, would it be insignificant, minor, major, or catastrophic? You can rate each member of staff individually.

3. **Assess the likelihood of the risk of staff absences due to illness or injury.**

   Would it be rare, unlikely, moderately likely, likely or almost certain?

4. **Put the ratings from Steps 2 and 3 together and score the overall risk.**

   This could be low, moderate, significant or high.

5. **Tailor your contingency action plan commensurate to the level of the risk.**

Note: The strategy outlined in the preceding steps is similar to risk analysis for workplace health and safety — see Chapter 14 for more.

Your contingency action plan for covering leave should include different responses to the different contingencies that you have identified in the risk analysis. For example, you can address the risk of financial ruin to your business by investing in back-up or fully automated systems that can continue during absences of key staff. The cost of covering other absences may be addressed through spreading or rearranging work among available staff who have the skills and knowledge to perform them. Importantly, have a plan in place for the inevitable absence of staff on personal/carer's leave.

See the sidebar 'Working out a contingency plan for covering leave' for an example of how this action plan might work.

Compassionate leave

Chapter 4 covers compassionate leave entitlements. You can't plan for this type of leave and your employees can't fake it. When a family member or member of their household dies or is seriously ill, you must allow them to take the entitled paid leave and bear the cost.

Community service leave

Generally community service leave is unpaid, meaning the cost to you is your time when covering the work while the employee is absent or, in the case of a replacement employee, the wages.

Jury service is an exception to the general rule — an employer must pay a full-time or part-time employee absent on jury service their ordinary rate of pay for a maximum of ten days absence. Casual employees are not entitled to payment.

Working out a contingency plan for covering leave

Go to Hell Travel Services specialises in travel packages to extreme sporting events held in remote and often dangerous locations throughout the world. The owner employs a core staff of three who coordinate all of the marketing, sales, packaging and delivery of the travel experience to customers. When a sporting event is scheduled, the owner employs another ten casual staff to answer the phones, transact sales, physically package the travel and ticketing information and then place the packages in dispatch form ready for Australia Post to pick up and deliver.

The systems that enable all of this to occur aren't automated, nor are they documented in an operating procedures manual. The system works because the three core staff know what to do, have the contact with suppliers and are authorised to handle the

receipt and expenditure of money to operate the business.

The risk rating for absences of one or more of the three core staff is likely to be significant or high because, were one or more of them to be absent during the period leading up to an event, the consequences would be major. If all of them were absent due to illness, the consequences would likely be catastrophic. On the other hand, the risk rating for absences of the casual employees is likely to be low to moderate because they don't carry any intellectual property around in their heads.

The contingency plan to minimise the risk to Go to Hell Travel Services would be to automate the operating procedures as far as possible and document them so that anyone called in to fill the vacancies could pick the procedures up and implement them. Simple!

Refer to Chapter 4 for a full explanation of the entitlement and management of community service leave.

Long service leave

The cost of long service leave to your small business varies depending upon where your small business operates. The NES doesn't expressly provide a national standard of long service leave, but covers this type of leave indirectly — that is, employees are entitled to long service leave in accordance with the terms of applicable pre-modern awards, agreements or state legislation.

Chapter 4 provides a summary of long service leave entitlements. In this section, I cover calculating the cost of long service and what you should do to ensure that you're able to meet the obligation when the employee becomes entitled to the leave.

Making provision for long service leave

Generally, employees are entitled to long service leave of two months duration on their ordinary rate of pay after 10 years of continuous service. South Australia and the Northern Territory are more generous, with the entitlement being three months long service leave after 10 years continuous service, paid at employees' ordinary rate of pay. Additional long service leave accrues normally in five-year blocks, at the same rate as it does for the first 10 years.

Table 6-1 outlines by state or territory what elements of remuneration are considered part of employee's ordinary rate of pay.

Notwithstanding that employees are entitled to take leave after ten years, they are entitled to payment for the leave if their employment terminates before ten years. (The entitlement to payment on termination is not automatic — refer to Chapter 4 for more details.)

Whatever the entitlement to payment on termination is, understanding the cost to your business, and when that cost kicks in, is important because you need to make provision for it.

Long service leave represents 1.67 per cent of ordinary pay salary for each year of continuous service in all states and territories except South Australia and the Northern Territory, where it represents 2.5 per cent of ordinary pay salary for each year of continuous service. (***Note:*** The Australian building and construction industry is the exception to long service leave rules in both entitlements and how they administered — see the section, 'Building and construction industry exception', later in this chapter, for more details.)

You don't have to make provisions for long service leave from the first day of employment. Once staff have been employed by you for a substantial period and are likely to qualify for long service, you can begin to make provisions in the accounts (and, more importantly, the bank) for payments that will occur in the future.

The long service leave provisions you need to make depend on the state or territory your small business is based in. For example, in NSW you don't need to set aside money for an employee's long service during the first 2.5 years of their employment. During the next 2.5 years of employment, you need to put aside 1.7334 weeks pay each year to cover the amount of leave they may be entitled to if they were to leave after five years of employment. Over the next five years, you need to put aside 0.8667 weeks pay per year to cover the amount of leave that they will be able to take after 10 years continuous service.

Table 6-1	Elements of Remuneration Considered Part of Ordinary Rate of Pay							
Remuneration	*NSW*	*VIC*	*QLD*	*SA*	*TAS*	*WA*	*ACT*	*NT*
Base or award salary	Yes	Yes	Yes	Yes	Yes	Yes	Yes	Yes
Over-award payments	Yes	Yes	Yes	Yes	Yes	Yes	Yes	Yes
Allowances (skill/performance)	Yes	Yes (if part of normal rate)	Yes (if part of normal rate)	Yes	Yes	No	Yes	Yes
Allowances (disability, site, tool)	No	No	No	No	No	No	No	No
Penalty rates	No	No	No	No	Yes	No	No	No
Shift work loading	No	No	No	No	Yes	No	No	No
Overtime payments	No	No	No	No	No	No	No	No
Board and lodgings	Yes	Yes	Yes	Yes	Yes	Yes	Yes	Yes
Bonus or incentives	Yes (averaged over >12 months or 5 years)	Yes (averaged over >12 months or 5 years)	Yes (averaged over >12 months or 5 years)	No (unless part of normal wages)	No (unless part of normal wages)	Yes (averaged over 12 months)	Yes (averaged over >12 months or 5 years)	Yes
What if ordinary pay or hours is not fixed?	Receives > average of 12 months or 5 years	Receives > average of 12 months or 5 years	Receives > average of 12 months or 5 years	Receives average of 3 years	Receives average of 12 months	Receives average of ordinary hours/pay	Receives average of 12 months (PT or Casual) 5 years if FT	Receives > average of 12 months or 5 years

Table 6-2 outlines the provisions that you should make towards your long service leave liabilities, depending on the state or territory your business is based in.

	For Each Completed Full:		
State/Territory & Period of Service	*Year of Service*	*Month of Service*	*Week of Service*
NEW SOUTH WALES			
0–2.5 years	Nil	Nil	Nil
2.5–5 years	1.7334	0.1444	0.0334
5 years +	0.8667	0.0722	0.0167
VICTORIA			
0–3.5 years	Nil	Nil	Nil
3.5–7 years	1.7334	0.1444	0.3334
7 years +	0.8667	0.0722	0.0167
QUEENSLAND			
0–3.5 years	Nil	Nil	Nil
3.5–7 years	1.7334	0.1444	0.0334
7 years +	0.8667	0.0722	0.0167
WESTERN AUSTRALIA			
0–3.5 years	Nil	Nil	Nil
3.5–7 years	1.7334	0.1444	0.0334
7 years +	0.8667	0.0722	0.0167
SOUTH AUSTRALIA			
0–3.5 years	Nil	Nil	Nil
3.5–7 years	2.6	0.2166	0.0500
7 years +	1.3	0.1083	0.0250
TASMANIA			
0–3.5 years	Nil	Nil	Nil
3.5–7 years	1.7334	0.1444	0.0334
7 years +	0.8667	0.0722	0.0167
NORTHERN TERRITORY			
0–3.5 years	Nil	Nil	Nil
3.5–7 years	2.6	0.2166	0.0500
7 years +	1.3	0.1083	0.02500
ACT			
0–2.5 years	Nil	Nil	Nil
2.5–5 years	1.7334	0.1444	0.0334
5 years +	0.8667	0.0722	0.0167

Table 6-2   **Required Long Service Leave Provisions by State and Territory**

Cashing out long service leave

Many state laws prohibit the cashing out of long service leave for the obvious reason that it's designed as a paid break from work, not a bonus payment for long service. However, some exceptions to the rule exist in Queensland, Western Australia, South Australia and Tasmania. These exceptions provide a little more flexibility to manage the cost of long service leave, especially where the employee is vital to the business and would prefer to be paid rather than take the leave. Refer to Chapter 4 for more on long service leave.

Building and construction industry exception

The Australian building and construction industry is an exception to the rule of human resource management and regulation in many ways. The entitlement to long service leave and its administration is a case in point.

Building and construction employers are businesses that employ construction workers on sites, engaged in construction, erection, installation, reconstruction, re-erection, renovation, alteration, demolition or (in some limited cases) maintenance or repairs.

If your small business operates in the building and construction industry — whether as a self-employed tradesperson or sub-contractor to the industry — the following arrangements apply to your employees:

- ✔ Long service leave accrues for employees working in the building and construction industry throughout Australia based on their continuous service in the industry. Service is not tied to one employer.

- ✔ The entitlement to long service may vary and isn't necessarily the same as that for other employees in the state in which the work occurs. For example, in Victoria it is more generous than the state's general entitlement (three months after 10 years of service instead of two months).

- ✔ Employers contribute to a fund established under complementary state laws for eligible employees based on either their hours of work each month or payment of a levy tied to the cost of the construction work.

- ✔ Agencies in each state collect the levy or fee set by regulation that funds the entitlement to long service leave of employees.

As an employer you need to register with the applicable fund and make contributions in accordance with the rules of that fund. The agency will pay employees when they're eligible for long service. You don't have to make provision in your accounts.

Agencies administering the portable long service scheme for the Australian building and construction industry can be located through the following websites:

- Australian Capital Territory: www.actlslb.act.gov.au
- New South Wales: www.longservice.nsw.gov.au
- Northern Territory: www.ntbuild.com.au
- Queensland: www.qleave.qld.gov.au
- South Australia: www.cbserv.com.au
- Tasmania: www.tasbuild.com.au
- Victoria: www.coinvest.com.au/StaticContent/index.jsp
- Western Australia: www.myleave.wa.gov.au

Workers Compensation Insurance and Payroll Tax

Taxes, levies and charges on employment are the stone in the shoe of small business. Why they're imposed is beyond the scope of this book. (My advice is always try to change the things that you can control and accept the things that you can't control.) Understanding how taxes, levies and charges work, and when they apply, empowers you to organise your employment arrangements in a manner to minimise the cost.

Workers compensation

The Australian Bureau of Statistics estimates that 640,700 workers suffered a work-related injury or illness in 2009. Safe Work Australia reckons around 135,000 claims are accepted each year involving one week or more off work, a permanent incapacity or fatality.

All small-business employers must have workers compensation insurance. Each and every claim for compensation means someone has to pay for the injury. Premiums charged by your nominated workers compensation insurer are the result of these claims. Your challenge is to minimise the cost to your business of the premiums charged. As a small business, your influence may be minor but you may be able control premiums to a minor extent if you know how they're established.

Factors influencing your premium

The factors affecting your workers compensation insurance premiums may vary depending upon which state your business is operating from within. However, in general the following factors are taken into account to establish the insurance premium:

- ✔ Remuneration, including wages, salaries, superannuation and other benefits you pay to your workers

- ✔ Your industry classification and rate (these reflect the claims experience of the industry in which you operate)

- ✔ The average premiums for your industry (if you have a remuneration of $200,000 or less)

If your remuneration is over $200,000, your workers compensation insurance premium is calculated using:

- ✔ The average rate of your industry

- ✔ Your claims experience — if you perform better than your industry average, you pay less; if you perform worse, you pay more

- ✔ The size of your business, measured using your remuneration and industry rate

Your workers compensation insurance premium is subject to 10 per cent GST, which is added after the premium is calculated.

Paying the first two weeks of a claim

Normally, you're responsible for the first ten days of benefits paid to an injured employee who is off work and the first payment of medical expenses (up to a maximum payment indexed annually). You can remove the responsibility of paying this excess by taking up a buy-out option, which increases your insurance premium — for example, in Victoria this option adds 10 per cent to your workers compensation insurance premium.

Payroll tax

The Australian Government describes the nature and purpose of Payroll tax succinctly on its business.gov.au website as follows:

> *Payroll tax is a state tax on the wages you pay to employees. It's calculated on the amount of wages you pay per month. You need to pay payroll tax if your total Australian wages exceed the exemption threshold in your state or territory — this varies between states.*

Don't you just love it when one level of government (that doesn't collect the tax) describes other levels of government taxes with such brutal honesty?

Each Australian state operates its own scheme of arrangements for registration and payment of payroll tax. Rebates are offered from time to time to special categories including small business. So the calculation of the cost of payroll tax can be problematic.

Table 6-3 provides a summary of the payroll tax and the exemption thresholds applicable in the financial year 2013–14 by state or territory.

Table 6-3	Payroll Tax and Thresholds for 2013–14	
State	*Tax*	*Exemption Threshold*
NSW	5.45%	$750,000
VIC	4.9%	$550,000
QLD	4.75%	$1,100,000
WA	5.5%	$750,000
SA	4.95%	$600,000
TAS	6.1%	$1,250,000
NT	5.5%	$1,500,000
ACT	6.85%	$1,750,000

Watching out for the wages definition trap

You may have noticed that the calculation of your obligations to pay taxes, levies, charges and other payments associated with employment of staff doesn't apply a consistent definition of wages and salaries. The Australian Tax Office defines *ordinary time earnings* specifically for the Superannuation Guarantee and PAYG, and this is different to the *ordinary rate of pay* used for long service leave calculations. Workers compensation insurance premiums are calculated using a definition of *remuneration* that's different to the *remuneration* included to calculate payroll tax.

Don't fall into the trap of thinking one size fits all — that would be far too logical!

When calculating the cost of employment, including whether your business falls under statutory thresholds or qualifies for exemptions, you must apply the criteria specific to the payment, tax or levy.

Go to the applicable state revenue office for further information on your obligations to register and pay the tax or visit www.business.gov.au where all relevant links and information are provided.

Paying Fringe Benefits Tax

Have you handed out gifts to your staff lately? Maybe you paid for a holiday to a resort in Queensland. How about free meals or discounts on goods and services that you sell to the public? If you provide any of these types of benefits to staff (or other benefits), you may be liable to pay fringe benefits tax (FBT).

Explaining every aspect of the Australian fringe benefits tax system is beyond the scope of this book. However, in the following sections I can point out a few of the fundamentals and illustrate the cost to you from the tax.

Defining fringe benefits

A *fringe benefit* includes any rights, privileges or services provided by you to employees. These may include

- ✔ Allowing staff to use a work car for private purposes

- ✔ Giving a financial loan at less than the market rate

- ✔ Providing access to entertainment activities at no cost — for example, access to restaurant dining, movies, theatre and sporting events

- ✔ Reimbursing non-business related expenses incurred by employees, such as school fees, home loan mortgage repayments, weekly grocery shopping accounts or private health insurance

Fringe benefits are usually provided either as part of an agreed salary sacrifice arrangement with employees, or ad hoc to suit the often personal and informal rewards offered to employees for the valuable contribution that they make to the business.

The following are *not* fringe benefits and so not subject to FBT:

- ✔ Contributions you make to a first home saver account (FHSA) for an employee

- ✔ Employment termination payments

- ✔ Exempt benefits such as:

  - • Work-related expense items such as mobile phones, laptop computers, tools, protective clothing and footwear

  - • Car parking benefit if the total gross income of your small business for the financial year immediately before the relevant FBT year was less than $10 million and the benefit isn't provided in a commercial car park

- Taxi travel if provided to travel home from work on a single journey due to illness or late night work

- Benefits of less than $300 in value that are provided infrequently or where calculating a value is difficult because of the minor benefit to the employee

✔ Payments made by partnerships and sole traders to relatives and other associates that are deemed not to be assessable income

✔ Reimbursements you make to an employee for their personal FHSA contribution

✔ Salary or wages

✔ Share dividends

✔ Shares acquired under approved employee share schemes

✔ Superannuation contributions made by you for employees

Car fringe benefits

Private use of business-owned vehicles is a fringe benefit. If you allow your staff to drive the business car home from work each night, that trip is a taxable fringe benefit. You can calculate the taxable value of a car fringe benefit using either the statutory method or the operating cost method:

✔ **Statutory formula method:** The old progressive statutory rates have been replaced with a single statutory rate of 20 per cent, which applies regardless of the distance travelled. The taxable value of the car fringe benefit is the statutory rate multiplied by the car's base value (that is, the purchase price).

✔ **Operating cost method:** The taxable value of the car fringe benefit is a percentage of the total costs of operating the car during the fringe benefits tax (FBT) year. The percentage varies with the extent of actual private use. The lower the incidence of actual private use, the lower the taxable value.

The previous Australian Government announced changes to the calculation methods for car fringe benefits, commencing on 1 April 2014. The change proposed removes the statutory formula method for calculating FBT on both salary-sacrificed and employer-provided cars and so calculations will rely exclusively on the operating cost method. The change, if implemented, will affect salary-sacrificed and employer-provided car fringe benefits for new contracts entered into after 16 July 2013, and all car fringe benefits for new leases entered after the 16 July 2013 and existing contracts materially varied after 16 July 2013. The proposed changes won't affect existing exempt car benefit concessions that apply to certain uses of taxis, panel vans, utility vehicles and other non-car road vehicles (see Chapter 10 for more on the exempt car benefit concessions).

Unfortunately, using the operating cost method for calculating car fringe benefits means keeping detailed log book records of business and private travel over a three-month period.

Recording and reporting obligations

If you are providing fringe benefits, you must do the following:

- ✔ Calculate how much FBT you have to pay
- ✔ Keep FBT records including car travel log books
- ✔ Register for FBT
- ✔ Report fringe benefits on your employees' payment summaries and your FBT return
- ✔ Pay FBT to the Australian Tax Office

Calculating FBT

The FBT rate is 46.5 per cent of the grossed up value of the fringe benefits that you provide to employees, and paying this tax is your responsibility. In this section, I outline the Australian Tax Office's recommended procedure for calculating your FBT liability.

Working out your FBT liability isn't particularly easy. If at all unsure, ask your tax accountant or bookkeeper for help or to calculate it for you.

Here's how to calculate your FBT liability:

1. **Determine what type of fringe benefits you provide.**

   Examples could include allowing staff to use a work car for private purposes, providing access to entertainment activities at no cost or reimbursing non-business related expenses incurred by employees.

2. **Work out the taxable value of each fringe benefit you provide to each employee.**

   The rules for calculating the taxable value of a fringe benefit vary according to the type of benefit — check the ATO website (www.ato.gov.au) and with your accountant if unsure.

3. **Work out the total taxable value of all the fringe benefits you provide for which you can claim a GST credit.**

4. **Work out the total taxable value of all those benefits for which you can't claim a GST credit**

   For example, these benefits include supplies you made that were either GST-free or input-taxed.

5. **Work out the grossed-up taxable value of the benefits by multiplying the total taxable value of all the fringe benefits you can claim a GST credit for (from Step 3) by 2.0647.**

   Grossing-up means increasing the taxable value of benefits you provide to reflect the gross salary employees would have to earn at the highest marginal tax rate (including Medicare levy) to buy the benefits after paying tax.

6. **Work out the grossed-up taxable value of the remaining benefits by multiplying the total taxable value of all the fringe benefits you can't claim a GST credit for (from Step 4) by 1.8692.**

7. **Add the grossed-up amounts from Steps 5 and 6.**

   This is your total fringe benefits taxable amount.

8. **Multiply the total fringe benefits taxable amount (from Step 7) by the FBT rate (46.5 per cent).**

   This gives you the total FBT amount you're liable to pay.

Reducing your FBT liability

You can reduce your FBT liability in either of two ways.

- ✔ **Pass on the cost of FBT to the employee under a properly constructed salary sacrifice arrangement.** This means the FBT on the agreed benefits that you provide to the employee in lieu of salary is absorbed in the amount of salary sacrificed. However, FBT is set at the equivalent of the highest PAYG marginal tax rate and, therefore, except in relation to FBT-exempt benefits and vehicles employees are unlikely to see a net tax benefit from the salary sacrifice arrangement under that arrangement.

- ✔ **Only provide FBT-exempt benefits to staff.**

Refer to the section 'Defining fringe benefits' for examples of FBT-exempt benefits.

In Chapter 10, I discuss how you can construct a tax-effective salary sacrifice arrangement for your employees. For further information in relation to fringe benefits tax check out the 'Fringe benefits for small business' section of the Australian Tax Office website (www.ato.gov.au).

Don't Forget Superannuation!

A major cost of employment is mandatory superannuation contributions to compliant superannuation funds on behalf of your employees. Commencing at 9 per cent of ordinary time earnings when introduced in the 1990s, the payments will progressively increase to 12 per cent by 1 July 2019. Understanding how much super, and when and where it must be paid are the fundamentals of superannuation for small business.

How much and how often?

As an employer, you have an obligation to pay super contributions on behalf of all your eligible employees. These contributions are in addition to your employees' salaries and wages. This compulsory contribution is called the Superannuation Guarantee and it requires you to:

- ✔ Pay super for your eligible employees
- ✔ Contribute to the correct super funds
- ✔ Pay contributions by the cut-off date each quarter

Table 6-4 shows the increases to the minimum super contributions you must pay on each eligible employee's earnings base occurring over the next few years.

At the time of writing, the Australian government planned to delay the scheduled superannuation contribution increases for two years. This would mean the increase to 9.5 per cent would not occur until 1 July 2016, and the other increase would follow yearly from that date.

Table 6-4	Required Superannuation Guarantee Contributions to 2019
Year	*Super Guarantee*
1 July 2013	9.25%
1 July 2014	9.5%
1 July 2015	10%
1 July 2016	10.5%
1 July 2017	11%
1 July 2018	11.5%
1 July 2019	12%

In relation to the super guarantee, your employees' earnings base is their *ordinary times earnings*, which includes all earnings for ordinary hours of work and may include a wider range of employee payments than the wages provided under a modern award or individual contract. For example, ordinary time earnings includes

- ✔ Allowances
- ✔ Commissions
- ✔ Over-award payments
- ✔ Paid leave
- ✔ Shift loadings

Also, various elements of remuneration aren't included in ordinary time earnings for the purpose of superannuation guarantee contributions, as follows:

- ✔ Fringe benefits
- ✔ Overtime
- ✔ Termination payments
- ✔ Workers compensation payments

Exceptions and inclusions to the ordinary earnings rules

Some exceptions to the ordinary earnings rules exists, as well as some payments that you might think would be excluded but are included, as follows:

- ✔ **Annual leave payments:** Unused annual leave payments on termination are specifically excluded from the definition of ordinary time earnings and so no superannuation is payable. However, superannuation is payable on annual leave taken while employed.

- ✔ **Expense allowance:** An expense allowance paid with the expectation that it will be fully expended in producing income, such as a car allowance or travel and accommodation for sales staff, isn't considered by the Australian Tax Office to be part of ordinary time earnings and so doesn't attract superannuation.

- ✔ **Meal allowance:** A meal allowance paid during a period of overtime isn't considered ordinary time earnings.

- ✔ **Non-expense related allowances:** Allowances paid other than a reimbursement of expenses or expense allowance are considered to be part of ordinary time earnings. For example, a site allowance isn't paid as expense allowances and therefore superannuation is payable.

✔ **Overtime payments:** Overtime payments are generally excluded, but in some circumstances they may be included. Employees required under a contract of employment to regularly work in excess of the standard 38 hours per week (in other words, overtime) may be entitled to superannuation on those hours. For example, an employee who is employed to regularly work 40 hours per week and paid a salary to cover all hours is entitled to superannuation on those additional two hours because they're regular, normal or customary. On the other hand, if an employee is contracted to infrequent and unspecified 'reasonable additional hours' in excess of the standard 38 hour week, superannuation isn't paid on those hours.

✔ **Payment in lieu of notice of termination of employment:** Awards and agreements often provide that, instead of giving notice of termination, the employer may simply pay an amount equivalent to the ordinary time rate of salary or wages that the employee would have earned during the notice period — that is, payment in lieu of notice. Such payments are considered to be ordinary time earnings and, therefore, superannuation is paid in addition to the payment.

✔ **Redundancy pay:** Redundancy pay isn't considered a payment for the performance of work. It is compensation for the loss of employment and so doesn't attract superannuation.

✔ **Unfair dismissal compensation:** Payments in respect of unfair dismissal claims are to compensate an employee for the loss of employment and/or to settle a dispute in respect of the employment. Such payments don't require superannuation contributions.

✔ **Workers compensation payment:** Workers compensation payments, including top-up or make-up payments, are considered to be ordinary time earnings where some work is performed, but not if the employee does not perform any work.

Eligibility

Generally, you have to pay super for your employees if they

✔ Are aged 18 years or over

✔ Are paid $450 (before tax) or more in a calendar month

✔ Work full-time, part-time or on a casual basis

An employee under the age of 18 who works at least 30 hours per week must receive superannuation. You may also have to pay super for any employees who are visiting Australia on an eligible temporary resident visa.

As of 1 July 2013, no upper age limit exists for paying super for an employee.

An employee is anyone who receives salary or wages in return for their labour or services. For super guarantee purposes, employees may also include

- ✔ Contractors
- ✔ Directors of the business
- ✔ Family members of the employer who work in the business

Frequency of contributions

The superannuation contributions must be paid at least quarterly. The Australian Tax Office publishes the quarterly deadlines for payment into a compliant fund. If the quarterly cut-off date falls on a weekend or public holiday, you should make the payment by the next working day.

You can choose to make super payments more regularly than quarterly — for example, fortnightly or monthly — so long as the total amount you owe each quarter is paid by the quarterly cut-off dates.

Table 6-5 shows the superannuation contribution quarterly cut-off dates (current as at 28 February 2013).

Table 6-5	Superannuation Contribution Quarterly Cut-off Dates
Quarter	*Dates*
1	1 July–30 September
2	1 October–31 December
3	1 January–31 March
4	1 April–30 June

Payments must be made no later than 28 days after the end of each quarter. You can generally claim a tax deduction for super contributions you pay on time. However, if you pay late you can't claim a tax deduction for the amount you pay.

Super choice: It's an employee's right

Under Superannuation Guarantee laws, employees are entitled to choose the superannuation fund they want their employer to contribute their mandatory payments into, unless an enterprise agreement is in place that prescribes a fund or funds into which all contributions must be made. If your small business has such an enterprise agreement in place, you must comply with the requirements of that agreement. For everyone else you are required to provide a choice to your employees — see the sidebar 'Three steps to offering super choice' for more on this.

Three steps to offering super choice

You're obliged to offer employees their choice of super fund. Here's how you do so. *Note:* This information is based on the Super Choice section of the ATO website www.ato. gov.au © Australian Taxation Office for the Commonwealth of Australia.

Step 1: Identify your new eligible employees

Your employees can generally choose their super fund if they're:

✔ Employed under a modern award

✔ Employed under another award or agreement that doesn't require superannuation support

✔ Not employed under any state award or industrial agreement (including contractors paid principally for their labour)

Your employees may not be eligible under the superannuation guarantee to choose a super fund if:

✔ You pay superannuation for them under a state award or industrial agreement or under certain workplace agreements, including an Australian Workplace Agreement (AWA) and collective agreements (although choice can also be provided under these awards or agreements)

✔ They're in a particular type of defined benefit fund or they've already reached a certain level in a defined benefit fund (unlikely for most small businesses)

Step 2: Provide a Standard choice form to eligible employees

If you have new employees who are eligible to choose a super fund, you should provide them with a Standard choice form (NAT

13080) within 28 days from the day they started working for you. You can download the form from the Australian Tax Office at www. ato.gov.au/content/downloads/ SPR56761NAT13080.pdf.

Employees aren't required to complete the form if they don't want to nominate a fund, but you do have to give them the choice if they're eligible.

If your employee does not choose a fund, you must pay the superannuation contributions for that employee into the fund you have identified as your employer nominated fund (also known as the *default fund*).

If a modern award applies to your employee, your nominated default fund must be one of the funds listed in the modern award.

You also have to provide a Standard choice form within 28 days if:

✔ An existing eligible employee asks you for a form

✔ You're unable to contribute to an employee's chosen fund, or it's no longer a complying fund

✔ You change your employer nominated default fund

Make sure the Standard choice form includes your employee's tax file number so that any contributions you pay aren't returned to you by the super fund.

Step 3: Act on your employee's choice

Once eligible employees choose a super fund, you have two months to arrange to pay contributions into that fund. After this time, any superannuation contributions must be paid to their chosen fund.

Using a default fund

You need to start paying superannuation contributions to your employer-nominated default fund if

✔ An employee doesn't choose a fund within 28 days of starting employment with you

✔ You haven't accepted an employee's choice of fund because he hasn't yet provided all the information you need

Your employer-nominated fund must offer minimum life insurance for members.

Small businesses are eligible to use a service provided by the Australian Government that makes the superannuation guarantee payments on your behalf. The Small Business Superannuation Clearing House is a free online superannuation payments service that helps small businesses with 19 or fewer employees meet their superannuation guarantee obligations. For more information, go to www.humanservices.gov.au/business/services/medicare/small-business-superannuation-clearing-house.

Making Use of the Real Cost Ready Reckoner

A simple way to calculate the real cost of employing staff is to identify each of the elements (such as wages, allowances, fringe benefits and on-costs) as a percentage of the salary or wage, and so calculate the amount of money in dollars that each element represents for each employee. Then add up these elements to obtain the Total Employment Cost (TEC).

Spreadsheets are the friend of every small business owner so in this section I outline how to create a spreadsheet ready reckoner that helps you calculate the real cost of employment of staff in your small business. The spreadsheet is simple to set up, enabling you to easily see the real cost of employing staff.

Follow these steps to create your spreadsheet:

1. **Identify the correct modern award applicable to the employee (if one applies).**

2. **Identify the appropriate wage classification, allowances, penalties and loadings.**

3. Set up a spreadsheet with two or more pages.

The first page should include the formulae and percentages to calculate the TEC as per the example shown in Figure 6-1.

Figure 6-1 shows a sample spreadsheet, using the example of a part-time food and beverage attendant employed in a small catering business.

Total Employment Cost Calculation Sheet - Tasty Catering Pty Ltd

EMPLOYEE DETAILS				
Employee Name	Jimmy Waitstaff			
Address	1 Super Highway Hipsterville VIC Australia			
Date of birth	1-Jul-95			
Tax File Number	111 222 444			
Superannuation Fund	Super Delicious Employees Industry Fund			
Date of Commencement	1-Jul-14			
Position and Award				
Occupation	Food & Beverage Attendant			
Award	Hospitality Industry (General) Award 2010			
Classification	Level 2 (Food & Beverage Attendent Grade 2)			
Status	Part-time			
Wages, Loadings, Penalties Overtime	Award clause	Award Rate	Weekly Hours	Weekly Wages
Adult Minimum Hourly Wage	cl 20.1	$17.05		
% Adult Rate (Junior)	cl 20.5	70%		
Casual Loading	cl 13.1	0%		
Ordinary Hourly Wage		$11.94	0	$0.00
Penalties				
M-F 7pm - Midnight	cl 32.3	$13.13	5	$65.64
M-F Midnight - 7am	cl 32.3	$13.73		
Saturday	cl 32.1	$14.92	10	$149.19
Sunday	cl 32.1	$20.89	10	$208.86
Public holiday	cl 32.2	$29.84		$0.00
Sub-Total			25	$423.69
Allowances	Award clause	Award Rate	Frequency	Amount
Meal Allowance	cl 21.1 (a)	$11.45	overtime meal	
Clothing Equipment & Tools	cl 21.1 (b)	$1.55	day	
Uniform Laundry Allowance	cl 21.1 (c)	$2.05	item	
Vehicle Allowance	cl 21.1 (e)	$0.75	kilometre	
Sub-total				$0.00
Accrued Leave	NES and Award	Rate %		Amount
Annual leave	NES	7.7%		$22.97
Personal/Carer's leave	NES	3.8%		$11.34
Long Service leave	NES	1.7%		$4.98
Annual leave loading	cl 34.2	1.3%		$3.88
Sub-total				$43.17
Taxes, Levies, Charges & Other	Rate %			Amount
Workers Compensation	3.0%			$12.71
Superannuation	9.0%			$38.13
Payroll Tax	0.0%			$0.00
Uniform	1.0%			$4.24
FBT	0.0%			$0.00
Other	0.0%			$0.00
Sub-total	13.0%			$55.08
Total Employment Cost				$521.95

Screenshot reprinted by permission from Microsoft Corporation.

Figure 6-1: Sample total employment cost calculator spreadsheet.

4. **When the rates change each year, update these pages of the spreadsheet.**

   Your formula on the main page should remain unchanged and, therefore, when the data on the modern award wages, allowances and penalties pages change, the results will automatically be updated.

On the second and subsequent pages of your spreadsheet enter the applicable modern award data of wages, allowances, penalties and any other payments, and mark it accordingly.

Go to www.dummies.com/go/hrsmallbusinessau to access the sample spreadsheet shown in Figure 6-1 and get more of a feel for the formulae used.

Chapter 7

Hiring: The Importance of the Employment Contract

. . . .

In This Chapter

▶ Making the job simple and clear with employment contracts

▶ Selecting the right terms and conditions

▶ Ensuring confidentiality and privacy

▶ Taking advantage of checklists to keep you on the right path

. . . .

A verbal contract isn't worth the paper it's written on.

Commonly misattributed to Samuel Goldwyn

*E*mployment contracts were once the domain of senior managers in big business. Very few people earning award wages had their terms and conditions put in writing and signed off by the boss — indeed, in the good old days a small-business owner would simply tell the new employee 'You can start Monday'. No longer. Australian laws now impose so many rights and obligations on employers and employees that detailing the employment arrangements in an employment contract is an absolute necessity.

In this chapter, I explain the intricacies, benefits and pitfalls of employment contracts while including tips for keeping it simple, fresh and relevant. Creating an employment contract that's satisfactory to your employees and suitable for your business isn't necessarily a simple matter of handing over a document and having employees sign it. I discuss the task of explaining terms and conditions, when parents and guardians may need to be involved and when you may need to adjust the contract to accommodate the specific interests and requests of employees.

I also show you how to draft your own employment template to use in your business, and explain how protecting the confidentiality of information critical to your business success is a matter that should be prominent in the employment contract.

The process of preparing, negotiating and then signing an employment contract can be daunting so I finish the chapter with a step-by-step checklist of action to keep you on the right path.

Working with an Employment Contract

No standard contract of employment can apply to all employment relationships. In fact, you're not required by law to place all of the terms and conditions of employment in writing. However, I don't recommend leaving the detail to chance — just too many aspects relating to employing staff really should be included in a clear, concise and simple document that reflects the myriad statutory obligations imposed on the employment relationships and the terms and conditions that you have agreed.

I won't bore you with the interminable legalese surrounding the nature of employment relationships but you should be aware of some fundamentals about the formation of the employment contract. Suffice to say that the employment contract isn't dissimilar to any other contract that you might make with another person or business.

The employment contract has five elements:

- Offer
- Acceptance
- Intention to enter into legal relations
- Valuable consideration
- Capability of making legally enforceable contract

You offer people a wage to perform a job that they duly accept. They perform the work and you pay them the wage. You, as employer, and another person, as employee, are adults capable of making a legally enforceable contract with each other. Voilà, you have an employment contract!

Unfortunately, the actual process isn't that simple. What about the promises made at the interview? The advertisement? Are they part of the employment contract? The employment relationship contains more grey than black and white and, therefore, formation of an employment contract can be a bit tricky. Lawyers love grey, but I don't. So in the following sections I explain aspects of the contract in a way that hopefully makes sense — and means you don't have to pay a lawyer to write the employment contracts for your small business.

Express and implied terms of employment

Every employment contract (whether in writing or not) includes both express and implied terms. *Express* terms are the one that are written into the employment contract by you and the employee. *Implied* terms are those that Australian courts say are part of the contract whether you like it or not.

Express terms

Letters of offer of employment usually provide a statement of the title of the job, the wage or salary, the hours of work and the date on which the person is expected to commence employment. These are express terms of the employment contract.

When formulating the express terms of the employment contract (whether in a simple letter of offer or a detailed contract) try to be as clear and precise as possible. Often that's a bit tricky but, let's face it— you're running a small business, not writing a novel. So, in formulating the express terms of the employment contract, you need to think about how it's likely to be understood by others and, in particular, how it's likely to be applied in reality over the course of the employment relationship.

Aspects of the employment relationship such as salary and hours of attendance you would naturally include in an employment contract. However, other elements aren't as clear cut. For example, employment contracts frequently refer to the application of various policies and procedures related to the business. Not all of them are intended to form part of the terms and conditions of employment and may be changed occasionally. They might be guidelines for behaviour or communication or simply administrative procedures. How then should they be expressed in the employment contract?

Judges with grey beards and serious demeanours have contemplated this question *ad infinitum* (that means *endlessly* in Latin — judges love speaking Latin). The good judges of the Australian High Court in a 2004 case (*Toll (FGCT) Pty Ltd v Alphapharm Pty Ltd*) summed up the situation as follows:

> It is not the subjective beliefs or understandings of the parties about their rights and liabilities that govern their contractual relations. What matters is what each party by words and conduct would have led a reasonable person in the position of the other party to believe ...

In other words, the express terms of the employment contract will be interpreted by others in light of what you do as much as what you write in the contract.

Implied terms

Some terms of employment are automatically *implied by law* where they have not been expressly provided, and some terms may be implied into an employment contract to give *business efficacy* to the contract.

Terms that are automatically implied in an employment contract where none are expressly provided include the notice that either party must provide to terminate the employment relationship. If you don't provide some period of notice, a period that the courts consider to be *reasonable* notice will be implied into the employment contract. Since the *Fair Work Act 2009* commenced on 1 January 2010, reasonable notice is normally no less than the period of notice prescribed in the National Employment Standards (NES) (refer to Chapter 4 for more).

Australian courts protect the interests of employers by implying into every employment contract terms that impose obligations on employees such as the following:

✔ Acting in good faith toward their employer

✔ Complying with reasonable and lawful directions of the employer

Equally, obligations on employers to their employees are also implied, such as:

✔ Acting in good faith toward the employee

✔ Being good and considerate and not deliberately damaging the trust and confidence between employer and employee

✔ Indemnifying employees against liabilities and expenses incurred in the course of performing work for the employer

✔ Taking reasonable care of the health and safety of employees

Courts are reluctant to imply other terms, unless these terms are necessary to ensure that the contract makes sense — that is, the implied term is necessary for the reasonable or effective operation of the contract.

The implied term may be inferred from custom and practice in an industry or may be so obvious that if the subject had been raised with the parties at the time of making the contract they would have replied 'Of course ...' and included it in the contract. For example, of course concierges at a hotel would dress and groom themselves in a manner appropriate to the nature of the clients that the hotel caters to. Or employees required to use their own vehicles to deliver pizzas would, of course, be compensated for the petrol and other running costs associated with the use of the vehicle.

Impact of statutory laws

Remember that old adage you learnt about the law at school: 'Ignorance is no excuse'? The relationship between the written *common law* employment contract and *statutory obligations* imposed on employers in modern awards, the NES, unfair dismissal, anti-discrimination, superannuation and health and safety laws is often misunderstood. Statutory laws — that is, laws enacted by Australian and state parliaments — operate alongside the common law applied by the Australian courts.

Statutory law overrides the common law of the employment contract where the two jurisdictions cover the same subject matter but with conflicting obligations or responsibilities.

Normally, the statutory laws impose minimum rather than absolute obligations and, therefore, the common law can continue to apply subject to compliance with the minimum statutory requirement. This means, for example, that employers and employees can make and enforce the terms of one contract of employment simultaneously through Australian courts through the common law *and* enforce statutory obligations that are referred to in the contract such as modern awards, the NES, superannuation, workers compensation and any other law created by Australian and state parliaments.

The relationship between statutory laws and the common law of the employment contract can be summarised with a few basic rules:

✔ You and your employee can agree on payment of wages in excess of the minimum wages prescribed in a modern award but you can't enforce a contract for payment of wages less than the minimum wages prescribed in a modern award or the national minimum wage.

✔ You're not permitted to make an agreement, willingly or otherwise, with an employee excluding statutory obligations such as the modern award system or the NES, workers compensation, superannuation, anti-discrimination and other laws made by Australian parliaments.

✔ Your employees can enforce the over-award terms of the employment contract in Australian courts claiming breach of contract if underpaid. They can also enforce minimum wages owed to them prescribed in modern awards through the government regulatory agencies such as the Workplace Ombudsman.

For more information and advice about Australia's workplace rights and rules, including awards and national employment standards, go to the Fair Work Ombudsman website (www.fairwork.gov.au).

Creating Your Own Employment Contracts

Using a template for employment contracts saves you time and ensures that you consistently apply terms and conditions that are compliant with applicable statutory obligations.

The two streams of statutory and common law operate in parallel, so your template for your employment contract should reflect both elements, sometimes by expressly stating required points and sometimes by referring to the statutory rule. (Refer to the preceding section for more on statutory and common law obligations.)

Your template should encapsulate all of the elements of the employment relationship that should be expressed in written form, as well as make clear to your employees what they can expect from you.

Setting out the terms and conditions

You should create as many employment contract templates as necessary to reflect the different circumstances of employees. For example, create separate templates for

- ✔ Award-covered casual employees
- ✔ Award-covered part- and full-time employees
- ✔ Award-free casual employees
- ✔ Award-free part- and full-time employees

Your templates should have a common set of headings covering all of the applicable terms and conditions that you would expect to see and are regulated in an employment relationship — see the following sections for the headings that should be included in the employment contract.

The content under each of the headings in the employment contract templates may necessarily differ to reflect the individual circumstances of the employee. However, you can construct your templates in a way that allows you to insert most of the individual circumstances, such as the job title, wage, employment status, commencement dates, period of employment and hours of work in the schedule, to the contract, leaving the rest of the document generally as standard provisions.

Once you have the templates ready, all you need to do is provide a covering letter welcoming new employees and inviting them to read, sign and return the employment contract before they actually start work for you. Simple!

Creating templates

I've created four templates that should suit most small-business employment relationships. The templates are tailored to award-covered and award-free employees including full-time, part-time and casual employees.

Go to www.dummies.com/go/hrsmallbusinessau to access the four employment contract templates. You can simply save the templates to your computer, and add your small business logo and address. Each time you employ a person, you can just open a new document using the templates. Open up a sample template and keep it handy as you go through the following sections. These sections will help you complete the employment contract template for a new employee.

Filling out the template to create a new contract

Here's how to complete an employment contract template for a new full- or part-time employee (using the template for full-time and part-time award employees):

- ✔ **Parties:** Insert here the name of the business that actually employs the employee and the employee's name and address.

- ✔ **Definitions and interpretation:** Choose from the options available in the template, which enable consistent use of key terms that are clear and well defined.

- ✔ **Relationship to awards and the NES:** Identify here the particular modern award that applies to the employee (if one applies).

The employer and employee can't agree to forego the minimum entitlements provided by any applicable awards and the NES, but they may agree to additional entitlements known as 'over-award' entitlements.

✔ **Job title:** For convenience the job title is inserted in Schedule A — Employment Arrangements. This is the title defined by the employer, not the award classification title.

✔ **Employment status:** Go to Schedule A — Employment Arrangements and insert either Full-time or Part-time. (If the employee is a casual employee use the Employment Contract — Award Employees (Casual) template or Employment Contract — Award-Free Employees (Casual) template.)

✔ **Period of employment:** You have three choices, as follows (select only one and delete the remainder):

- **Employment is ongoing:** If the employment has no particular expiry date, choose the first option

- **Employment is for a temporary period:** Use the second option and insert an expiry date

- **Employment is temporarily to fill a vacancy due to parental leave:** Choose the third option (the employee on leave has an entitlement (with agreement of the employer) to either extend the leave or return to work earlier than was expected)

A casual employee may be dismissed without notice and, therefore, does not require an expiry period. However, in some circumstances it may be convenient to provide a clause indicating the expected period in which the casual employee is likely to be employed. For example, you may want a person to work for the busy period leading up to Christmas or to replace an employee on short periods of leave. Casual employment is convenient in these situations and a clear indication of how long you want staff for is appropriate.

✔ **Duties:** Include here a thorough position description.

✔ **Hours of work:** Insert here the actual hours of work required of the employee, including the daily commencement and finish times and the days of the week on which the employee is employed (keeping in mind minimum hours of work boundaries set by the NES and, if applicable, the modern award).

✔ **Meals and rest breaks:** See the applicable modern award for what to include here. In the absence of the modern award, meal and rest breaks are negotiable. Insert here what you and your employee have agreed to.

✔ **Remuneration:** This section of the template first covers the commencement salaries. Fill out this section as follows:

- For award employees paid no more than the modern award salary, use the first option provided.

- For award employees paid in excess of the modern award minimum salary, use the second option. This ensures that the award entitlement to allowances, loadings, penalties and overtime is set off against the over-award payments. (This is subject to the over-award payment being at least equal to or in excess of the payment that the employee would have received if paid the modern award entitlement.)

If paying over-award payments to employees to offset these payments against other entitlement, this arrangement should also be reflected in a separate individual flexibility arrangement (IFA) signed by award employees once they commence employment. You don't need to provide an IFA to an award-free employee.

The remuneration section of the template also includes non-salary benefits. Include here any fringe benefits provided, whether as salary packaging or in addition to the salary. If no fringe benefits are provided, insert 'Not Applicable' in the relevant section of Schedule A — Employment Arrangements.

The salary review section reflects the usual eligibility criteria and procedure. However, these may be altered to include any local arrangements or policy. Include here any additional processes you and your employee have agreed to.

Casual employees aren't normally eligible for salary reviews and are paid hourly rates of pay rather than salaries. The minimum casual loading for award casuals is 25 per cent and award-free casuals 23 per cent.

✔ **Annual leave:** This section refers to the application of the NES and the modern award as the entitlements are described in detail in those instruments. You don't need to replicate the entitlement in the employment contract but can prescribe conditions that complement or are in addition to the NES and the modern award. In particular, you can amend the clause to reflect the local arrangements such as Christmas closedowns or other periods of the year in which annual leave is expected to be taken.

Award-free employees aren't entitled to annual leave loading. Casual employees are paid a loading in lieu of annual leave.

✔ **Personal/carer's and compassionate leave:** This clause refers to the application of the NES as the entitlements are described in detail in those instruments. You don't need to replicate the entitlement in the employment contract but can prescribe conditions that complement or are in addition to the NES. In particular, employers may choose to provide additional leave. The section should also over the conditions when medical certificates for absences need to be provided.

✔ **Community service leave:** Provided in the NES and applicable to all employees.

✔ **Long service leave:** Provided in the NES and applicable to all employees.

✔ **Parental leave:** Provided for in the NES and applicable to all employees.

✔ **Public holidays:** Provided for in the NES and the modern award.

✔ **Notice of termination and redundancy:** Provided in the NES and the modern award.

✔ **Employment policies and procedures:** This clause is designed to ensure employees are aware they must comply with the various policies and procedures related to their employment. However, only the obligation to comply forms part of the contract — not the actual detail of the policies. This is because the detail of the policies will vary and evolve over time in accordance with changing circumstances. Highlight here any policies and procedures the employee must be aware of.

✔ **Performance management and appraisal:** This clause ensures that employees are aware that they must participate in periodic reviews of their performance. Employers that have particular policies prescribing how individual performance is measured and reviewed should describe them at orientation (see Chapter 8). Otherwise informal performance appraisal is okay. Include details of your appraisal system in this section.

✔ **Confidentiality:** Confidentiality is important to employers and as such it is protected by requiring the employee to maintain the confidentiality of information obtained of key aspects of the employer's business during and after the employment ends. Include the details of requirements for your employees here. You can also include specific clauses in respect of intellectual property, copyright, moral rights and/ or other matters that may be important to you.

✔ **Dispute resolution:** Disputes in respect of the terms and conditions of employment prescribed either in the modern award, NES or the employment contract are subject to the resolution procedure. *Note*: The contract does not provide Fair Work Australia the right to arbitrate unless the employer and employee in any particular circumstance allow it to do so.

✔ **Signatories:** The employment contract should be signed by both parties prior to the commencement date of employment. A copy should be provided to the employee for her personal record. Junior employees normally require a parent or guardian to sign on their behalf.

✔ **Schedule A — employment arrangements:** For convenience, Schedule A allows the employer to insert the terms and conditions that are pertinent to the individual employee. The Schedule may also be used (in conjunction with a simple covering letter) to record variations to the employment arrangements during the course of the employee's employment.

The NES and any applicable modern awards cover your minimum employment obligations, and these can't be overridden by the employment contract. Refer to Chapters 4 and 5 for more on the NES and modern awards.

Staying on top of important attachments

Your employment contract refers to other business policies and related documents such as the staff handbook, anti-discrimination policies, workplace health and safety and the Fair Work Information Statement. You must provide these documents to the employee with the employment contract if you wish to rely on them once the employment relationship commences — you can't expect people to comply with a policy if they don't know what it contains.

Many of these policies can and should be explained in detail during the induction procedure but, nevertheless, providing them before employees commence employment is also good business practice. Access to the documents can be in a hardcopy version or online. This means when employees sign the employment contract and have had the detail explained to them, they will be acknowledging that they have read and understood how other policies and documents apply to their employment.

Here are some of the other items you may need to provide to new employees before, or as soon as practicable after, they commence work:

- ✔ A copy of the applicable modern award, if one applies (or direct employees to where they may access a copy)
- ✔ The Fair Work Information Statement
- ✔ A copy of the signed individual flexibility arrangement (IFA), if applicable
- ✔ A Superannuation Choice form

Knowing who should sign the employment contract

Employment contracts should be signed by both parties prior to the commencement date of employment, or at least no later than on completion of the induction. The period prior to signing the employment contract is the period for the employee to ask questions or request amendments. Once the contract is signed, you and the employee each implementing every aspect of the employment contract in good faith is expected.

Once signed, a copy of the employment contract should be provided to employees for their personal records.

Junior employees — that is, young persons under the 18 years of age — normally require a parent or guardian to sign on their behalf. If the employee is entering into a formal training agreement while employed by you, the training agreement and the employment contract should both be signed by the parent or guardian, preferably at the same time.

Witness signatures may be included but aren't necessary on employment contracts.

Confidentiality

Confidentiality is important to business success and, as such, is often protected by requiring employees to maintain the confidentiality of information obtained about the employer's business during employment and after the employment ends.

The employment contract plays an important part in the strategy to protect your confidential information. The contract is a means of making clear to staff that certain information must be remain confidential, and is an opportunity to list the type of information this may include.

Not every piece of information that's produced or shared in a business needs to be confidential. Lots of facts, figures, maps, plans, recipes, formulae, pictures, methods and systems that your business uses, for example, are already in the public domain. Binding employees to secrecy about something your business competitors already know about is pointless. Therefore, identify the information that you have created or acquired or that has a unique and beneficial quality that's valuable to your small business — the kind of information that enables you to compete in the market place for your goods and services.

Information you ask your staff to keep confidential may include the following:

- ✔ **Genuine intellectual property:** This includes the information, systems and methods you use to operate your business and that are capable of being copyrighted, patented, registered or accredited. See Chapter 8 for more on protecting intellectual property.

- ✔ **Business financial information:** This may include information on loans, investments, cash flows, expenditure and revenue, debtors and creditors, pricing and supply contracts, taxation records and other items relevant to the balance sheet. Unlike a public company, your financial performance is private and may remain so (except to the Australian Tax Office).

- ✔ **Business intelligence:** This includes client lists, customer data and market knowledge acquired through the course of operating your business.

- ✔ **Business plans and strategy:** These are important to the way you intend to compete in the market place. Competitive advantage is created through how well you apply your resources and capability in a coherent business plan — this is valuable and worth protecting.

- ✔ **Staff information of a personal and sensitive nature:** This must not be disclosed for any other purpose than the reason for which it has been collected. Although employment records such as salary, hours of work, applicable award, annual leave accruals and sick leave aren't subject to the Privacy Principles, ensuring staff who have access to such information don't disclose the information outside of the business environment is respectful to your employees.

Attending to Privacy

Privacy isn't the same as confidentiality. Confidentiality in employment isn't regulated by any statutory laws and, therefore, is generally subject only to the terms of the employment contract.

The privacy of personal information that's collected by businesses is subject to the ten Privacy Principles in the *Privacy Act 1988*. The Privacy Principles regulate how personal information gathered by businesses is collected, stored, used and accessed by others.

Small businesses don't have to comply with the Privacy Act unless they have an annual turnover of $3 million or more or are

- Contractors that provides services under a Commonwealth contract
- Health-service providers
- Operators of a residential tenancy database
- Related to a business that's not a small business
- Reporting entities for the purposes of the *Anti-Money Laundering and Counter-Terrorism Financing Act 2006* (AML/CTF Act)
- Trading in personal information (for example, buying or selling a mailing list)

Employment records are exempted from the Privacy Principles but that doesn't mean all personal information collected by businesses on their staff is exempted. For example, employees receiving and sending personal information over the business email, such as banking notices, messages from family and invitations to attend personal events, is common practice. This is not information that forms part of the employment record.

You may also collect personal information as part of your business social club or employees may just share personal information about themselves and their lives because that is what people do when then get together. Perhaps you do not allow staff to use the business IT equipment to engage in personal matters (or at least discourage them from doing so) but that's another issue. The point is that information will always be shared of a personal nature — this information is private but may not be subject to the Privacy Principles. In those cases, confidentiality provisions in employment contracts and policies addressing acceptable use of business IT and the like are useful means to protect the disclosure of this information — see Chapter 8 for more on these.

Using a Checklist to Stay Organised

As well as being able to draft an employment contract (refer to the section 'Creating Your Own Employment Contracts', earlier in this chapter, for more detail), you also need to make sure that you stay on track and apply contracts to staff consistently and effectively. To help you with this, in this section I provide a version of one of the small-business owner's best friends — the checklist. You can use the checklist provided in Figure 7-1 to reduce your risk of doing something wrong. Once you've checked off all items on the list, you can rest assured that you've started the employment relationship on a good footing.

Select a template appropriate to the nature of the employment — that is, award full-time, award part-time, award-free casual	☑
Using the guidance notes to completing your employment contract template*, insert the required details into the template	☑
Amend or delete irrelevant provisions in the employment contract	☑
Append applicable policies such as a staff handbook, Fair Work Information Statement	☑
Write a covering letter formally offering the job to the person and inviting him to read, sign and return the employment contract	☑
Copy the signed contract and provide it to the employee on the day that she commences employment	☑
Place the signed employment contract in a Staff Personal File ready for the first day of employment and the induction	☑

Figure 7-1:
Employment
contract
checklist.

*Provided in the section 'Filling out the template to create a new contract', earlier in this chapter.

Part III
Putting the Employment Relationship to Work

Five Ways of Focusing Your Staff on High Performance

- **Link day-to-day performance to the bigger picture:** Explain the connection between simple tasks and business success. Staff are more likely to take particular care to do well in everything they do when they understand and believe in your vision for a successful business.

- **Remove the barriers holding back your staff:** Everyone is capable of doing well with the right equipment, knowledge, tools and attitude. Get rid of the stuff that's holding back your staff from being the best they can be. Upgrade equipment, improve communication and empower them to make decisions.

- **Encourage and reward good performance:** Motivation mainly comes from within the person, but encouraging good work sets the right tone, and providing valuable and meaningful rewards for effort reinforces high performance.

- **Measure the things that matter:** Identify the tasks that contribute to successful performance and regularly measure performance against these benchmarks. Don't be distracted by the things that don't matter.

- **Learn from every success and failure:** Take time to reflect with staff on what makes a high performer. High performance doesn't just happen by chance. It occurs when your staff learn the lessons of experience and apply their skills, knowledge and ability in a manner better than they have done before.

Check out more tips about the employment relationship with a free article at
www.dummies.com/extras/hrsmallbusinessau.

In this part ...

✔ The most important stage of the employment relationship is at the beginning. Learn how to implement an orientation program that systematically builds performance and sets the standards expected throughout the life of the employment.

✔ Performance standards don't just fall down from the sky. Design a structured system to define, measure and reward good work performance. And use a checklist of action to effectively address poor performance, get employees back on track or move them inevitably toward end of the employment relationship.

✔ Minimum wages aren't negotiable but market rates and incentives are important to attract and retain good staff. Discover how to find out what to pay and how best to structure the package of remuneration and align it to really good work performance.

Chapter 8

Making a Good Impression: Orientation Programs

- -

In This Chapter

▶ Establishing expectations from the start with the orientation program

▶ Documenting the rules of engagement in a staff handbook

▶ Using employment policies to guide working lives and protect your intellectual property

- -

You never get a second chance to make a first impression

Anonymous

*M*aking a good impression isn't just a task for the new employee, but should also be your aim when introducing a person into your business. You have invested time and money in recruiting this person and you want to get a good return on that investment. Besides, getting on well with the people you work with is good enough reason in itself to make the effort at the start.

In this chapter, I explain how you can use a structured orientation program to make a good impression on new employees, establish the expectations for performance and provide the best opportunity to commence work with confidence in the future. Orientation commences before new staff begin employment so I explain the work that should be completed early, such as creating a package of information about the business and ensuring equipment and other work materials are ready for staff's arrival.

You should be ready to implement a structured orientation program over the first few weeks of employment, not just the first day. I discuss the elements of this structured program starting with the tour of the business and introductions to the people your employee will be working with, through to an explanation of employment policies, and behavioural and dress standards that should appear in your staff handbook.

Finally, I explain how you should manage the use of business internet and social media, and intellectual property. These two important issues have the greatest potential to put at risk the employment relationship and so should be addressed at the commencement of employment.

Setting the Tone for the Future with Orientation

Staff orientation (or staff induction) is the process of welcoming your new employees into your small business. *Orientation* means providing information, guidance and support to enable your new employees to adjust to the work environment, understand your vision for the business and commence working productively and cooperatively with you as soon as possible. The benefits of an effective orientation are real and measurable, as are the drawbacks of an ineffective orientation — refer to Chapter 1 for the top three of each. So don't think you can go without providing an orientation.

Start preparing for your new employee as soon as the offer of employment has been accepted. Certain tasks can (and should) be undertaken as soon as possible. Other elements are essential for all employees to learn. The following sections cover these tasks and elements.

Preparing and providing a welcome pack

Putting together a welcome pack for new employees is a good way to provide all the information and forms they may require in the one place. Make sure you include some general information about the business in the pack, and send the pack out to new employees before they commence work.

Your welcome pack should include all of the information that you're required to provide, and all the forms the employee is required to complete, such as:

- Bank account number for payroll form
- Fair Work Information Statement
- Superannuation Standard Choice form
- Tax File Number Declaration form

All of the forms in the preceding list (except the bank account number for payroll form, which you can create yourself) are readily available to download from the Australian Tax Office website (www.ato.gov.au).

You should also include specific information about your business in the welcome pack, such as:

- Business plan or overview
- Employment policies, including
  - Confidentiality
  - Access and equity
  - Health and safety
  - Intellectual property rights
  - Performance review
  - Unsatisfactory performance and dismissal
  - Use of internet and social media
- Staff handbook

Getting the welcome pack to new employees before they commence work allows them an opportunity to read the material prior to the first day of work and, where necessary, obtain advice from the ATO or other government agencies that are responsible for regulating the area covered in the information. This means they have a chance to digest the information, obtain advice and ask questions before they sign off and acknowledge that they have read and understood the information (see the following section). When employees commence work you can explain in detail the information and answer any questions they may have of you.

Reading, acknowledging and signing

In your welcome pack, you should include a form that asks employees to acknowledge they have read and understood the employment policies provided in the welcome pack. This form should also provide a space for employees to sign, to indicate they agree to adhere to these policies.

The form should be signed and returned (together with the employment contract) no later than the day on which new employees commence employment during the initial orientation.

If you've provided the welcome pack prior to the commencement of employment (refer to preceding section), and so given new employees enough time with the information before they sign off on it, you're then entitled to rely on that signed acknowledgment if ever a dispute arises about one of the issues covered in the pack.

Talking about and facilitating performance

During orientation you can build the foundations for successful performance from your employees, first through making your expectations clear and then through providing the appropriate levels of instruction and supervision.

Talking to your new employee about your expectations for performance should form the core substance of your orientation program for the next few weeks, and you can start these discussions as soon as the orientation paperwork is completed.

The five key themes for successful performance are:

- ✔ Defining
- ✔ Facilitating
- ✔ Rewarding
- ✔ Evaluating
- ✔ Learning

Implementing these themes effectively is a process. Depending upon the nature of the job that your new employee is performing, you should increase the expectations for performance gradually over an extended period, somewhere between four and eight weeks. Over this period you can adjust the level of supervision and instruction commensurate with the increases in your expectations of performance. In this way, you can implement a graduated program to achieve a fully informed, capable and productive employee.

Figure 8-1 illustrates this graduated program over a six-week time frame. During the first week of the orientation most of your time with the new employee should be spent defining and facilitating performance. This includes instruction on how the job should be performed and the results that are expected from successful performance. You and your employee should agree on the measurable standards or indicators of performance for the next 6 to 12 months. You may provide instruction on use of equipment and tools necessary for the performance of the job and resolve potential or actual barriers to successful performance. In weeks two to five, you should provide a graduated balance of supervision and autonomy over the performance of the job as the employee grows in confidence and competence. In the sixth week you may review performance and make some adjustments to the performance standards and facilities to enable the employee's performance.

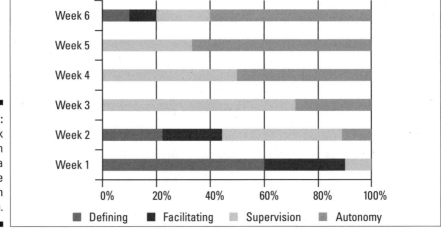

Figure 8-1:
Six-week
breakdown
for a
performance
orientation
program.

Over the following weeks and months the employee can work to the performance standards set during the orientation program, under varying mixes of supervision and autonomy.

See Chapter 9 for detailed information about the elements of effective performance management systems.

Following an orientation checklist

I mention throughout this book the importance of checklists to small-business owners. Working through a checklist of tasks that must be undertaken for the orientation program ensures a thorough and consistent approach. Figure 8-2 provides a simple orientation checklist, using the example of a small supermarket.

PREPARING FOR THE NEW EMPLOYEE

☑ Supervisors and staff informed of new employee start date

☑ Work area prepared, protective cloth, tools and supplies provided

☑ Name badge and uniform ordered

WELCOME

☑ Store manager/supervisor meet new employee on arrival

☑ Explanation of the aims and objectives of the business, customers and 'how we do things'

EXPLANATION OF TERMS OF EMPLOYMENT

Terms of employment explained including:

☑ Contract of employment

☑ Policies and procedures of staff handbook

☑ Employment equity and access policies

☑ Acceptance of offer of employment confirmed

PAYROLL INFORMATION & EMPLOYMENT DETAILS

☑ Tax file number declaration completed

☑ Employee bank account details for payment of wages provided

☑ Superannuation Choice forms completed

☑ Roster of hours of work forms completed

☑ Promotional goods/bonus stock form completed

ATTENDANCE RECORD, SECURITY, EMERGENCY & EVACUATION PROCEDURES, AND FIRST AID

☑ Time keeping system for attendance explained and electronic time card provided

☑ Building security, emergency and evacuation procedures explained

☑ Workplace health and safety policy explained

☑ Customer incident/accident procedure and, where relevant, armed robbery survival rules explained

☑ First aid procedure explained

☑ Leave application procedures explained

Figure 8-2:
Sample staff orientation checklist.

☑ **TOUR OF STORE AND WORK AREA**

☑ Tour of store including lunch rooms, bathroom facilities and personal locker (provide keys)

☑ Introduction to other staff

☑ Introduce to specific work area, such as store room, meat room, delicatessen

WRITTEN MATERIALS

☑ Copy of signed acceptance of offer of employment provided to employee

☑ Ensure employee has retained the package of information including staff handbook, employment policies, job description and roster of work hours

Name of Employee: _____ Date _____

Manager conducting orientation: _____

ACKNOWLEDGEMENT

I acknowledge that the orientation process and the information referred to in the checklist have been delivered as recorded above.

Signature of Employee: _____

Comments: _____
_____
_____

Evaluating orientation: Don't be scared of constructive criticism!

Self-reflection is very difficult for all of us, and it can be particularly difficult for self-reliant small-business owners. Criticism of any sort can be hard to take and often isn't welcomed. Nevertheless, I'm telling you to 'suck it up' and be prepared to listen and learn from your staff. Learning what works and what doesn't will outweigh any misgivings about criticism from the newcomer.

Orientation evaluation is a simple method to learn what you're doing well and not so well. The process doesn't have to be elaborate or overly complex — simply provide your new employee with an Orientation Evaluation form to complete and return to you once the orientation process has been completed.

Figure 8-3 provides a sample orientation evaluation form for the same small supermarket used in Figure 8-2.

The following questionnaire has been implemented as part of a quality-assurance process to ensure that the orientation of new employees is of a consistently high standard and relevant to their needs. Please indicate your response by circling the appropriate statement and providing comments where possible. Your responses will remain strictly confidential.

Do you feel that the manager conducting the orientation was well organised and professional?

    Yes   No

Do you believe that the manager conducting the orientation had a good understanding of the subjects he or she was delivering?

    Yes   No

Was the orientation delivered in a way that was clear and easy to follow?

    Yes   No

Was the content of the orientation you received relevant to your needs?

    Yes   No

Did the manager conducting the orientation answer all of your questions to your satisfaction?

    Yes   No

On a scale of 1 to 10, how would you rate the orientation procedure?

Poor	1	2	3	4	5	6	7	8	9	10	Excellent

If you have any further comments that you would like to make about the orientation procedure, please feel free to provide further comments below.

_____
_____
_____
_____
_____
_____
_____
_____

Figure 8-3:
Sample staff
orientation
evaluation
form.

The Staff Handbook: Setting the Rules of Engagement

Whether you like it or not the modern Australian workplace is characterised by multiple layers of rules and regulations. These are often cumbersome, burdensome, obtuse and unhelpful — and, unfortunately, mostly unavoidable. On the other hand, some customs, protocols and behavioural standards are healthy and beneficial to the way we work with each other in business. I recommend that you deal with the required rules of engagement in a simple and concise publication that I have dubbed the staff handbook.

The staff handbook for your employees should be a summary of the key aspects of the employment relationship that can be read as a companion to the individual employment contract and the various employment policies applicable to the employee and your small business. In the following sections, I cover each of the headings or themes that you should include in your handbook. Of course, you can always add more.

Values, philosophy, goals

I revisit this theme throughout the book but your employees knowing and understanding what your business is all about is very important to the success of the employment relationship. Your values, philosophy and business goals must be open for all to see. Otherwise, how are you going to get staff to engage with you in building the business?

List in the staff handbook the personal values that you wish to see reflected in your business and in the behaviour and attitude of staff — for example, honesty, integrity, compassion and initiative. Explain in no more than 250 words your business philosophy and your long-term goals. Believe it or not, the modern generation are genuinely interested in working for businesses that reflect their own values, philosophies and personal goals.

Behaviour standards

The behaviour standards you outline in the staff handbook as being required from all employees can range from simple statements such as, 'Staff are expected to speak and act toward customers and each other in a courteous and respectful manner', through to detailed descriptions of your anti-discrimination and anti-bullying policies, and procedures for making a complaint.

To keep your staff handbook clear and concise, summarise the key message about your required behavioural standards in the handbook, and then reference the more detailed policy and procedural matters in your employment policies. For example, all employees have a duty to ensure that, as far as practical, they perform their work in a manner that's safe and that doesn't place them or anyone else at risk to their health and safety. However, you don't include your entire policy and procedure to manage risks to health and safety in the handbook. The actual policy could be maintained on a common hard drive or accessible on the business's network, or via hardcopy files.

The following is a list of the themes that should be covered under the general heading of Behavioural Standards in your staff handbook:

- Acceptable use of internet and social media
- Attendance hours and notice of absence
- Bullying and discrimination
- Confidentiality and privacy
- Dress code
- Grievance resolution procedure
- Health and safety
- Private use of company vehicles
- Professional conduct toward customers
- Respect for others and behaviour
- Sexual harassment
- Smoking in the workplace
- Use of company equipment and property

Unfortunately, the rules of engagement in Australian workplaces tend toward the censorious — that is, 'DO this' 'DON'T DO that' type of rules. You can't do much about the negative vibe this creates, except perhaps balance the negative with a few words of encouragement prefacing the message such as

We all expect to be treated with respect and dignity. As such, staff are expected to respect personal boundaries, not to engage in sexual innuendo, abusive or hurtful gossip or otherwise behave in a manner that would reasonably be construed as offensive to others. Please refer to our policies on sexual harassment, prevention of bullying, and anti-discrimination for a detailed commentary on the standards of behaviour expected of each other and the procedures to respond to incidents and complaints. We are all responsible for our behaviour and, therefore, we will be held accountable pursuant to those places where they may be breached or behaviour falls short of the acceptable standard.

Dress codes

I don't know about you but I really hate those ties and socks with silly cartoon characters printed on them that blokes wear in the office. That was the sort of gift children gave their hapless fathers on birthdays and at Christmas back in the 1980s. Thank goodness that era has passed!

Unfortunately, every generation brings forth a new set of crimes against fashion, with Generation Y (or is that Z?) now seeming to think having multiple tattoos and body piercings is compulsory. Thankfully, you can do your bit to reduce what can be appalling episodes of bad dress sense by setting out some reasonable standards in your staff handbook — otherwise known as the company dress code.

Figure 8-4 shows some possible dress codes against some example businesses or employees. Re-organise the items listed to match the acceptable dress code to the type of work or business in the second column. You can grant yourself a prize if you get most of them correct. The answers to this quiz are pretty obvious and so are the lessons for your own dress codes. Be sensible and apply standards that are appropriate to the nature of the work performed, its context, regulations and the expectations of your customers.

Figure 8-4:
Matching
dress
standards
and
businesses
challenge.

Dress Code	Business/Employee
Suit and tie	Restaurant waiter
Black skirt or trousers and white shirt	Butcher shop
Safety boots, hard hat and protective glasses	Hairdresser
Multi-coloured hair, excessive jewellery and make-up	Timber and hardware store
Apron and hair net	Medical clinic
Fluoro jacket, sunglasses on head	Sales representative
Rubber gloves, thermometer and stethoscope	Metal foundry

General housekeeping

Have you ever opened the fridge at work and not been able to find the milk, butter or delicious birthday cake for all of the notes in the way warning you under threat of summary execution not to touch the stuff in the fridge? What about that thing at the back of the fridge that has grown its own full-length beard, or the 500 unwashed coffee cups sitting in the kitchen sink? Yes, I thought so, horrible!

Including points on general housekeeping in your handbook is a way to cover staff responsibilities in relation to this sort of stuff and more.

Here's a list of suggested topics you can cover under the theme of general housekeeping in your staff handbook:

- ✔ Building access and security
- ✔ Cleaning and hygiene in common areas
- ✔ Emergency procedures
- ✔ First aid kit
- ✔ Fundraising activities
- ✔ Staff amenities
- ✔ Staff social club

Employment Policies

Employment policies are the fourth important element in the compendium of employment documents that you should create and apply to staff (for more about the employment contract, refer to Chapter 7, and welcome pack and staff handbook, refer to the preceding sections). You can create no end of employment policies to cover situations that may arise at work. However, you must retain certain policies to comply with Australia's array of health and safety, workplace rights and equal employment opportunity laws.

You should have employment policies covering the following:

- ✔ Equal employment opportunity/anti-discrimination
- ✔ Sexual harassment prevention
- ✔ Workplace bullying prevention
- ✔ Rehabilitation and return to work
- ✔ Workplace health and safety

See www.dummies.com/go/hrsmallbusinessau for some sample model policies you can replicate, or create your own using similar headings and content relevant to your business.

Certain employment policies are desirable not because of laws imposed by the government but because of situations that can occur in modern businesses that benefit from a bit of order or guidance. I consider two areas to potentially be of high risk to your small business, and I cover creating employment policies in these areas in the following sections.

Acceptable use of internet and social media policies

If your business relies upon staff using the internet for communication, you need to have a policy explaining the acceptable use of the electronic equipment and facilities provided. The temptation to use your equipment to access social media such as Facebook and Twitter and other favourite websites such as YouTube seems to be irresistible to employees, and the risk of it being misused is very high. Think sexual harassment, cyber bullying, pornography, and offensive and obscene conduct. If these are not sufficient reason for a policy, think about the time wasted by staff on this stuff.

Privacy considerations

When politicians make a law regulating one area of life or business they rarely think about the impact on other laws that they have made, such as the relationship between privacy laws and laws prohibiting harassment and cyber-bullying. Your policy on the acceptable use of internet and social media must satisfy the Privacy Principles (refer to Chapter 7 for more), as well as the general duty to provide a workplace free from risks to health and safety, harassment and discrimination. In New South Wales laws also control surveillance of employees in the workplace, extending to monitoring of internet use. Consequently, simply prohibiting unacceptable use of company internet and computer facilities isn't sufficient. If you intend to monitor the use of communication equipment to ensure it's not misused, you must warn staff of this intention.

In most instances where action is taken against employees who misuse computer equipment, Australian courts don't shy away from upholding employment policies that seek to eradicate misconduct in circumstances where the employee has been warned about the consequences of non-compliance with the policy.

The Australian Privacy Commissioner says it receives many enquiries from employees regarding the privacy of workplace email and web-browsing activities. The level of enquiries seems to suggest that Australian employees have a general expectation that there must be laws to protect their privacy in the workplace. However, no general constitutional, statutory or common law right to privacy in Australia extends to employees. The Privacy Act exempts employee records from the definition of personal information that's covered by the privacy principles in the law. But the Act does apply to staff emails that contain personal information, other than employee records, in certain circumstances, and also applies to logs of staff web browsing activities. Refer to Chapter 7 for further commentary on the difference between employment records and other personal information in Australian workplaces.

Drafting your acceptable use of internet policy

Your employment policies should clearly outline the acceptable use and monitoring of email and internet. Your policy should:

- ✓ Communicate the policy to staff in a manner that can be clearly understood

- ✓ List the activities that are permitted as well as forbidden

- ✓ Clearly set out what information is logged, and who in the business has rights to access the logs and content of staff email and browsing activities

- ✓ Highlight that improper use of email may pose a threat to system security, the privacy of staff and others, and the legal liability of the organisation

- ✓ Outline how you intend to monitor or audit staff compliance with the policy on acceptable usage of email and web browsing

Your acceptable use of internet policy should be reviewed on a regular basis to keep up with the accelerating development of the internet and information technology. The policy should be re-issued whenever significant change has been made.

Protecting intellectual property rights

The genuine intellectual property of your small business should be protected from misuse, and where it is created in the normal course of the business duly accredited to you as the owner of the business.

The risks of damage to your business from the theft and/or misuse of your intellectual property are very high and the consequences potentially catastrophic — and trying to recover damages after the fact is pointless if no business is left to recover.

A well-constructed intellectual property policy, making clear to employees who owns the silverware, is a good idea. You can create a simple intellectual property employment policy covering the areas included in this section.

Refer to Chapter 7 for information on how confidentiality clauses in employment contracts also protect the genuine intellectual property of your business.

Inventions and designs

Patent laws give the owner of the patent exclusive rights to exploit an invention and authorise other persons to exploit the invention. The owner of the patent is normally the inventor; however, where the invention occurs during the course of employment, the employer (that is, you) is entitled to the benefit of the invention. Similar principles apply to unique designs in terms of the visual style or features.

The sorts of issues the courts will take into account when addressing disputes over whether an invention occurred in the course of employment include the following:

- ✔ Expectations of the employer and employee regarding inventions
- ✔ Nature and seniority of the job held by the inventor
- ✔ Normal duties of the inventor
- ✔ Specific directions or assignments of the inventor
- ✔ Whether the inventor was an employee or independent contractor

The law generally protects your interests in a dispute of ownership. Nevertheless, you don't want to get into an argument with staff over who is entitled to patent inventions and register designs that you have paid them to develop during the course of employment.

Your policy in this area should make it clear that inventions and designs will be considered to have been created during the course of employment at any time during employees' employment, particularly where such inventions or designs are related to the nature of your business or industry.

Copyright

Copyright covers literary, dramatic, musical and artistic works, including computer software and applications. The general rule of copyright is that the author of the work is the owner of the copyright subsisting in the work. The author is the person who creates the work, originates it and first reduces it to material form. However, an exception exists in relation to works created by an author in pursuance of the terms of his or her employment by another person. In other words, material made in the course of the employment relationship is owned by you as employer unless the staff member who created the IP has a contract of employment expressly stating otherwise.

Your employment policy should clarify this aspect for all staff.

Moral rights in copyright

Moral rights have been recognised in relation to copyright but not patents and designs. Three types of moral rights for authors of literary, dramatic, musical and artistic works are protected under the *Copyright Act 1968*. These cover:

- ✔ Correct attribution of authorship — that is, the right to be identified as the author

- ✔ Authorship not being falsely attributed to another person

- ✔ Integrity of authorship being maintained — that is, the right not to have the work subjected to treatment that results in a material distortion, mutilation or alteration that is prejudicial to the author's honour or reputation

Consequently, you should include a section in your intellectual property employment policy that outlines that you as the employer are absolved in relation to any omissions or infringement of the moral rights of employees where they may have created material that's subsequently copyrighted by the employer.

Refer to Chapter 7 for further commentary on protecting your intellectual property through confidentiality clauses in the employment contract.

Chapter 9

Performance Expectations: The Wage–Work Bargain

. . . .

In This Chapter

▶ Setting the right standard for the wage–work bargain

▶ Understanding what performance measures to pay attention to

▶ Giving feedback and making changes

▶ Analysing performance within the first 6 months

▶ Managing poor performance with warnings and procedures

. . . .

Anyone can do any amount of work, provided it isn't the work he is supposed to be doing.

Robert Benchley

*Y*ou set the standards of performance, provide the necessary tools, direct employees in how to perform work and pay wages for the time employees spend performing this work. In exchange, employees apply their knowledge, skills and experience diligently and conscientiously in the interests of your business. This describes, ladies and gentlemen, the fundamental *wage–work bargain*.

In this chapter, I explain how to get the best value from that bargain by creating an effective system to manage performance. I cover how you can improve your business by defining, facilitating and encouraging good performance, and measuring and learning precisely how well your employees are performing their work.

The first 12 months of employment are an important time, during which you invest time, energy and money in your employees. You need to make an important decision during this period about whether or not to continue to employ beyond these initial 12 months. Often known as the *probationary* or *qualifying* period of employment, I explain how you should approach this decision. I also look at how to address any poor performance issues, keeping in mind the best interests of your small business, and in a manner that minimises any risk of claims of unfair dismissals.

Lastly, I set out a checklist procedure that should be followed when addressing poor work performance to get employees back on track.

Defining, Facilitating and Encouraging Performance

You can manage the performance of your staff in two ways: Informal and ad hoc supervision, or the correct way, which is what this section is all about.

Introducing a structured system of managing the performance of staff serves three important purposes:

- ✔ **Strategic:** Taking a strategic approach to performance management helps ensure your staff's daily activities are consistent with your businesses values, goals and objectives. Everyone should be working for the same objectives, and doing so in a manner that reflects how you want them to work. Defining the tasks and work standards in this way gives you a better chance of actually achieving your business goals.

- ✔ **Developmental:** Using a structured management approach in your staff's performance enables you to focus on the specific skills, knowledge and abilities required to achieve your business goals. By doing so, you can then work to develop each person's capacity to succeed and to grow in the job.

- ✔ **Evaluative:** Applying a well-structured system enables you to accurately evaluate performance so that you and the staff learn from experiences and improve in the future. Having both individual and collective performance accountability makes it easier to address deficiencies and reward success.

A structured performance management system has five stages and works in a continuous cycle designed to improve performance over the life of the employment relationship (refer to Chapter 1 for a figure showing this performance management cycle). The five stages in the cycle are defining, facilitating, encouraging, measuring and learning.

I cover the early stages in this cycle in the following sections and then talk about the later stages further on in the chapter in 'The Art of Measuring the Right Stuff' and 'Providing Feedback'.

Defining performance standards

The first step in the performance management process is defining the key performance indicators (KPI) for employees. This means describing the results that you want staff to achieve in a manner that can be easily followed and measured. For example, you may want your receptionist to greet telephone callers in a friendly and courteous manner such as:

> 'Good morning, you have contacted ABC industries. How may I help you?'

You may also want your receptionist to answer the telephone within five rings. Congratulations — you've just defined two KPI for your receptionist:

✔ KPI 1: Greet telephone callers in courteous manner

✔ KPI 2: Answer all telephone calls within five ring tones

Both KPI are simple indicators of performance that can be achieved by the employee applying his knowledge, skills and abilities to the tasks described in the job description (refer to Chapter 2 for more on writing job descriptions). The KPI are consistent with the business goals and values, are measurable indicators of performance and are integral to the success of the wage–work bargain that you have with your employee.

Performance indicators can include a combination of results, processes, personal attributes and behaviour. An effective system of performance management measures everything from the way in which employees do the job through to the revenue generated from sales to customers.

One of the most successful businesses in the world is McDonald's Restaurants. Its performance management system isn't a secret, and its system of defining and managing the restaurant staff's performance has been replicated throughout the world. Staff are required to follow a very simple operating procedure for every customer that they serve:

✔ Provide a friendly and attentive greeting

✔ Take the order promptly

✔ Provide an accurate recounting of the order

✔ Hand over the meal within a short period

✔ Say thank you to customers as they leave

All of these actions are carefully defined tasks requiring a combination of personal qualities, attributes, skills and a focus on results to achieve the ultimate objective of selling fast-food meals to the customer. Both the employer and the employee know precisely the standard of performance required to achieve the business goal.

It's a good idea to work collaboratively with your employees to define and agree upon no more than ten suitable KPIs for their job, and then measure how well employees perform in those areas for 6 to 12 months.

Start with five KPIs for new employees, just to get things going, and focus these KPIs in particular areas. You should have a KPI that's result-based, one that's quality-focused and one that's task-oriented. One should also cover the attribute and another the behaviour you want to see continually displayed. You can record the agreed KPIs on a form known as a *performance plan*. This form captures the specific KPIs, the timeline to achieve them, the assistance that will be provided, how success will be measured, and any other comments that you and your employee may wish to add.

Rather than taking a broad approach to the KPIs, focus on specific measurable requirements for each one. For example, a KPI could be 'Make five sales per week', 'Greet all customers who enter the shop', 'Ensure a ten-minute response time for customer enquiries', or 'Ensure a failure rate of no more than 3 per cent on dispatching goods within 24 hours to customers'.

Visit www.dummies.com/go/hrsmallbusinessau for a sample performance plan worksheet.

Removing the barriers to performance

You can't expect people to succeed in any area of life — whether it be work, school or sport — if they don't have the basic equipment required to perform in that area. The required tools include more than just, say, a computer, driver's licence, apron, recipe, hammer or nails. They include skills, knowledge and ability. At this stage of the performance management cycle, you and your employees being able to identify not only the things that employees need to perform the job but also the things that will hold them back is critical. I call anything that can hold staff back *barriers to success*. This stage of the system is aimed at removing those barriers.

Plan to discuss and identify at the outset any barriers that may inhibit the individual employee's capacity to achieve the agreed KPIs. Cost, develop and implement strategies to address barriers — such as gaps in professional or product knowledge, poor or inadequate skills, and inadequate equipment. Changes required may be something as simple as upgrading computer software, providing new tools and equipment, sending your payroll officer to a class to learn a new payroll system or providing financial support so she can improve her bookkeeping qualifications.

Record the strategies for removing barriers on individual performance plans (refer to the preceding section) so that you can return to them and check them off as they're completed and during the regular review meetings. This also enables you to assess the success of these strategies (see the section 'Learning from the experience', later in the chapter, for more).

Encouraging performance

Motivation to perform well in a job is influenced by various factors, with financial reward not the only means of encouraging performance. In fact, once employees receive a level of remuneration that they believe to be fair and equitable, additional payments to encourage greater performance have little impact on motivation.

Many experts in the field of human behaviour now argue that, beyond remuneration, other motivators are at work, including the desire for autonomy (that is, being able to control how you perform the work), for mastering the work performed or for an affinity with a greater purpose to the work other than just making money.

Keeping possible other motivators in mind, you can encourage employees to achieve better performance through focusing on the following areas:

- **Leadership:** Motivation comes from the top as well as from within. Good leadership contributes to good performance. Model the behaviour that you want others to display, whether it be honesty, diligence, humour, initiative or teamwork.

- **Valuable encouragement:** The encouragement and reward that you provide has to be valued by employees. Think about what motivates the person, and what she views as important and valuable, and provide encouragement accordingly.

- **Timely reward:** Immediate positive reinforcement of an employee's performance is more likely to see the same performance repeated. Wait too long to thank employees and they're less likely to continue along the path that you want.

- ✔ **Fairness and equity:** Employees compare their rewards (financial and non-financial) with their peers both in the broader working population and with their immediate work colleagues. Motivation doesn't come from money but it sure can dampen enthusiasm if employees believe they're not treated fairly or their wage is inequitable. Get online occasionally and check out the job advertisements to see what your competitors are offering in wages and conditions.

- ✔ **Compatibility:** Rewards given to staff should encourage behaviour that leads to the desired performance standards. Say that your small business relies upon cooperation and teamwork to produce and sell your products and services. Offering individual incentive payments in this situation is pointless, because such payments may encourage staff to act selfishly. Bar and restaurant staff, for example, need to work as a team no matter which part of the bar or restaurant is experiencing high demand. It would be counterproductive to divide customer tips only between those who serve on tables because it takes more than one person to prepare and deliver the order, serve the customer, manage the money and clean up at the end of the night.

For greater detail on the wage side of the wage–work bargain, see Chapter 10.

The Art of Measuring the Right Stuff

Being able to measure performance is integral to achieving high-level performance. Defining performance standards that you want staff to work toward is pointless if you can't measure their performance correctly and precisely.

Duh, pretty obvious … but how do you measure it?

Well, firstly, the number of actual products and services sold, either individually or collectively, is easy to measure. You have the sales receipts to help you calculate and report on sales. However, success may also occur because of excellent after-sales service. In that case, you may wish to measure the quality of the action taken by sales staff to ensure customers are satisfied with the product they purchased from you. This could include slightly more sophisticated measures, such as measuring the quality of customer feedback provided in after-sales surveys. Another area critical to your business success may be persistence and consistency in sales methods such as pursuing and nurturing new customers. In that case, you may want to measure work behaviour such as diligence, initiative and customer relationship-building. Add to the mix product knowledge, and you can see that performance can and should be measured from various perspectives.

Here are some common methods or approaches that you can use to measure employee performance:

- ✔ **Comparative:** This involves techniques that require you to compare an individual's performance with that of others. This approach typically uses some overall assessment of an individual's performance or input in the business, and seeks to develop some of the employees within a given work group. For example, you could establish a friendly competition between staff to try to encourage better performance.

- ✔ **Attributes:** This approach focuses on the extent to which an employee has particular characteristics or traits believed to be desirable for the businesses success. Specific traits are measured, such as initiative, leadership, empathy, teamwork, problem solving, and employees are evaluated on these. A simple way to measure attributes is using a performance scale such as the example shown in Figure 9-1.

You and your employee rate how apparent the attribute is in the way in which the employee performs his job on a scale of 1 to 5. Try to reach agreement on the rating because such attributes are unlikely to be displayed in the future where your employee views his performance differently to you.

<table>
<tr><td rowspan="2"></td><td rowspan="2">**Attribute**</td><td colspan="5">**Rating**</td></tr>
<tr><td>Always Evident</td><td>Frequently Evident</td><td>Adequate</td><td>Occasionally Evident</td><td>Never Evident</td></tr>
<tr><td>Initiative</td><td>5</td><td>4</td><td>3</td><td>2</td><td>1</td></tr>
<tr><td>Leadership</td><td>5</td><td>4</td><td>3</td><td>2</td><td>1</td></tr>
<tr><td>Empathy</td><td>5</td><td>4</td><td>3</td><td>2</td><td>1</td></tr>
<tr><td>Problem solving</td><td>5</td><td>4</td><td>3</td><td>2</td><td>1</td></tr>
<tr><td>Teamwork</td><td>5</td><td>4</td><td>3</td><td>2</td><td>1</td></tr>
</table>

Figure 9-1: Attribute performance scale.

- ✔ **Behavioural:** This approach defines behaviour that an employee must exhibit to be effective in the job. Some really complex mathematical methods are available to measure behaviour but I suggest you and your employee can measure the type of behaviour that you would like to see on display by identifying *critical incidents*. These are incidents at work in which you believe the employee has displayed the desired behaviour during the period in review. For example, displaying initiative in after-sales service, always attending work on time, following up on customer enquiries and complaints promptly, or managing difficult customers calmly and effectively. Keep a diary or notes as and when you witness the incidents so you can remember them during reviews. You should also document poor behaviour.

✔ **Results:** In this approach, you focus on managing the objective, measurable results of a job. This approach assumes that subjectivity can be eliminated from the measurement process and that results are the best indicator of an employee's contribution to business success. The method that the employee uses to achieve the result is less important. Using this approach encourages creativity and innovation in employees, particularly in jobs that require a reasonable level of expertise and knowledge and where autonomy and mastery over the work is important to successful performance.

✔ **Quality:** Characteristic of this approach is customer-orientated action or measures. For example, action of staff that takes a preventative approach to errors. Customer satisfaction is the primary goal and risk management and quality assurance are the key techniques or methods to achieve quality. To measure these goals, you could run a customer survey once a year and include questions that are likely to give you an insight into quality. Error or complaint registers are also useful tools.

✔ **Means-based:** This approach focuses on the way in which performance outcomes or results are achieved, and provides a way of determining the extent to which performance outcomes are the result of the employee's behaviours rather than due to external or environmental influences. This approach is the opposite to the earlier Results approach to measuring performance. It assumes that tightly controlled operational methods followed by employees will lead to the desired result and, therefore, performance measurement focuses on the method of work and making sure certain processes are followed. I refer earlier in the chapter to McDonald's Restaurants, which provide a perfect example of this approach to performance measurement (refer to the section 'Defining performance standards').

Providing Feedback

No-one likes sitting down for a bit of one-on-one discussion and reflection. The situation is often unpleasant and usually embarrassing and sometimes can go pear-shaped! Nevertheless, measuring and appraising performance is critical to the management of staff work performance. Plus, I guarantee that if you manage this phase of the performance cycle properly, it can be painless and, importantly, productive.

Regular appraisal of the individual employee's performance is designed to

✔ Assess past performance against agreed standards

✔ Analyse the reasons contributing to the performance

✔ Reward good performance

✔ Adjust future KPIs

When you focus on these aims, the appraisal interview experience should be beneficial to you and your employee. You must, however, get yourself organised beforehand, and be prepared to also learn from the experience.

Handling appraisal interviews

Sitting down with staff to formally review their performance should occur more than once a year, preferably quarterly for the following reasons:

✔ The data measuring performance is more manageable for shorter periods.

✔ The feedback is more immediate.

✔ The reward for good performance will be more effective.

✔ You have greater chance of rectifying unsatisfactory performance if picked up earlier on.

You should provide information that you have collated measuring staff performance in advance of the appraisal to your employees. In fact, they should be able to see how they're progressing whenever they need to via regular informal reporting and feedback.

The appraisal process is a reflective process and, therefore, you should be as honest as possible in your analysis of satisfactory and unsatisfactory performance, and encourage your employees to be so as well. The process can then inform the next step, which is the review and re-alignment process occurring through the learning stage of the cycle (see following section).

You should collate and discuss performance results. You must also record the results and comments and keep them on the individual employment record.

The performance appraisal process isn't a de facto disciplinary procedure. Poor work performance or conduct justifying warnings or dismissal should be dealt with separately and as the need arises. If you indicate that your employee's performance has been satisfactory in an appraisal and subsequently initiate action to formally warn or dismiss the employee on the same set of facts, you may risk a claim of unfair dismissal against you. Therefore, honestly appraising the performance of your employees is much more sensible.

Learning from the experience

One of the primary purposes of managing staff performance in a structured manner is the development of the staff and the business. Consequently, the performance management cycle is a dynamic model that has been designed to promote continual improvement in staff and your small business.

Information acquired or learnt through the appraisal process that contributes to your understanding of the strengths and weaknesses of each employee should be recorded on the performance plan and fed back to allow adjustments to improve employee effectiveness.

Upon the completion or shortly after completing an employee's appraisal, you should create a new or revised performance plan for the employee.

Reviewing the First Six Months

You want employees to repay your confidence in them with good to really good work performance. In other words, you want a good return on your investment. After the formal orientation program has been completed, the best method of achieving good performance from staff is to support them and provide regular feedback on their performance. You should also let them know for how long the employment is *probationary*. This means new employees must satisfactorily perform to the standards set at the commencement of employment in order for the employment to continue beyond the probationary period. Continuing employment is often a hard decision where the performance has been borderline satisfactory. However, unless you make a hard decision during the first six months, you will pay for it in frustration and money when you tolerate unsatisfactory performance for too long.

Applying a formal qualifying period

Once you have determined what your probationary period is for new staff — I recommend six months, but you can choose one, two, three or six months — make this clear to your employees at the commencement of employment. Also clarify that continuing employment beyond the probation (or qualifying) period depends upon you being satisfied with their performance over that period.

Employees engaged by small businesses (that employ fewer than 15 employees) in Australia aren't entitled to claim unfair dismissal and apply for reinstatement or compensation if they're dismissed within the first 12 months of employment. (The period is six months for every other business.) However, this isn't an opportunity to ignore the signs of poor or inadequate performance, safe in the knowledge that you can just dismiss employees before they achieve 12 months' service. The performance expectations established during the orientation program should be reinforced, measured and reviewed, just as you would with other staff in your business. See Chapter 17 for an explanation of unfair dismissal laws.

If any of you has reasons why ... speak now or forever hold your peace

You have window of opportunity of either 6 or 12 months as a small business (depending on how many employees in your business) to thoroughly assess the performance and suitability of your new employee. Whether the performance has been good, bad or indifferent, you should formally assess the suitability of the employee to continue in your employ.

Assessing an employee's suitability includes using the objective measures of performance (refer to the section 'The Art of Measuring the Right Stuff', earlier in this chapter) and also an assessment of the person's general suitability. Answer the question: *Is this person a good fit for my business?* This is often difficult to answer because it relies on your intuition, balancing the emotional factor of the equation against the objective measurement of performance. Give yourself some time to reflect on performance measurements and your 'gut feel'.

If you don't think the person is a good fit, end the employment. Not every person is suitable to your business. Thank the person for her time and assist her to move on to other employment.

On the other hand, where employees are suitable, confirm their value to the business by formally writing to them that they have successfully completed the probation and have qualified for continuing employment. This act may also coincide with a pay increase, cake or other reward to mark the occasion.

Reinforcing employees' performance and value to the business builds loyalty, and the true value of loyalty to a business can't be measured by any system of performance appraisal.

Addressing Poor Performance

The aim of defining, facilitating, measuring and rewarding performance is to create a culture of continuous improvement that benefits your small business. When managing poor or unsatisfactory work performance, your dilemma may be how far you should go to remedy the underlying problems.

Reprimanding an individual can have a sobering effect on an employee's performance, but it may also create resentment and further poor performance. People don't like being told they're not working to the required standard. Nevertheless, you must address poor work performance and behaviour when it occurs, because serious risk to the business occurs from the failure to act on poor work performance. Nothing sends a good business toward insolvency more swiftly than the act of putting your head in the sand and hoping the problem will go away.

Warnings, warnings and more warnings!

Issuing warnings or counselling to staff is a necessary procedure, because failing to go through this process before sacking staff may result in liability for compensation to disgruntled employees who sue for unfair dismissal. Nevertheless, warnings should be the last resort because, undoubtedly, such action can have a negative impact on the individual and the general work culture. You're aiming to remedy poor work performance not contribute to the problem.

Okay, you may be thinking this is easy for me to say, but difficult for you to implement. Table 9-1 provides a breakdown of the type of poor work performance scenarios possible, and responses that you could use where appropriate.

Running through a simple checklist and procedure

The responses suggested in Table 9-1 are designed to provide a response commensurate with the underlying problem. However, performance problems rarely fit preordained patterns. The issue usually involves a lot more than is immediately apparent. Therefore, your response must include a procedural stage that will inform the remedial action to improve performance.

Table 9-1	Responding to Unsatisfactory Work Performance
Scenario	***Response***
Poor work performance during probation period but putting in effort to achieve expected performance standard	Additional supervision and instruction. Where performance doesn't improve sufficiently over the period of the qualifying period, you need to assess whether or not it's likely to improve to the expected standard. If in doubt, consider terminating the employment.
Performance problems affected by personal factors unrelated to work	Offer opportunity to disclose personal factors. Where practical to do so, offer assistance to overcome the factors. Look at offering annual or personal leave or leave without pay. ***Note:*** Personal issues do affect what action you can take against employees not performing to expectations.
Performance affected by poor attitude, behaviour	Issue warning indicating the problem and the attitude and behaviour expected of the employee. Be very clear about the attitude and behaviour that's unacceptable. Provide a reasonable opportunity for the employee to improve attitude and behaviour.
Performance improves for a short period and then deteriorates once close supervision is withdrawn	This is the most frustrating scenario for employers. A formal performance improvement plan (PIP) with very specific standards of behaviour and performance, combined with frequent reviews is the best response because it both places pressure on the employee and reduces the risk of successful claims of unfair treatment.
Serious and repeated poor performance where employee has been given opportunity to improve	Final warning or dismissal. Prior to dismissal you must offer the employee an opportunity to defend himself. This means offering a face-to-face interview.

The checklist of action provided in Figure 9-2 is a guide to addressing unsatisfactory work performance, with the aim of remedying the problems and enabling the employee to improve performance to a standard where you will be satisfied. Follow the checklist and you can reduce the risks to your business from claims made against you of unfair dismissals.

Everything that you do with employees is connected. This means the action you take to address unsatisfactory performance during the course of employment affects the final decision on that employment, including whether to dismiss an employee. In Chapter 17, I explain the way in which you need to manage terminating employment in detail, because you need to consider additional issues if dismissal is considered the appropriate response.

Identify the performance issue: *(Describe the tasks, duties, attitude or behaviour that's an issue affecting staff performance)* _____ _____ _____	☑
Notify employee of intention to discuss the performance issues: *(Organise time away from the direct work environment to ensure uninterrupted and private discussion.)* *(Provide employee with outline of issues. The discussion isn't a court case so you don't have to provide everything in writing. However, the employee should know in sufficient detail the subject matter of the discussion.)* *(If dismissal is a real possibility, offer employee opportunity to bring a support person.)* *Insert date of notification here* _____	☑
Meet with employee to discuss the issues: *(Explain the issues and the reasons you believe the performance is unsatisfactory. Back these up with work reports or other applicable data.)* *(Offer the employee an opportunity to respond. If you need to reflect or follow up on certain matters, allow time for you to do so before deciding on remedial action.)* _____ _____ _____	☑
Decide on remedial action: *(Warnings should include specific description of the standard of performance or behaviour that you require.)* *(Provide deadlines for achievement of the required standard of performance or behaviour.)* *(List the action taken to facilitate performance.)* *(Describe the level of supervision that will be provided over the review period.)* *(Set a date to meet again to review performance.)* _____ _____ _____	☑
Sign the record of interview and invite employee to do so as well: *(You can't require employees to sign the document. However, you can offer them an opportunity to add their own comments to the record.)* *(File the record of interview in the staff personal file.)*	☑

Figure 9-2:
Performance improvement checklist.

Chapter 10

Pay Increase? You Must Be Joking!

. . . .

In This Chapter

▶ Increasing wages according to the law

▶ Understanding that rewarding good performance is more than a stab in the dark

▶ Considering the market when setting base wages

. . . .

Money can't buy happiness, but it can make you awfully comfortable while you're being miserable.

Clare Boothe Luce

*O*ne side of the wage–work bargain is obviously wages. Money for living. Money rewarding good work. Money for skills. Money for holidays and money to compensate every conceivable eventuality. In Chapter 5, I explain the impact of statutory minimum wages, allowances, penalties and loadings underpinning all Australian employment relationships. In this chapter, I explore how you should establish your own policy on how much you pay to attract and retain employees, and the mix of cash, bonus and fringe benefits that may entail.

Decisions on wages and salaries shouldn't occur in a vacuum. I describe how to find out how much your competitors are paying staff and where you should place your wages policy in the broader wages market.

Finally, I tie the disparate threads of minimum wage obligations, over-award payments, fringe benefits, and incentive payments together to explain how you can meld the inevitable wage increases to rewards for good to excellent work performance, retain key staff and place your business in a good position to recruit and pay the right people for your business.

Adjusting Base Rates of Pay

Nobody offers small-business owners a regular pay increase but staff are rarely satisfied with a wage that never changes. Employees expect that the wages paid at the commencement of employment will be adjusted regularly to at least keep pace with inflation. This expectation is fuelled by the traditional Australian spectacle of regulatory authorities such as the Fair Work Commission reviewing and adjusting minimum wages and allowances every year.

These serious and august bodies listen to all sorts of employers, industry represents and trade unions on the subject of what is right and fair, and take into account various economic and social factors in deciding to adjust the minimum rates. You have little to no control over these decisions but you must ensure that your small business pays staff in accordance with these ever moving statutory minimum standards.

A lot of mystery and misunderstanding surrounds this process of minimum rate adjustment and what it actually means for business, so in the following sections I unravel it for you.

Modern award minimum rates and the national minimum wage (NMW) are not negotiable (refer to Chapter 5 for more on these). Both minimum rate mechanisms are also regularly adjusted (never downwards) and usually apply from the nearest pay period commencing on or immediately after 1 July each year.

Recognising skills and experience

Some modern awards prescribe multiple pay points within each wage classification, reflecting the acquisition and application of new or enhanced skills as employees continue their employment in that job. Where a wage classification in a modern award applicable to your staff has multiple pay points, your staff are eligible for progression to the higher pay points only where they have completed 12 months of continuous service in a classification level and have satisfactorily demonstrated their competence in the job. These wage increments are also minimum base rates.

Focus on identifying the modern award that covers your business and the classification description that applies to your employees. This is a skill that will help you comply with the law and save you money in the long term.

Paying above minimum wages

Minimum wages are just that — the minimum. You may pay employees more than the statutory minimums prescribed by modern awards and the NMW. This is the realm of *over-award payments* and here you have the greatest opportunity to link wages to performance and, therefore, extract the best value from the cost of employing staff and obtaining good work performance.

You may pay over-award wages for the following reasons:

- To attract the best person to perform the job
- To cover the extra hours of work that the person is expected to perform
- In recognition of higher qualifications
- To provide some incentive to better performance

Unlike statutory minimum wages, over-award payments to staff are negotiable. This basic fundamental fact has several implications for the way in which you can manage over-award payments.

Absorbing minimum wage adjustments

Adjustments to the basic minimum wage prescribed in modern awards and the NMW may be absorbed by the higher over-award component of the wage or salary you already pay to your staff. For example, an employee in charge of a fast-food shop or delivery outlet was entitled to a minimum wage of approximately $745 per week in 2013–14 under the Fast Food Industry Award. If you actually pay that employee in charge $800 per week, any yearly adjustment of the minimum award wage (for example, $12), up to the amount you already pay, isn't required to be added to the actual wage. The $12 increase may be absorbed in the over-award payment of $55 per week unless you agree to pass it on to your staff.

Rolling-up penalties, loading and overtime

Administrative simplicity is another reason to pay more than the minimum award wage. Employees may work evenings, weekends, public holidays, or more than 38 hours per week. Unless an over-award payment is made, the employees are entitled to penalties, loadings and overtime payments, which can be complex.

As long as the over-award payment amounts to the same or more than what employees would have received in penalties, loadings and overtime, rolling-up the obligations in the single hourly, weekly or yearly wage is a convenient and simple method of employing staff. The periods in which to measure the rolled-up wage with the award rates is usually 12 months.

Recognising skills and experience

Modern award minimum wages often prescribe higher rates or higher commencement rates for employees who hold qualifications in a specialist field or area of expertise. As well as this, you also have a good opportunity to apply your own policy of paying higher amounts of wages, or allowances to employees who hold or acquire qualifications in a field that assists your business and leads to better work performance.

Such payments provide an incentive to employees to develop their knowledge and improve their competence in the areas of work that contribute to business success.

Rewarding Good Performance

Whether the wage is a minimum rate prescribed by the modern award or contains over-award payments, the total package of wages or salary is a substantial contributor to the cost of running a business and, therefore, your challenge is to extract value from the expenditure.

The way to do this is to design and apply a remuneration policy tailored to reward good performance. Sounds simple? Well, of course, you don't want a policy that rewards poor performance. However, unless you think about the way in which employees earn money, this may be exactly what you end up with.

For example, a small factory producing component parts for automobiles may employ staff on minimum rates during Monday to Friday and overtime rates on Saturdays. Saturday overtime is worked to satisfy the fluctuating demands of customers for car parts. Staff may work out pretty quickly that the best way to reap the best reward is to ensure that production levels during the week remain low or static so that regular overtime is offered on Saturdays at the higher rates of pay. If you were the owner of this business, you'd need to re-engineer your wages policy to reward behaviour that produces more component parts during Monday to Friday.

A job well done is its own reward ... sometimes

Your task is to ensure your wages policy complements the other measures you have in place to motivate employees to produce good work performance (refer to Chapter 9 for more on these other measures). You can break it down as follows:

✔ Offer a basic wage that's compliant with statutory minimum rates and is considered fair and equitable when measured against the broader market of remuneration for the applicable occupation or profession.

✔ Design over-award payments for administrative simplicity, to compensate effort that goes beyond the standard working week, and to recognise additional or specialist expertise that produces higher level work performance.

✔ Adjust the basic minimum rates to keep pace with statutory obligations and cost of living and, therefore, maintain the real value of the remuneration package for the employee.

✔ Offer allowances to compensate for expenses incurred during the course of performing work for your business.

✔ Provide fringe benefits to encourage loyalty and reward very good performing staff, such as private use of business vehicles and access to corporate hospitality (seats at sporting venues, theatres and cultural events — see the following section).

✔ Use incentives and bonus payments to reward exceptional performance that increases the revenue of the business (see the section 'Paying bonuses and incentives', later in this chapter).

Providing fringe benefits and other rewards

Once upon a time you could reward employees with a mixed bag of benefits that were not necessarily in the form of cash and did not attract taxation. No longer is that the case as most fringe benefits attract the highest marginal rate of personal taxation and — worse — you, the employer, must pay the fringe benefit tax (refer to Chapter 6 for more on this, and for a list of the types of benefits that aren't fringe benefits and so aren't subject to FBT).

Nevertheless, you can organise the salary package to maximise the net benefit to you and staff.

Salary sacrifice

Fringe benefits are often provided either as part of an agreed *salary sacrifice* arrangement with employees, or ad hoc to suit the often personal and informal rewards offered to employees for the valuable contribution that they make to the business. The most common benefits that employees sacrifice part of their pre-tax salary for are superannuation and cars (that is, the payments into superannuation or to pay off their car come out before tax, meaning the employees' taxable amount is reduced). The most common ad hoc fringe benefits are hospitality and travel gifts such as movie tickets, dinner vouchers and holiday packages.

An *effective* salary sacrifice arrangement is subject to fringe benefit tax (or superannuation guarantee) rather than income tax, including the exemptions and tax-free thresholds applicable to particular benefits.

An 'effective salary sacrifice arrangement' satisfies the following conditions:

✔ The arrangement must be entered into before the work (that is to be remunerated) is performed. The ATO will not accept as effective an arrangement to sacrifice salary for work that has already been performed by the employee.

✔ Subject to the terms of any contract of employment, the arrangement can be renegotiated at any time. Where a renewable contract is in place, you and your employee may renegotiate amounts of salary or wages to be sacrificed before the start of each renewal.

✔ The sacrificed salary must be permanently forgone for the period of the arrangement. If a fringe benefit that has not been provided is cashed out at the end of a salary sacrifice arrangement accounting period, the amount cashed out is salary and is taxed as normal income.

Salaries and wages, leave entitlements, bonuses or commissions that accrued before the arrangement was entered into cannot be part of an effective salary sacrifice arrangement. Similarly, if you make payments to a third party from salary that has been earned for things such as health insurance premiums, loan repayments, union fees or credit card repayments, these payments do not constitute an effective salary sacrifice arrangement. They are made from after-tax or net amounts of salary.

You and your staff should document all the terms of any salary sacrifice arrangement. This may take the form of a term of the employment contract, or a separately documented agreement.

Providing business vehicles for private use

Providing a company car, truck or van for private use of an employee can be complicated where such use attracts FBT.

According to the ATO (www.ato.gov.au), an employee's use of a taxi, panel van, utility or other commercial vehicle (that is, one not designed principally to carry passengers) is FBT-exempt if the employee's private use of such a vehicle is limited to:

- ✔ Travel between home and work

- ✔ Travel that is incidental to travel in the course of duties of employment

- ✔ Non-work related use that is minor, infrequent and irregular (for example, occasional use of the vehicle to remove domestic rubbish)

The exemption also applies to non-work related use by an employee's wife, husband or other family member that is minor, infrequent and irregular.

The ATO says dual cabs qualify for the work-related use FBT exemption only if:

- ✔ They're designed to carry a load of one tonne or more, or more than eight passengers.

- ✔ While having a designed load capacity of less than one tonne, they're not designed for the principal purpose of carrying passengers.

Providing a car or allowing private use of business vehicles can still be a tax-effective means of remuneration for an employee under a salary sacrifice arrangement. See the sidebar 'Tax impact of salary sacrifice' for an example that works through the various issues.

Paying bonuses and incentives

Bonuses and incentives are paid to reward above average or exceptional performance. They can be paid for past performance that was exceptional or unexpected (bonuses) or in recognition of targeted and precisely measured performance that delivers a quantifiable result for the business, usually sales revenue (incentives).

No perfect formula exists for such payments. The only rule is that the payment should be made in recognition of performance that delivers a clear and quantifiable benefit to your small business.

Tax impact of salary sacrifice

Bob is paid $65,000 a year, and is entitled to sacrifice part of his salary with his small business employer for use of a business vehicle. Under this arrangement, Bob's employer allows him exclusive use of a $35,000 business car for private use. Bob's employer pays all the running expenses of $11,500 (including a GST-free payment of $600 for registration). Subtracting the GST paid on the remaining expenses means the GST-exclusive car expenses total $10,509.

The following table shows how to calculate the taxable value and FBT payable on the car fringe benefit provided to Bob. *Note:* I have included in the third column of the table an option for Bob to contribute $7,000 (the taxable value of the car, assuming for the purposes of this example that the operating cost method leads to the same taxable value of the car fringe benefit) from his after-tax income to eliminate the requirement to pay FBT. This means that Bob has two tax-effective methods to sacrifice an amount from his salary of $65,000 to have the private use of the business vehicle. One option is to sacrifice pre-tax salary only and the second option is to combine pre-tax salary sacrifice with a post-tax contribution.

FBT calculations (using either statutory or log book method)	Without employee contributions	With employee contributions
Base value of car	$35,000	$35,000
Multiply by applicable statutory % for kilometres travelled	20%	20%
Taxable value of car benefit	$7,000	$7,000
Less employee contributions	NIL	$7,000
Multiply by gross-up rate	2.0647	2.0647
Equals grossed-up taxable value	$14,453	NIL
Multiply by FBT rate	46.5%	46.5%
FBT payable by employer	$6,720	NIL

The following table shows how the salary sacrifice amount is calculated for both options.

		Salary plus car (no employee contribution)	Salary plus car (employee contribution)
Add	GST-exclusive value of car expenses paid by the employer	$10,509	$10,509
Add	FBT payable	$6,720	NIL

		Salary plus car (no employee contribution)	Salary plus car (employee contribution)
Add	GST payable on employee contributions	NIL	$636
Less	Employee contributions (GST-inclusive) to employer (paid for out of employee's income after tax has been deducted)	NIL	$7,000
Salary sacrifice amount		$17,229	$4,145

As the preceding table shows, Bob has the choice to sacrifice the following amounts (inclusive of FBT) from his salary:

✔ $17,229 if no employee contributions are made

✔ $4,145 if employee contributions of $7,000 are made

Applying the 2013 personal tax rates, Bob's disposable income after salary sacrifice is $1,821 higher if he makes a contribution of $7,000, and only $458 higher without the $7,000 contribution to obtain the same benefit.

Individual incentives and bonuses

Payment of individual incentives and bonus payments is sometimes a philosophical decision as much as a practical business choice. You want to recognise individual effort, which is fine as long as you understand that the reward truly must recognise and reward individual effort. No man or woman is an island and so don't forget that the individual result may occur due to collective effort — for example, the office-based staff who supports the sales staff. Failure to recognise and reward the support team may lead to resentment, conflict and lessening of performance from those who have not been rewarded.

Individual incentives are usually paid to sales-type employees who rely on sales to justify continuing employment — that is, no sales, no job.

Collective bonuses and incentives

If your business performance relies upon teamwork, and your capacity to deliver quality products and services is only as strong as the weakest link, collective incentives and bonus payments are more likely to lead to the performance that you have aimed to achieve. They can also have an impact on the morale of all staff and encourage the better performers to support and lead others in the team to achieve higher levels of performance. One in, all in.

Keeping Pace with Market Rates

The old saying 'Pay peanuts and you get monkeys' is not a bad way to introduce this topic. Paying an employee the base minimum wage prescribed in a modern award is the easiest way of managing rewards, and may also be the most affordable method for your business. Nevertheless, in a competitive market for skilled staff you will be certain of only one thing: Your business competitors won't be paying less (unless doing so illegally!). However, you can't know for sure how much more they will be paying than you. Consequently, you may find yourself at a competitive disadvantage where attracting and retaining skilled staff is important to business success.

The answer to this dilemma is threefold:

- ✔ Get the base wage right for your business circumstances
- ✔ Understand where you want to compete in the market for staff
- ✔ Know when and how to negotiate wages with staff

Getting the base wage right

The base wage or salary provides the basis upon which all other remuneration is calculated, including overtime, superannuation, penalties and bonuses. This wage should be compliant with the statutory minimum rates as well as sufficient to attract and retain quality staff. You can reference the applicable modern award for the correct minimum base wage.

Competing in the market for wages

Believe it or not, a market exists for skilled and experienced staff that operates independently of the system of statutory of minimum wages and allowances. You need to decide how you intend to compete in this market, and that means deciding the level of base wages and other remuneration you are prepared to pay to attract and retain skilled staff above the statutory minimum.

You can look at three key elements when determining the salary for an employee:

✔ Market rates

✔ Work value

✔ Personal value

The market for wages

Deciding where you wish to pitch your business in the market for salary and wages means working out where you sit in the market. Think of wages as falling within a spread of four quartiles. The first quartile contains the bottom range of salaries for a given job. The second quartile represents wages paid by businesses that are between 25 and 50 per cent of the highest rates. The third and fourth quartiles obviously represent wages that are above the mid-point of the market.

For example, retail shops and supermarket owners in Australia pay an adult shop assistant an hourly wage ranging from the award minimum (approximately $18) to approximately $30. Therefore, the market for wages in the general retail industry is characterised by a spread of $12 with a bottom end of the market at $18 per hour. If we assume that 50 per cent of retail businesses pay their shop assistants $25 or more, any small business that pays less than $25 per hour may not be able to attract or retain shop assistants who are attracted to the higher end of the market.

Most small businesses aren't able to compete with the larger industry leaders — that is, the big businesses that hold large market share in total business activity for the industry. Therefore, rather than paying the highest wages you may offer a wage at the mid-point. In the preceding example that means $25 per hour. This should ensure that you are at least able to compete against the lower 50 per cent of your competitors to attract and retain staff while maintaining cost competitiveness with your larger competitors that may be paying higher wages.

You can find out what the market is paying by scanning the job advertisements online and in newspapers. You can also contact industry and professional associations to get an idea.

Work value

Australia has a long tradition of differentiating wages on the basis of the inherent value of the work performed. For example, a surgeon is paid more than a hospital orderly. A chef is paid more than a kitchen hand. This is because of the complexity of the work, the required years of education and application of skills and knowledge that aren't easily replicated by the lesser skilled persons.

However, work value is not always a good indicator of how much salary or wage should be paid to an employee. Although modern award wages are loosely determined on work value, actual wages and salaries are increasingly determined by the fluctuating demands of the Australian economy. A fitter and turner, a boiler maker and truck driver, for example, can all make more money than a university professor by working in the iron ore mines of Western Australia or coal mines of Queensland. Therefore, work value is not necessarily a good indicator of the wages that you should pay to attract and retain good staff. Market rates and personal value may be better indicators in some circumstances, especially where the relation between traditional professionals and occupations has been skewed by market shortages such as in the Australian mining industry.

Personal value

If you find a person who works well for your business, paying a higher wage to retain that person is often a good investment. An employee's personal attitude, aptitude, loyalty and competence are valuable traits that should be rewarded with a wage or salary commensurate with the person's value to your business.

Negotiating with unhappy staff

Negotiations for a wage or salary is usually done at the time the offer of employment occurs. In many small businesses negotiations never occur. The wage is the wage and if employees don't like it then they can resign and/or go elsewhere. This is not an attitude that is likely to engender loyalty from staff.

Negotiations don't need to be formalised affairs with each party sitting on either side of the table with lawyers and union officials fighting it out to extract the best result for their respective clients. I suggest you review the wage or salary package each year on the anniversary of staff employment or coinciding with the adjustments to the NMW and modern award wages.

The factors that you can take into account when negotiating wages and salary are:

- Changes in the cost of living (consumer price index)
- How employees values their contribution to the business
- Movements in market rates of wages — that is, how much your competitors are paying staff
- Rewards that will motivate better performance
- The personal value of the employee to the business
- Any other issues on your mind and the mind of the employee

Whatever factors you consider when negotiating wages and salary, keep in mind that you can only pay (above statutory minimum rates) what the business can afford. Do your sums before you commit to any increases and also be creative with your negotiations. You don't have to just offer wages. Bonuses, incentives and fringe benefits (as discussed earlier in this chapter) may be valued more highly by staff and can be linked to performance more readily than wages or salary.

Many negotiators talk about the concept of *win–win* outcomes. This is important because the employment relationship is not a winner take all relationship. Both you and your employee need to leave any wage review with a sense of mutual satisfaction. As far as possible, you should ensure that your employee is satisfied that you have considered their interests seriously and that the results of the review or negotiations are fair and equitable. A happy employee is more likely to be a productive employee. Good luck!

Part IV
The Non-Discriminating Employer

Five strategies for harmonious working relationships

✔ **Live your values:** The single most important thing you can do to prevent bad behaviour is to model good behaviour. Respect, honesty, politeness, empathy and diligence aren't just words on a mission statement. When you live those values, you can expect others to do so as well.

✔ **Understand the underlying causes of conflict:** Treat the cause and not the symptoms of conflict to help resolve problems affecting the harmony in your business. Personality clashes, inequitable treatment, unfulfilled expectations, bad behaviour and competition for attention can contribute to conflict between staff.

✔ **Keep in mind it's not always what you say but what you do:** Speaking about personal differences, disabilities and personal characteristics isn't discrimination when it shows an interest in the person, is done respectfully and relates to the work that staff are expected to perform. Prejudicing a person's employment because of personal attributes is usually unlawful — and just wrong.

✔ **Don't be afraid to give someone a go:** Just because a person has a disability doesn't mean she can't do the job. A person who overcomes life's hurdles just may have the resilience, creativity and determination you need in your business. A few practical adjustments to the work environment may be a really good investment.

✔ **Create your own policies to guide everyone on acceptable conduct:** Bullying, harassment and discrimination are difficult issues to explain. Having policies in writing are essential tools for thorough orientations that set staff off on the right path.

Find out more about avoiding discrimination and handling conflict in your small business with a free article at www.dummies.com/extras/hrsmallbusinessau.

In this part ...

- ✔ Work out the underlying causes of conflict at work, how to resolve conflict if it does occur in your business, and when you might need third-party help.

- ✔ Understand what your and your employees' responsibilities are when looking at anti-discrimination, and how to get proactive and develop a strategy that works for your business

- ✔ Learn what bullying and sexual harassment mean in the workplace, and how to use policies and practice to educate staff.

Chapter 11

Managing Workplace Conflict

. . . .

In This Chapter

▶ Working out what may be behind workplace conflict

▶ Understanding the laws controlling how employers and employees behave

▶ Taking advantage of simple resolution techniques

▶ Picking the correct resolution method and facilitating discussions

▶ Keeping in mind that external agencies have a role

. . . .

Always forgive your enemies. Nothing annoys them so much.

Oscar Wilde

C onflicts among your staff and with your staff are inevitable. Some conflicts may be bad, some less so. Your challenge is to work to resolve them so that a positive result is achieved (even if you're not always doing so with kindness in your heart, as Oscar Wilde so cleverly observed).

In this chapter I explain contemporary methods you can use to prevent and resolve workplace conflict. I start off by covering how to identify the underlying reasons for conflict — to give you a better chance at firstly preventing conflicts and then, when they do occur, successfully resolving them.

Australian laws regulating or indirectly impacting on the resolution of workplace conflict are many and varied. I provide an overview of the laws so that you can navigate a safe path through the conflict without breaching personal rights and the obligations imposed. Importantly, I explain practical methods of conflict resolution that you can apply in your own small business.

Finally, I explain how external agencies such as the Fair Work Commission and the Human Rights Commission can sometimes impose their powers to resolve conflicts in the workplace.

Understanding the Causes of Conflict at Work

Conflicts in the workplace arise in the same way that conflicts occur in everyday life. They may be caused by issues such as personality clashes, changes to the way work is done, bad attitudes and behaviour and insufficient communication. Whatever the context, a common factor — people — runs through all conflicts.

Conflict commonly occurs between small-business owners or managers and the staff they oversee. Of course, it can also occur between colleagues working alongside each other, within groups of employees and between groups. For example, Betty doesn't get along with Bert in administration. The accounting team don't like the sales staff. Fred objects to the way his supervisor speaks to him and the kitchen staff all dislike the chef.

Problems, problems, problems. Time to get to the bottom of the conflict or else it will only get worse.

Sources of conflict

Here's a list of the common reasons for conflict in the workplace (you may have other examples to add):

- Behaviour — for example, misconduct, bullying and harassment
- Perceptions of inequity
- Personality clash
- Power struggles
- Unfulfilled expectations
- Unsatisfactory performance

Behavioural standards

Bad behaviour occurs in many ways. Dishonesty, bullying, harassment, abuse, insensitivity and even simple rudeness to others can poison relationships in a workplace. Often you may not even notice bad behaviour in others because you're so busy running your business. Worse, it could be your behaviour that's the source of conflict!

Interpersonal behaviour is a highly regulated area of the employment relationship. People enter the workplace from diverse cultural, national, racial, social and religious backgrounds. Governments seem to think that they can control socially unacceptable conduct by imposing financial penalties and other obligations on employers to prevent behaviour that offends, discriminates, harasses, bullies or otherwise prejudices the working lives of employees. Therefore, this area of the law is one that you must get to know, so you can apply policies to prevent bad behaviour in your small business. See the section 'The Heavy Hand of the Law', later in this chapter, for more.

You set the standards of behaviour in your business so take time to reflect on your own conduct from time to time. Modelling good behaviour is one way to prevent bad behaviour, and this is a theme I return to throughout this book.

Unfulfilled expectations

Everyone enters a job with certain expectations. Sometimes it doesn't quite work out the way employees wanted. Frustration with the wage, other people, the nature of the work, the lack of opportunities can all lead to conflict when these differ from what was expected.

Outline the job requirements very clearly before you even offer a job to a person, and also provide a good picture of the work environment and the people that person will be working with. Your small business more closely resembles the family unit than it does a major corporation, so frustrated ambitions, or unfulfilled or different expectations can be a significant source of conflict and these are very difficult to resolve once entrenched. Your regular performance reviews (refer to Chapter 9) are an ideal opportunity to have an honest discussion about how satisfied both you and your employee are with working life.

Inequity

People believing they're sometimes treated unfairly or unequally at work is natural. Although the belief may only be perception rather than reality, it's often the cause of conflict. People compare their arrangements with others in the workplace and against benchmarks in the wider world. If a person believes he's treated unfairly, he's less likely to display the commitment, loyalty and effort that you would expect.

Have a keen sense of what's fair and reasonable and apply it consistently, particularly in relation to recognition and reward. Playing favourites has an upside for the favourite employee but may be viewed unfavourably by others.

Personality clashes

Personality clashes are undoubtedly the most common cause of conflict in a workplace. Personalities, unlike behaviour, can't be changed. Therefore, where two or more people conflict for this reason, you need to find means to channel the conflicting personalities into productive areas of work, avoiding situations that fuel the conflict.

A helpful way of looking at a personality clash is to view it essentially as a difference in interpreting the other person's motivations. For example, Betty may falsely attribute Bert's behaviour because it has adversely affected her. In other words, the employee thinks the other person's behaviour was intended to harm or adversely affect them at work. Understanding this as the source of conflict enables you to apply resolution techniques appropriate to the underlying cause.

Power struggles

Power struggles between individuals can occur where employees are competing for your attention and admiration. You know the type of employees who may get involved in a power struggle — often they're ambitious, determined and a little bit ruthless. A little bit of competition is good but it can also degenerate into open hostility, affecting the wellbeing of other employees and the productivity of the business.

Think about how you want working relationships to operate. Teamwork is difficult to achieve where the team members are working to undermine each other.

Poor work performance

I would love to have a dollar for every time an employer attempts to hold employees accountable for poor work performance and the employees then complain that they've been bullied or are (seemingly suddenly) suffering from stress and anxiety.

Don't get me wrong — I'm not casting judgement on the sincerity of these claims. My point is, poor work performance is of itself a source of conflict and you cannot ignore performance that's less than satisfactory and is harming your business.

Poor work performance is definitely a major area of conflict that requires your undivided attention, both in terms of implementing a program to improve performance and, if necessary, the application of disciplinary action that's not going to expose your business to successful claims for compensation citing unfair dismissal, harassment, bullying or workers compensation. (Refer to Chapter 9 for more on managing performance, and see Chapter 17 for more on unfair dismissal.)

Don't ignore the signs of conflict (they won't go away)

Knowing what causes conflict is one thing. Seeing the signs of these causes before the conflict gets ugly is quite another. Conflict manifests itself in various forms of behaviour not always evident to the unsuspecting eye. The symptoms of conflict can be

✔ Grievances such as claims of bullying and harassment

✔ High levels of absenteeism

✔ High staff turnover

✔ Industrial action such as strikes

✔ Poor work performance

✔ Workers compensation claims of stress and anxiety

Every medical practitioner in the world is likely to tell you to look for the signs of illness through the symptoms that are exhibited. In business, you need to monitor the prevalence of the symptoms of conflict and read them as the sign of a potential major blow up among staff or with yourself. Treat the underlying cause of the symptoms of conflict if you want a healthy and productive workplace.

The Heavy Hand of the Law

The law of the land often has a very large hand in how conflict is addressed in Australian businesses, with an array of laws in place to control and modify behaviour in Australian workplaces. Some of those laws, such as the anti-discrimination, unfair dismissal, and health and safety laws, are explained in subsequent chapters. However, certain laws also prescribe how you may prevent, manage and resolve conflicts that occur in your workplace. These laws include

✔ *Age Discrimination Act 2004*

✔ *Disability Discrimination Act 1992*

✔ *Fair Work Act 2010*

✔ *Human Rights and Equal Opportunity Act 1986*

✔ *NSW Anti-Discrimination Act 1977*

✔ *QLD Anti-discrimination Act 1991*

✔ *Racial Discrimination Act1975*

✔ *Sex Discrimination Act 1984*

✔ *South Australia Equal Opportunity Act 1984*

✔ *Tasmanian Anti-Discrimination Act 1998*

✔ *Victorian Equal Opportunity Act 2010*

✔ *Western Australia Equal Opportunity Act 1984*

✔ Various state health and safety laws

Of course, I don't expect you to become expert in each of these areas of the law. However, you do need to be aware of the duties and obligations imposed by the laws on how conflicts of various forms must be addressed. The regulations mostly follow a similar pattern of rules, procedures, preventative measures and remedies, as shown in Figure 11-1.

Figure 11-1: Common principles of conflict resolution in Australian workplace laws.

Rules	Procedures	Prevention	Remedies
• Entitlements • Obligations – Subjective – Objective	• Resolution methods • Fairness	• Education • Consultation • Risk management systems and action	• Compensation • Reinstatement • Dismissal

Each law establishes rights and obligations, such as the right to a healthy and safe workplace or the obligation not to take adverse action against a person for exercising a workplace right. Breaches of such rights and obligations open up paths for resolution of the conflict and interventions of external authorities where your attempts at resolution are unsuccessful. Integral to the legal frameworks are the obligations to treat people fairly in the investigation and resolution of conflict, and a duty to implement education programs and other preventative measures. So, if you think about all the laws regulating workplace conflicts in this manner, you can start to see through the fog of regulation with a structured and rational method of classifying the nature of the conflict and working through the procedures, education, consultation and remedial action to prevent and resolve the conflict.

In the following section, I cover the resolution side in more detail.

Resolving Conflict: Simple Methods that Just Might Work

Thousands of experts, academics, business gurus (and others) claim to have the simple answers to resolving conflicts. I don't make any such assertions and I don't believe conflict is easily resolved with a magical formula. So ignore anyone who tells you that they have a guaranteed simple method for resolving workplace conflicts. That's the bad news. The good news is that conflict can be resolved — doing so just requires hard work, a clear mind and, sometimes, a lot of time.

Over the course of my career, I've found successful conflict resolution techniques usually exhibit five processes:

✔ Examining the issues thoroughly

✔ Understanding the regulatory constraints

✔ Establishing the preconditions for resolution

✔ Applying the right method to resolve the issue

✔ Working through fair procedures to achieve a fair outcome

The first three processes in the preceding list are covered in the following sections. The final two are covered in the section 'Selecting the Right Method', later in this chapter.

Examining the issues

Finding out the facts is the first and most important task to perform when looking to resolve conflict. Without facts you can't move forward. The questions for which you need answers are: Who? What? Where? When? How? Why?

For example, find out who is involved in the conflict — it may involve more people than immediately evident. What is the conflict really about? What is the source of the conflict? Where is the conflict occurring and when did it occur? The conflict may be ongoing or it may relate to personal relationships or incidents outside of work. Ask yourself how this conflict got to the stage it has. It may be that particular reasons are fuelling the conflict, such as failures of leadership, pressure to perform, unhappy work culture, inadequate support to employees and clashes of personalities.

Question the people involved and check answers with your own independent investigation. As you write down the answers to each of these questions, a picture of the facts should begin to emerge.

Fact can sometimes be a slippery term. Don't worry if you have conflicting perspectives or gaps in the story. You won't always obtain a perfect picture of every fact at this stage. You will have an opportunity to fill in the gaps and weigh the various stories when you move on to resolve the conflict.

Understanding the legal constraints

Understanding the policy parameters and regulatory limitations means you can assess (and revise, if required) the policies and procedures that you have created to manage these types of workplace conflicts.

For example, in Chapter 8 I explain the importance of creating employment policies that describe behavioural expectations and the procedures to investigate and resolve issues that commonly occur in the workplace, such as sexual harassment and discrimination. In the situation where a conflict occurs that includes issues of this nature, you must go back to the policy, read it and make sure that the rules and procedures for dealing with these issues are strictly adhered to, because the law sets the boundaries or constraints within which you can resolve the conflict. Your policy and procedure should faithfully apply the underpinning regulation.

Refer to the section 'The Heavy Hand of the Law' earlier in this chapter for more on the underpinning regulation.

Pre-conditions for resolution

HR specialist AC Tidwell has identified three preconditions for successful resolution of conflicts. They are:

- ✔ **Opportunity:** This involves having the right environment to resolve the dispute. For example, conducting the investigation, interview and mediation outside of the immediate work environment (away from the 'battlefield') often has a calming effect on people.

  Timing is everything with conflict resolution. Once you become aware of a problem you must decide whether to wait until the end of the working day, at a break, immediately or otherwise depending upon the circumstances of the particular incident or complaint. You should follow your instincts on this as no one can provide an all-encompassing rule to guide you. Suffice to say that if the grievance alleges serious misconduct then acting swiftly to remove or separate the complainant from the person complained about is prudent until the matter is resolved. If the complainant is suffering some illness or injury because of the bullying or harassment then you might offer them time off work until the matter is resolved.

✔ **Capacity:** This covers the ability of the parties involved in the conflict to communicate, understand and respond to the issues, see things from other peoples' perspectives, and think rationally, devoid of emotional responses. There may be circumstances whereby, for example, language is a barrier, or religious or cultural attitudes impede the efficient resolution of the grievance. These barriers must be removed, reduced or set aside before the conflict can be resolved. For example, a translator could be brought in to remove a language barrier. If cultural attitudes are a barrier, you need to find a way for employees to set these aside while at work.

Capacity is probably the most difficult precondition to establish because conflicts such as harassment and bullying complaints are highly emotional issues and challenge personal reputations, integrity and honesty. Personality clashes, by definition, are extremely difficult to resolve because of the inability of conflicting parties to see other's perspective. Nevertheless, an attempt must be made to get the parties to open their minds to the possibility of compromise and resolution.

✔ **Volition:** Perhaps a word you don't hear in everyday conversation, *volition* means the willingness of the parties to participate in a process to resolve the conflict. The people involved have to be personally prepared to work together to find solutions to the matter. It must be a give and take process. As an employer, you can use both the carrot and the stick to achieve this precondition. For example, an accused employee is normally willing to participate because failure to do so may lead to dismissal. Unwilling complainants sometimes need cajoling because they fear recriminations. In these circumstances, you need to be very strong on ensuring that you won't hold complaining or 'whistleblowing' against the employee.

Most of the laws impacting on conflict resolution usually prohibit action against complainants.

Each of the preconditions in the preceding list should be in place to give you the best chance of resolving the conflict effectively.

A simple checklist to determine whether these preconditions are in place before you decide to tackle a complaint can enable you to assess the likelihood of successful resolution.

Selecting the Right Method

You can use various formal methods in the resolution of conflicts, and not all of these methods require specialised skills or qualifications. However, some alternative dispute resolution methods may need to be conducted by trained experts, such as

- Conciliation
- Facilitation
- Mediation
- Arbitration

I cover the various techniques — both those that don't require expert help and those that may — in the following section.

Working through conflicts with your employees

You may be able to work through some conflict resolution techniques with your staff, without the involvement of outside experts. These include the following:

- **Collaborative problem-solving:** This requires you and the parties involved in a conflict to work together to find a solution to the conflict. The key to collaboration is to work from people's real needs, not from their stated position. For example, employees may state that they're dissatisfied with the attitude or behaviour of another employee, but may in fact really be seeking some recognition of their contribution to the business. In other words, you need to explore the underlying needs of the people who are conflicted. Collaboration involves people working together to find creative solutions. Often no magic solution is possible and you need to use another approach, but at least concentrating on personal needs gives you the chance to satisfy everyone. You should take notes and document any agreed action so that all parties have a confidential record of the resolution.

- **Self-managed resolution:** This is where the conflict is resolved by the parties directly involved. For example, where one employee has a grievance with another employee, you can encourage the two people involved to sort it out themselves. This sometimes takes courage, particularly if the grievance is a claim of bullying or harassment. However, in many situations the issue may be a minor misunderstanding or a case of unintentional offence. In cases such as these, asking the employee to first address the matter with the work colleague before contemplating a formal complaint may be appropriate (and may provide the most likelihood of success). Don't suggest this process if it may put an employee at further risk.

✔ **Disciplinary action:** Situations will arise where an initial investigation suggests that one or more of the staff may be involved in serious misconduct. For example, allegations that an employee has physically assaulted an employee or has engaged in conduct that poses a serious risk to the health and safety of the employee. Initiation ceremonies of apprentices and other new employees are notorious examples. In these types of circumstances, you should commence disciplinary action and an investigation of the complaint as soon as practicable — just as you would any other situation that suggests an employee has breached a fundamental obligation or employment policy that places continuing employment in question.

✔ **Managerial directive:** This is probably pretty obvious, and involves you telling employees to get on with it, placing an employee on a warning or otherwise deciding for the parties to a conflict how it will be resolved. This is the last resort power that you can exercise to resolve conflicts where the parties are unable to resolve the conflict themselves, a risk exists of bullying or harassment continuing or escalating, or the solution isn't readily apparent. A possible directive could be separating staff to different work locations or different working hours or days. You could also require one employee to apologise or something of that nature. Alternative dispute resolution methods are discussed in the section 'Third-Party Interventions and the Role of Government Tribunals', later in this chapter.

Considering alternative approaches

You can take other approaches to conflict resolution beyond the methods listed in the preceding section. The following sections cover some alternative behaviour-based approaches, and the pros and cons of each.

Contesting

When people contest options, they're attempting to have their idea accepted at the expense of other ideas. The danger with adopting this style of conflict resolution is that it often leads to further conflict, because contesting ideas while still listening to others requires great skill.

Many people avoid contesting because they're concerned about offending others. Although this is a valid concern, you must be careful not to let it stop you arguing for an idea which you believe is the best solution.

Contesting is appropriate when the issue is important to you but unimportant to the other party. It is also valid when quick, decisive action is needed — for example, the building is burning down so everyone better get out.

Accommodating

Accommodating is letting other parties have their way at the expense of your view. This style is inappropriate when it's simply a way of avoiding conflict. Accommodating is appropriate if you find out you are wrong or when maintaining harmony is more important than satisfying your personal needs.

Withdrawing

Sometimes people will withdraw from a conflict situation. This is inappropriate if designed to manipulate people or avoid discussing difficult issues. Withdrawing is appropriate when the issue being discussed is none of your business or is trivial. It can also be used to let people calm down.

Compromising

Compromising is one of the most popular approaches to resolving conflict. It involves both parties working toward a solution that's somewhere between their initial stated positions. Compromising is popular because everyone gets part of what they want. However, the approach involves two significant weaknesses:

✔ Producing the best solution (if such a solution exists) is unlikely

✔ No-one is going to be completely satisfied, which can cause serious problems if the solution isn't a success — nobody owns the solution and so nobody takes responsibility for making it work

Compromising is a good style to use on minor issues when the goals aren't worth the possible disruption or to achieve temporary solutions. Getting some of what you want now and working toward improvement in the longer term is a better approach than 'all or nothing'.

Offering facilitation

Facilitation means helping people work through a process to improve communication and facilitate a resolution that meets the interests of each party. The primary responsibility of a facilitator is to provide the structure for the discussion, whether it is one-on-one or between a large group of people.

Facilitation is a technique often associated with third-party interventions. However, you can master the technique yourself — that is, you can be the facilitator. Figure 11-2 shows how it works.

Figure 11-2: Facilitating conflict resolution.

Getting started
Building rapport
Agreeing on norms of behaviour
Agreeing on agenda

Uncovering issues
Asking questions
Acknowledging views
Clarifying points

Identifying options
Brainstorming
Identifying pros and cons
Keeping discussion on track
Summarising points

Deciding
Evaluating options
Staying focused on outcome
Agreeing on timeframe
Getting real commitment

'A fair go all round'

An old Australian legal principle is often recognised and quoted when the question of fairness is raised in employment situations: 'A fair go all round'. The phrase was coined by his Honour Justice Sheldon in a court case brought by the Australian Workers Union in 1971, and means that, whenever assessing the merits of a case (in that instance a dismissal), the court should apply a fair go all round to both employer and employee.

To provide a fair go all round in the resolution of conflicts in your small business, you need to adhere to the following:

- ✔ Explain the problem to everyone in sufficient detail to enable each person to understand what is precisely the problem

- ✔ Provide opportunity to respond so the affected persons have sufficient time to consider the issues before responding

- ✔ Allow opportunity for employees to improve or meet the expectations — that is, you offer a way to redeem themselves before leaping to action and penalising employees

- ✔ Allow representation and advice to employees facing action as result of the conflict so they're able to adequately participate and respond to grievances underlying the conflict

Don't solve one problem while creating another. Complaints must be resolved but the way in which you resolve them must include a fair procedure. This means

- ✔ Ask questions: Who? What? When? How? Why?

- ✔ Ask the complainant how he would like the matter resolved

- ✔ Be open and frank with the person who is the subject of the complaint

- ✔ Draw your conclusions from the facts and not what you think might have happened

- ✔ Emphasise confidentiality to all parties

- ✔ Listen to the complaint and take notes

- ✔ Be patient — don't promise anything to any of the parties until you have fully investigated the facts

- ✔ Stay impartial — don't jump to conclusions

You may believe one party over the other if it comes down to 'He said/she said', although you must base your conclusion on sound reasoning. For example, if one employee's explanation is more plausible or one person is more trustworthy based on an analysis of the arguments and prior experience with each employee. If unsure, ask a colleague with no direct involvement and test your conclusion as to who should be believed.

Third-Party Interventions and the Role of Government Tribunals

Asking an independent third party to broker a resolution of a conflict in your business is sometimes prudent — and sometimes the decision is beyond your control. For example, where the conflict is of a serious nature and you want to ensure that a higher level of expertise is applied to the problem, you might engage a consultant to investigate, facilitate or mediate the resolution.

Where an employee complains to a regulatory authority, you have no choice but to respond to the authority and participate in the proceedings dictated by that authority. In the following section, I provide a very simple explanation of two methods that are applied by regulatory authorities such as the Australian Human Rights Commission and the Fair Work Commission. Normally you will need representation if you are directed to respond to complaints filed with these authorities, but knowing the methods that they apply is useful.

Mediation

The role of mediator includes establishing ground rules for negotiation, opening channels of communication, ensuring that the needs of each party are clarified and identifying key issues. Mediators are usually legally trained or at least well versed in the laws regulating the issues underlying the conflict.

Mediators don't decide who is right or wrong. Their role is to assist the conflicted parties to reach an agreed settlement of the dispute. Nevertheless, mediators may recommend or suggest particular courses of action that may or may not have some bearing on the outcome of the conflict.

You can appoint your own mediator to assist in the resolution of a conflict. A good mediator should be able to display clear, rational and innovative thinking, as well as empathy, self-awareness and self-control, among other interpersonal and problem-solving skills.

The courts use mediation before directing parties to litigation to attend court for a full hearing and judgement.

Conciliation and arbitration

Conciliation is another third-party process commonly used in Australian workplace relations tribunals, and bodies established to enforce anti-discrimination and human rights laws.

Conciliators investigate complaints brought against employers where an employee makes an allegation that a statutory right or obligation has been breached. Conciliators make an initial assessment and investigation of the complaint and may then compel disputing parties to attend a conciliation conference (similar to a mediation session).

In the Fair Work Commission, conciliation is initiated by an employee or their union notifying the Commission of a formal dispute or claiming that the employee has been adversely affected or unfairly dismissed.

The conciliator runs a meeting in which an attempt is made to reconcile the parties and address their conflict. Where the parties agree on a settlement, the conciliator formally records the result and the matter is ended. If a conciliation conference fails, the conflict may sometimes be taken to the next level, where the case is heard and a decision is arbitrated.

Arbitration is a formal process in which a third party, such as an individual Commissioner, makes a decision on the legal merits of the dispute. Arbitrators make this decision after a hearing that generally involves the presentation of evidence and oral argument. Arbitration is sometimes mandatory — such as in the resolution of claims of unfair dismissal.

You can also agree to private arbitration as an alternative to going to court. This requires all parties to the conflict to agree to abide by the decision of the private arbitrator. A private arbitrator could be someone from the Fair Work Commission or a person appointed by you and the aggrieved employee, such as a local lawyer or the person who mediated the dispute. Private arbitration is entirely up to the conflicted parties.

Keeping a clear head through conflict resolution

While no simple answers exist to preventing conflict in your small business, conflict resolution is certainly not all doom and gloom. Getting to know the underlying sources of conflict by monitoring the symptoms, and understanding your legal obligations and setting them out in your employment policies provides a solid framework from which to work toward resolution. Conducting thorough investigations by asking the right questions allows you to focus in on the real issues. Applying conflict resolution techniques suitable to the particular situation, combined with a 'fair go all round' approach, should (with a bit of grit and determination) lead to a positive resolution. After that, it's back to business!

Chapter 12

A Journey through Australian Workplace Rights and EEO

In This Chapter

▶ Working out what unlawful discrimination means

▶ Treading carefully around workplace rights

▶ Creating your workplace strategy

▶ Respecting privacy and personal information

▶ Homing in on suitability, not disability

*A*ccording to the Australian Macquarie dictionary, to discriminate means (1) to make a distinction, as in favour of or against a person or thing: to discriminate against a minority and (2) to note or observe a difference; distinguish accurately: to discriminate between things.

Australian governments have implemented anti-discrimination law over many years to protect people from discrimination and harassment in their employment, their education and in other aspects of public and private life. However, not all actions that might be described as discriminatory are unlawful. In this chapter I explain what is meant by *unlawful discrimination* at work and discuss how the national, state and territory laws impact on the way you can employ people in your business.

While not every action that breaches the law is characterised as discriminatory, these actions may nevertheless contravene an employees' *workplace rights*. This relatively new area of employment regulation is a minefield for employers. I explain these workplace rights and what you can and can't do to stay on the right side of them.

Developing workplace policies that describe your expectations of staff behaviour, how you aim to educate the people under your control and your procedures to resolve complaints are a must for your small business. I provide some practical advice on using employment policies to achieve those ends.

You also need to be sensitive in the manner in which you ask prospective and current staff for personal information, and how you store and manage it confidentially. I explain how to do this properly.

Finally, I discuss the exemptions to anti-discrimination and workplace rights, explaining the concept of *inherent requirements of the job*, and providing some practical tips on how to manage difficult decisions where either current or prospective employees have disabilities affecting their capacity to perform work in your small business.

Understanding Unlawful Discrimination

Discrimination in employment is *unlawful* (rather than perhaps unfair) where an employee is disadvantaged or treated less favourably by an employer in some aspect of their employment because of a particular personal characteristic or attribute. Motivation for unlawful discrimination isn't relevant. The person only needs to show that he has been treated less favourably or been disadvantaged, and that a reason (not necessarily the only reason) for disadvantaging the person was because of the characteristic. National, state and territorial governments have enacted various grounds upon which discrimination is unlawful and the list seems to grow as the years progress.

In summary, the personal characteristics or attributes to which unlawful discrimination in employment applies across Australia are the following:

- Age
- Breastfeeding
- Carer status
- Colour
- Criminal record
- Disability
- Family responsibilities
- Gender
- Marital status
- Medical record
- Parental status
- Physical features

- Political belief
- Pregnancy
- Race
- Religious belief
- Sex
- Sexual orientation
- Trade union activity
- Personal association with anyone that possesses the preceding characteristics

Unlawful discrimination in employment can happen in various situations, including

- Decisions to offer or not offer employment
- Hostile working environments resulting from bullying and harassment
- Hours of work
- Overtime requirements
- Promotional and training opportunities
- Salary and other benefits
- Travelling overnight for work

Under Victorian equal opportunity law, for example, an employer must not unreasonably refuse to accommodate the parental and caring responsibilities of the employee. The majority of the Australian anti-discrimination laws recognise that discrimination can occur indirectly through imposing on people obligations that they are less able to comply with than others who don't share their particular characteristics.

I cover the nature of direct and indirect discrimination prohibited in Australian employment in the following sections.

Direct discrimination of staff

Direct discrimination in employment occurs when a person is treated less favourably than others because of a particular characteristic or attribute.

Three important elements are required to prove direct discrimination:

- ✔ **Less favourable treatment.** An employee must show that she has suffered some loss or disadvantage as the result of the action of the employer because of the less favourable treatment. For example, termination of employment or denial of a benefit that other employees are provided.

- ✔ **Treatment based on attribute or characteristic.** A link must be shown between the behaviour complained of and the prohibited ground. That is, the characteristic or attribute of the employee is the reason or one of the reasons for the treatment.

- ✔ **Treatment occurs in circumstances which are the same or not materially different.** In order to establish direct discrimination, the employee must show that his less favourable treatment has occurred in circumstances that are the same as, or similar to, the circumstances of the non-discriminatory situation — that is, the treatment of the other employees.

If your small business operates in Victoria and the Australian Capital Territory, direct discrimination can be proven simply if a person with a particular attribute can show she has been treated *unfavourably* because of that attribute — that is, the person doesn't need to compare the treatment with other staff or some hypothetical situation. This is also the case under the Australian *Racial Discrimination Act 1975*.

Indirect discrimination of staff

Indirect discrimination in employment occurs where the employer imposes a requirement or condition on an employee or employees that has, or is likely to have, the effect of disadvantaging people with that attribute, and that requirement is not reasonable.

For example, the age old practice of 'Last on, first off' to select people for retrenchment during downturns in business (where the last person hired is the first to be retrenched) can indirectly discriminate against some staff. Younger people are more likely to have shorter periods of service and, therefore, more likely to be retrenched.

Another example of indirect discrimination would be where an employer doesn't consider a request for part-time work from a female employee returning from parental leave, because this policy is more likely to disadvantage women (who are still usually the primary carer for younger children).

An explanation of the intricacies of how the various laws decide whether employees have been indirectly discriminated against in relation to their employment conditions is complex, legalistic and beyond the scope of this book. Suffice to say that in order for employees to show that they have been indirectly discriminated against, the following elements must be evident:

✔ The employer has imposed a condition or requirement on employees

✔ A substantially higher proportion of people without a relevant attribute or characteristic are able to comply with the requirement, as compared with those of the same status as employees with the attribute

✔ The employee(s) with the attribute cannot comply with that requirement

✔ The requirement or condition isn't reasonable, having regard to all the relevant circumstances

The final element of the test in the preceding list is important. A requirement — or condition or policy for that matter — is only unlawful if it's *unreasonable in all the circumstances*.

Reasonableness is a question of fact that can only be determined on a case-by-case basis. However, the following factors common to small business may be taken into account in assessing reasonableness in an employment context:

✔ Cost of implementing alternative measures

✔ Disadvantage disproportionate to the result sought by the employer

✔ Inherent requirements of the job in question

✔ Safety

Finally, the onus is generally on the person complaining to show that the indirect discrimination was unreasonable. However, to make things complicated, the onus is reversed in some situations. For example, employers (assuming they're the ones complained about) must prove the conduct or decision was reasonable where a complaint is brought under the *Sex Discrimination Act 1998*, Queensland's *Anti-discrimination Act 1991* and the ACT *Discrimination Act 1991*. The onus is also on the employer to disprove breaches of workplace rights under the *Fair Work Act 2009*.

Discrimination against prospective staff

The laws prohibiting discrimination aren't limited to the circumstances of your actual employees. People who may wish to work in your business — *prospective employees* — also have the right to complain of discrimination if you choose not to employ them because of one or other of the characteristics/attributes constituting prohibited grounds. The implications for the way in which you select people to work in your business are self-evident. For example, although engaging candidates in conversations about their lives is acceptable, you must be careful not to ask questions that give the impression that you would exclude them from employment on the basis of attributes such as political beliefs, religious attitude and race.

Asking prospective employees about personal attributes is acceptable only if the questions relate to the selection criteria and nature of the job. Stay away from conversations about personal appearance unless direct relevance to the job is clear. Telling a prospective employee she looks really great in that short skirt isn't acceptable. An explanation of the dress code of your business is acceptable.

Finally, if you ask a female job candidate whether she intends to have children, I hope your business is handling toxic chemicals or other material hazardous to unborn children. If it isn't, you will most certainly find yourself on the wrong side of anti-discrimination laws. A better way is to ask whether anything would prevent prospective employees from performing the job.

Refer to Chapter 3 for a more detailed discussion of recruitment.

Adverse Action and Workplace Rights

The *Fair Work Act 2009* contains *general protections* of employees from victimisation, discrimination and action that adversely affects them because they have exercised a workplace right.

The general protections are similar in nature to anti-discrimination laws. They are also similar to protections that have traditionally been available for employees against employers who prejudice their employment. For example, employees who were prejudiced against because they complained about their terms and conditions of employment, joined a trade union, or were absent from work due to illness or injury.

However, these general protections are significantly broader because they extend to

✔ Employees

✔ Employers

✔ Independent contractors

✔ Prospective employees

The main purpose of the general protections is to prohibit the taking of *adverse action* in connection with a person exercising a *workplace right*.

Understanding how the general protections work in practice is very important, because if you ignore this employment responsibility the cost of legal fees and potential compensation from successful claims against you could very well bankrupt your business.

Understanding adverse action

An employer takes *adverse action* against an employee if the employer:

- Dismisses the employee (see Chapter 17).

- Injures the employee in his employment — any injury of a compensable kind. That is, the employee suffers work-related injuries that entitle him to workers compensation payments.

- Alters the employee's position to the detriment of the employee — including not only legal injury but also any other form of disadvantage.

- Discriminates between the employee and other employees (refer to the section 'Understanding Unlawful Discrimination', earlier in this chapter).

The key question to answer when assessing adverse action is whether employees are worse off after you alter their employment arrangements. For example, not offering overtime to one employee or changing the working hours of an employee to night shift or weekends could be described as an alteration to the position of an employee to the employee's prejudice.

A prospective employer takes adverse action against a prospective employee by:

- Refusing to employ the prospective employee

- Discriminating against the prospective employee in the terms and conditions offered to the prospective employee

A principal contractor takes adverse action against a sub-contractor if the principal:

- Terminates the contract

- Injures the independent contractor in relation to the terms and conditions of the contract

- Alters the position of the contractor to the contractor's prejudice

- Refuses to make use of, or agree to make use of, services offered by the independent contractor

- Refuses to supply, or agree to supply, goods or services to the independent contractor

The extension of the general protections to independent contractors provides sub-contractors with an additional and very significant source of protection.

For more on how adverse actions can potentially get you into trouble, see the section 'Navigating the minefield of workplace rights', later in this chapter.

Understanding workplace rights

Employees (and independent contractors) have workplace rights derived from just about every law, order or contract that they have in place with a business. For example, a person has a workplace right if he is entitled to the benefit of an award, employment contract, workplace law or an order made by an industrial relations tribunal such as the Fair Work Commission. A person also has a workplace right where she has a role or responsibility, such as a union delegate or health and safety representative, and where she's able to make a complaint or inquiry to regulatory bodies such as the Fair Work Ombudsman under a law, order, award or employment contract. This pretty much includes everyone who is employed in a job or as a contractor in Australia.

Interpreting the legal mumbo jumbo of the *Fair Work Act 2009* into plain English, and putting it into the context of small business, the Act means the following:

✔ An employee or contractor that you engage or propose to engage has enforceable workplace rights under a modern award, employment contract, service contract, statutory employment laws such as the *Fair Work Act 2009*, workplace health and safety laws and even your small business employment policies.

✔ Workplace rights include the right for employees to complain or ask questions about their terms and conditions of employment and health and safety, the right to join trade unions, and the right to refuse to make an individual flexibility agreement, enterprise agreement, or to engage in lawful industrial action such as approved strike action.

✔ Prospective employees have the same workplace rights that they would have if employed by you.

In practical terms, workplace rights are really the same as terms and conditions of employment.

Navigating the minefield of workplace rights

You can infer from the definitions provided in the preceding sections that adverse action is very broadly defined and covers virtually any action that has a detrimental impact on an employee or independent contractor. However, small-business owner and employer problems *only* arise if the adverse action is taken because the employee or contractor has or proposes to exercise a workplace right.

Employees and contractors will invariably be unhappy with you when you do something that they perceive to be against their interests. Nevertheless, hard decisions are inevitable — you must make choices in the best interests of your small business and often those choices adversely impact on others. However, not all unhappy employees and contractors can pursue an action for compensation through the Australian courts claiming that you have adversely acted against them for exercising a workplace right.

Danger zones

Understanding that people have workplace rights, focusing on the operational and strategic needs of your business and not the person, honest communication and a sharp sense of the 'danger zones' enables you to see the hazards ahead and learn how to navigate your way safely through the minefield of workplace rights.

The workplace rights danger zone barometer shown in Figure 12-1 can help you with this. For example, your action in response to frequent absences from work due to illness or injury is potentially very dangerous because breaching workplace rights in these circumstances is easy to do and may result in substantial fines and penalties. Therefore, you will adopt strategies to minimise the risk of breaching workplace rights commensurate with the level of risk. This could include adhering to a written policy and procedure on how to manage such absences consistent with the workplace rights. The policy might include offering the employee an opportunity to confidentially disclose the health issues, or a request to speak to their treating medical practitioner to discuss how you can practically assist the employee to better health. These sorts of actions mitigate the risk of breaching workplace rights, and will work in your favour especially if subsequently you have to adopt more serious action such as dismissal. See the following section for tips on how to adopt appropriate strategies.

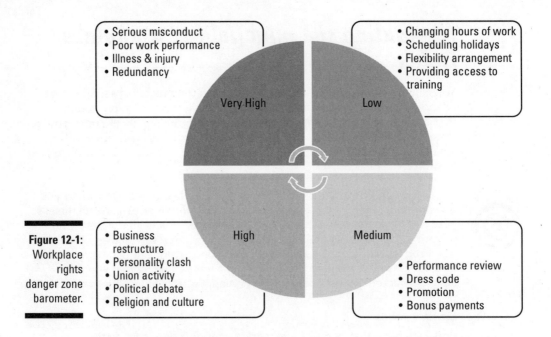

Figure 12-1:
Workplace
rights
danger zone
barometer.

The reverse onus of proof

Where an allegation is made that an adverse action took place, the courts
will presume that you took adverse action for a prohibited reason — that
is, because the person exercised a workplace right. In order for you as
employer to satisfy the *reverse onus* and remove the presumption that
you acted for a prohibited reason, you must provide evidence of an
alternative reason for the alleged adverse action. You should also tell
the employee the reason. This shouldn't be hard to do if you have taken
actions to protect the business and otherwise acted in accordance with
good management practice — such as documenting the warnings provided
and giving the employee an opportunity to respond (refer to Chapter 11 for
more on this).

If you dismiss employees or contractors because they haven't performed
the work satisfactorily, say so — even if you're unsure that you've
completely complied with every element of a fair procedure. Don't dress up
the dismissal in an explanation that isn't true. If you did dismiss someone
for reasons unrelated to performance and offer an explanation that you
think the judge wants to hear but is not true, you won't succeed. Tribunals
and courts have a talent for exposing dubious explanations and falsehoods.

Coercion and undue influence and pressure

One important point under this general topic of workplace rights is the
obligation not to coerce or exert undue influence or pressure on another
person to exercise a workplace right, or exercise the workplace right in a
particular way.

An example of this would be offering employment conditional on the person entering into an individual flexibility arrangement. This is expressly prohibited. Consequently, any arrangement that varies the operation of modern award conditions, such as the arrangement of the hours of work, payment of allowances, loadings, penalty rates and overtime, must be negotiated after employment has commenced.

The prohibition on coercion and undue influence and pressure also applies to action to prevent a person from exercising a workplace right.

Get Proactive: Develop a Strategy

As is the case with almost all aspects of employment regulation, the best strategy to ensure you're able to comply with the law is to develop policies and procedures to explain your objectives and the general principles that you intend to abide by in relation to the topic. And then update them regularly to ensure they're still current.

Secondly, prevention is better than the cure and, therefore, establishing an educative program during inductions and beyond to ensure that your staff understand and work in accordance with your policy is worthwhile.

Go to www.dummies.com/go/hrsmallbusinessau for sample access, equity and anti-discrimination, anti-bullying and sexual harassment policies that you can model your own on.

Each employment policy should cross-reference other related policies and forms that you use in dealing with this area of employment. Having specific policies is better than relying on a general code of conduct. Refer to Chapter 8 for more on employment policies.

Making reasonable adjustments for disability

As discussed at the start of this chapter, you're expected to make reasonable adjustments to accommodate persons with disabilities when offering employment in your small business. The expectation is limited to whether or not the accommodation is practical in all the circumstances. Thus your recruitment and employment strategy must include a procedure for considering the practicality of adjustments if faced with employees or prospective employees who have a disability that inhibits their chances of employment and successfully performing a job.

The Human Rights Commission publishes information on practical measures to make reasonable adjustments to accommodate employees and prospective employees with a disability. Here are a few examples of adjustments provided:

✔ Adjustments to the hours of work and use of leave entitlements to accommodate the person's capacity. For example, part-time work.

✔ Adjustments to work methods, such as use of better equipment that can be used by persons with physical disabilities.

✔ Adjustments to computer software and settings and telephone equipment that enables hearing- and sight-impaired employees to work as efficiently as others.

✔ Training co-workers or supervisors so they can understand the person's disability and, therefore, adapt their own working methods to accommodate the person with a disability.

✔ Provision of interpreters, readers, attendants or other work-related assistance.

Probably the most contentious issue for your small business is the cost of making adjustments to the facilities or property, and the provision of equipment. You may not have to pay for every adjustment to accommodate a person with a disability. Investigate the possibility of subsidies and grants from government agencies. The key to your strategy is making the effort to find out what's practical and then being prepared to implement what's reasonable for your small business and what gives the person a reasonable chance of succeeding in the job.

You're not obligated to adjust the inherent requirements of a job to accommodate people with a disability in employment. You can be quite clear about this with prospective employees. Just make sure you can explain the inherent requirements.

Educating staff

Educating yourself and your staff on the obligations and responsibilities under the law is probably the most constructive activity that you can undertake to both minimise the risk of claims against your business, and promote a workplace that's free from discrimination and harassment and a really good place to work.

If you are ever challenged by a person from the Human Rights Commission the first question they will ask you is, 'Where is your recruitment and employment policy and when did you last train your staff?'

Two stages of the employment relationship with regards to discrimination and workplace rights are vitally important to educate staff on, as follows:

- ✔ **The commencement of employment:** One of the purposes of providing formal induction programs for staff is to communicate the values that you wish to see applied in your business and set expectations for the way in which the business is conducted, including the interaction with fellow staff, customers and suppliers. Consequently, this issue is not something that you just require employees to 'tick the box' on. Reading and acknowledging the policy statement is only meaningful where it has been accompanied by a thorough explanation from you. Refer to Chapter 8 for more on formal induction programs.

- ✔ **Throughout employment:** The issue of discrimination and workplace rights is a topic that can usefully be raised from time to time with staff in order to reinforce the message that everyone is expected to conduct themselves in a manner that does not unlawfully discriminate against others in the workplace.

Serious incidents that attract media attention such as bullying and sexual harassment often raise the level of awareness of the subject and may be accompanied by a spike in complaints to regulatory authorities. These incidents are a good opportunity to conduct refresher courses on the subject of discrimination and workplace rights. Formalised training isn't always necessary. Instead, the refresher may be as simple as a five-minute agenda item in the weekly staff meeting. Or the training required may be a full review and induction of all staff. You can obtain resources from the regulatory agencies such as the Australian Human Rights Commission (www.humanrights.gov.au) and Fair Work Ombudsman (www.fairwork.gov.au).

Disclosing Personal Information Isn't Against the Law

A common misconception among small-business owners is that employment records are subject to privacy laws, meaning you can't ask prospective employees about their health or a disability. However, small businesses with an annual turnover of $3 million or less aren't covered by the *Privacy Act 1988*, and employment records aren't covered by privacy law even if your business does earn in excess of $3 million.

Privacy laws don't prevent you from obtaining personal and sensitive information about employees or prospective employees in order for you to fulfil your obligations under anti-discrimination laws.

Table 12-1 shows some legitimate reasons for collecting personal information from employees and prospective employees. I've included in the table the primary reasons that are permissible.

Table 12-1	Reasons for Collecting Personal Information from Employees and Prospective Employees	
Information	*Employees*	*Prospective Employees*
Pre-existing work-related illness or injury	Workplace health and safety, including rehabilitation and reasonable adjustments to work arrangements	Disclosure required for workers compensation insurance and reasonable adjustments to work arrangements
Physical illness and injuries	Capacity to perform inherent requirements of job	Capacity to perform inherent requirements of job
	Reasonable adjustments to work arrangements	Reasonable adjustments to workplace
Mental illness	Capacity to perform inherent requirements of job	Capacity to perform inherent requirements of job
	Reasonable adjustments to work arrangements	Reasonable adjustments to work arrangements
Disability	Capacity to perform inherent requirements of job	Capacity to perform inherent requirements of job
	Reasonable adjustments to work arrangements	Reasonable adjustments to work arrangements
Family and carer responsibilities	Hours of work	Hours of work
	Business travel	Business travel
	Individual flexibility arrangement (IFA)	

Asking questions of people is not generally discriminatory. You can ask almost any question and obtain almost any information from an employee or prospective employee if the information is directly relevant to the performance of the job. Discrimination and breaches of workplace rights generally arise from what you do with the information that you have obtained (for example, choose not to employ someone based on it). So focus on the job and not the person and you should stay out of trouble.

Focusing on Suitability Not Disability

Not all discrimination is unlawful. In fact, anti-discrimination laws nationally and in all states and territories contain exemptions. Religious organisations have a general exemption from the application of anti-discrimination laws as long as the action is taken in good faith and to avoid injury to the religious susceptibilities of adherents to that religion. Your small business may discriminate against employees and prospective employees where a genuine occupational qualification to perform a job exists and where a person is unable to perform the inherent requirements of a job in your business. I discuss both of those concepts in the following sections.

Genuine occupational qualification

Under most anti-discrimination law, a limited exemption exists to cover a *genuine occupational requirement*. That is, you have a genuine requirement that an employee must have certain abilities to perform a specific role. This limited exemption generally only applies to particular types of occupation, for example:

- Theatrical performances and, in some cases, in relation to food outlets selling food of a particular nationality
- Personal decency in relation to change-room attendants, or other persons required to work in areas where persons of a particular gender may be in a state of undress

Performing the inherent requirements of the job

Anti-discrimination law recognises that accommodating an individual at a workplace due to disability (also referred to as physical or mental impairment) is sometimes difficult. An employer discriminating on the grounds of disability is generally not unlawful if

- The employee can't perform the *inherent requirements* of the job as a result of the disability.
- Providing services or facilities required by the employee in order to carry out the inherent requirements of the job imposes an *unjustifiable hardship* on the employer.

This exemption is particularly important in the selection of a job applicant or the termination of an existing employee's employment where he has become unable to perform the tasks and duties of his role. I discuss the issue of when it is permissible to dismiss an employee who's no longer capable of performing the inherent requirements of the job in Chapter 17.

Understanding inherent requirements

The *inherent requirements* of the job are the *fundamental aspects* of the job that a person must be able to perform in order to do the job.

The nature of inherent requirements was explained by Chief Justice Brennan in a famous 1998 High Court case (*Qantas Airways Limited v Christie*) on whether compulsory retirement of airline pilots was unlawfully discriminatory:

> *The question whether a requirement is inherent in a position must be answered by reference not only to the terms of the employment contract but also by reference to the function which the employee performs as part of the employer's undertaking and, except where the employer's undertaking is organised on a basis which impermissibly discriminates against the employee, by reference to that organisation.*

In other words, no general rule determines inherent requirements in every instance. Each job function must be considered in the context of the particular business to uncover the fundamental or inherent requirements to successfully perform the work.

The best starting point is to answer the question: Is the job able to be performed to the minimum standard required if the particular task or duty at issue was not able to be completed by any person? If the answer is no, the tasks or duty is probably an inherent requirement.

An example would be a commercial sales representative job, where a requirement is to travel to customers' business premises to demonstrate products. A person who is visually impaired may not be capable of obtaining a vehicle driver's licence and, therefore, is unable to fulfil this function without considerable support provided by you. This means an inherent requirement of the job is the ability to drive a motor vehicle — otherwise, the job can't be performed to a satisfactory minimum standard.

The inherent requirements exemption also applies to the anti-discrimination provisions of the *Fair Work Act 2009*.

Unjustifiable hardship

The unjustifiable hardship exemption is difficult to establish. Whether unjustifiable hardship exists depends on all the circumstances of each situation, including the

- ✔ Cost and financial impact on the business
- ✔ Likely impact on the workplace
- ✔ Impact on other employees

These factors are weighed against the benefit that will accrue to the disabled employee.

Your small business is far more likely to be able to rely upon this exemption than a large company or government department.

You're not required to adjust the inherent requirements of a job to accommodate a person with a disability. Applying the example of the commercial sales representative from the preceding section, the question of whether or not an adjustment would cause unjustifiable hardship depends upon how much it would cost to provide the visually impaired person with a driver to attend customer business premises. I suspect this would cause unjustifiable financial hardship to most small businesses.

Chapter 13

Harassment and Bullying — Gee, Can't You Take a Joke?

. . . .

In This Chapter

▶ Understanding the importance of context and tone

▶ Working out what may be behind harassment and bullying

▶ Using education and workplace policies for prevention

▶ Picking up conflict resolution methods

. . . .

We just want it to stop.

House of Representatives,
Standing Committee on Education and Employment

A more emotionally charged issue in employment than staff claiming they have been bullied and harassed at work probably doesn't exist. The claim can arise from a physical act, emanate from individual or group behaviour, or come from something that was thought of as a joke shared among work colleagues. Wherever the complaint emanates from, if you manage it badly the consequences for your small business are potentially catastrophic.

In this chapter, I outline your responsibilities as an employer under equal opportunity, sexual harassment and anti-bullying laws, and place these responsibilities in the context of the innumerable list of regulations imposed on your small business. I discuss the possible underlying causes of conflict that grow into bullying and harassment, and explain effective strategies to prevent both situations.

I emphasise the importance of workplace policies and procedures when responding to grievances of this nature and, finally, I provide some useful tips in addressing this very challenging responsibility.

It's Not Always What You Say, But How You Say It

The 'Gee — can't you take a joke?' that forms part of the title of this chapter illustrates a common cry from people accused of offending or humiliating others through the statements that they make. In the modern workplace, what seems like an innocent conversation, quip, joke or aside can sometimes be taken by others as an act of bullying or harassment. The accused may be bewildered and often resentful of the work colleague who has complained. If the complaint is against you, you may feel angry and want to dismiss the complainant. The situation can become a real mess.

Of course, in many instances the bullying or sexual harassment is deliberate and, as such, the perpetrator is likely to face severe consequences when such behaviour is uncovered — either by you as employer or the courts with responsibility for enforcing the law. No matter how the issue begins, it's your responsibility to deal with it and resolve it. The days of telling people to just get over it are, themselves, over.

Your ability to address this very difficult issue depends, firstly, on how well you understand what these concepts mean and, secondly, how you frame your response (preventative and remedial) to address the risks of harm done to your business and the people you employ.

Defining harassment

Harassment is behaviour that's not wanted, not asked for and not returned, which is likely to offend, humiliate or intimidate a person in your business. Harassment may also be discriminatory where it is directed at a person because he has attributes protected by the law as explained in Chapter 12.

Sexual harassment is any unwelcome sexual advance, request for sexual favours or other conduct of a sexual nature likely to offend, humiliate or intimidate. Sexual harassment is expressly outlawed by the *Sex Discrimination Act 1984*.

Sexual harassment in the workplace can take various forms. The Australian Human Rights Commission (www.humanrights.gov.au) provides various examples of what it considers behaviour that could constitute sexual harassment, including

- Insults or taunts based on sex
- Intrusive questions about a person's private life or body
- Requests for sex
- Sexually explicit emails or SMS text messages
- Sexually explicit physical contact
- Sexually explicit pictures or posters
- Staring, leering or unwelcome touching
- Suggestive comments or jokes
- Unnecessary familiarity, such as deliberately brushing up against a person
- Unwanted invitations to go out on dates

Defining bullying

The term *bullying* is used to describe behaviour that may intimidate, humiliate or otherwise injure a person physically or mentally.

The *Fair Work Act 2009* was amended to incorporate a definition of bullying. It states that an employee has been bullied at work if you, another employee or a group of employees at work

> ... *repeatedly behaves unreasonably towards the employee, and that behaviour creates a risk to the health and safety of that person.*

On the other hand it states that:

> *Bullying does not include reasonable management practices including performance management conducted in a reasonable manner.*

In recent times, workplace bullying has risen in the consciousness of employers and employees alike as incidents are reported in the media, and as regulatory agencies such as the Human Rights Commission, Fair Work Commission and state-based workplace health and safety authorities prosecute businesses for failures to prevent bullying. In employment, the consequences for the bully, the bullied and the employer can be serious — careers and business reputations can be damaged.

Reasonable versus unreasonable management practice

In order to fully understanding the bullying definition, you need to keep in mind what distinguishes 'reasonable' from 'unreasonable' management practices.

Here are some examples of bullying behaviour cited by workplace health and safety agencies such as Safe Work Australia in guidance materials published:

✔ Assigning meaningless tasks unrelated to the job

✔ Changing work rosters to inconvenience particular employees or withholding information that's vital for effective work performance

✔ Excluding or isolating employees from team activities

✔ Giving employees impossible assignments

✔ Using offensive language, yelling, screaming, verbal abuse, rudeness

✔ Ridiculing, insulting, belittling opinions, nicknames

The Australian Human Rights Commission (www.humanrights.gov.au) lists even more graphic examples, leading me to the conclusion that it considers bullying to include everything from criminal assault, discrimination and sexual harassment through to school yard–type behaviour such as excluding people from work activities and information allowed or provided to others. Here are some examples from the Human Rights Commission:

✔ Allocating impossible jobs that can't be done in the given time or with the resources provided

✔ Allocating pointless tasks that have nothing to do with the job

✔ Attacking or threatening with equipment, knives, guns, clubs or any other type of object that can be turned into a weapon

✔ Deliberately changing work hours or schedule to make the job difficult

✔ Deliberately holding back information needed for getting the work done properly

✔ Excluding employees or stopping them from working with people or taking part in activities that relates to their work

✔ Initiation or hazing — where employees are made to do humiliating or inappropriate things in order to be accepted as part of the team

- ✔ Intimidation — making employees feel less important and undervalued
- ✔ Playing mind games, ganging up on employees, or other types of psychological harassment
- ✔ Pushing, shoving, tripping, grabbing in the workplace
- ✔ Repeated hurtful remarks or attacks, or making fun of an employee's work or her as a person (including family, sex, sexuality, gender identity, race or culture, education or economic background)
- ✔ Sexual harassment — particularly unwelcome touching and sexually explicit comments and requests that make employees uncomfortable

The difficulty with the preceding very broad list is that the examples invite quite extreme and sometimes contradictory interpretations to describe the phenomena. Reasonable conduct and reasonable management practice may be in the eye of the beholder but, ultimately, the strategy to address them both is going to be a matter of common sense. The remainder of this chapter is devoted to unravelling the mystery and explaining how you can adopt good management practice and common sense to reduce the risk and incidence of bullying and harassment in your small business.

Underlying Causes of Bullying and Harassment

The solution to providing a healthy and safe workplace free from harassment and bullying is largely in risk management. If you're going to reduce the risks of your employees suffering workplace bullying and harassment and the consequent impact on their health, you firstly need to understand the underlying causes.

In Chapter 11 I cover possible sources of conflict in the workplace, and the importance of understanding the underlying reasons that cause conflict. Bullying and harassment are forms of conflict and, therefore, the message in this chapter is the same — that is, you need to understand the underlying causes by monitoring the symptoms (in this case risk factors) to successfully prevent and respond to bullying and harassment.

Identifying the risk factors

Conflict that develops into bullying and harassment may occur for many and varied reasons, but these reasons can usually be categorised under two headings: Personal issues and management style.

For example, personal issues may include

- ✔ Competition for attention
- ✔ Maturity of staff
- ✔ Mental illness
- ✔ Personal problems, such as divorce or gambling
- ✔ Personality clashes
- ✔ Social relationships

While management-style reasons may include

- ✔ The boss's behaviour
- ✔ Change in management objectives
- ✔ Changes in management personnel
- ✔ Organisational restructure
- ✔ Workplace culture

Whenever I take a poll in workshops on harassment and bullying, participants always indicate that the two most frequently cited personal factors most likely to lead to bullying and harassment are personality clashes and mental illness. The two most frequently cited answers for management style factors most likely to lead to bullying and harassment are the boss's behaviour and workplace culture. Ask yourself what the top reasons in your workplace are likely to be. Your strategies to prevent workplace bullying and harassment can then focus primarily on these high-risk factors.

Reducing the risks

Once you know the risk factors most likely to lead to bullying and harassment (refer to preceding section), you can design your workplace policies to help stop them developing into full-blown conflicts and formal complaints.

Table 13-1 outlines some simple strategies for common risk factors.

Table 13-1	Bullying Risk Responses
Risk Factor	**Risk Response**
Personality clash between staff	Treat staff equally (avoid perceived favouritism)
	Proactively address rumours and rumblings
	Separate staff on different rosters
Mental illness	Provide honest and regular communication on work expectations and performance
	Invite staff to confidentially disclose health information
	Provide access to professional counselling services
	Be alert to symptoms such as high absenteeism and turnover
Behaviour of the boss	Seek honest and open feedback from reports, peers and superiors
	Self-reflect — see yourself from your staff's perspective
	Role model the behaviour that you expect of others
Workplace culture	Organise events where staff can share a positive experience together
	Focus on team work and cooperation to achieve business goals
	Reward behaviour that contributes to a positive work environment

Preventing Harassment and Bullying

According to the best research on the subject, the most comprehensive stress-intervention strategies are done on three levels, as follows:

✔ The primary level deals with prevention at the source of stressors in the workplace and is generally considered the most effective intervention.

✔ The secondary level of intervention provides control at the individual employee level, and includes measures that minimise the risk to employees.

✔ Tertiary intervention aims to provide treatment to employees who have experienced a work-related mental stress injury.

Mental stress is, among other things, an indicator of conflict, including incidents of bullying and harassment. So addressing the primary causes of bullying and harassment wherever possible makes sense.

According to a 2013 report published by Safe Work Australia, helping employees cope better with the existence of stress is a short-term solution. What's more effective is reducing the source of the stress, across the business. Focusing on stress reduction or removal can provide long-term benefits for employees and for your business. Better to prevent workplace bullying and harassment than having to try and fix it once it has occurred.

Educating your staff

The best way to educate staff on prevention of bullying and harassment is to formulate a workplace policy on the topic and incorporate that policy in all information about your business.

Go to www.dummies.com/go/hrsmallbusinessau for sample anti-bullying and sexual harassment policies that you can model your own on.

However, an employment policy is just empty words unless you apply it in a manner that produces real results.

Using the policy as an education tool

You must use your bullying and harassment policy as a tool to educate employees and managers in the standards of behaviour expected in the workplace, and provide a broader statement of your values to customers and stakeholders. Introduce the policy in recruitment, induction, and learning and development activities.

Spreading the message to prospective employees

You should draw the attention of every candidate for employment to your business's values, mission and attitudes to matters such as equal employment opportunity, discrimination, bullying and harassment. This could be a simple statement included in the position description and the job advertisement.

Using orientation to set the right standards

The orientation process is the best opportunity to educate new staff on your employment policies, including the procedures for responding to incidents of workplace bullying and harassment.

Every one of your staff must commit to workplace values and respecting the other people they work with. The best way to get that commitment is to fully document the process through the induction and to ask staff to sign and acknowledge that they understand and agree to work in accordance with those standards.

Refer to Chapter 8 for more on the orientation process.

Understanding once is not enough

During the course of employment opportunities will arise where conducting refresher training on employment matters, including bullying and harassment, is both useful and necessary. Incorporate this training as a regular item on the agenda of staff meetings or annual staff training.

A well-formulated bullying and harassment policy should also provide a checklist of action to cover situations where intervention is needed to resolve complaints. This is a very difficult task, so a clear policy checklist can assist you (or your nominee) to work systematically through the steps to investigate and resolve incidents of workplace bullying and harassment.

Notwithstanding the best intentions and the introduction of good preventative education programs, you may face a situation where an employee claims to have been bullied or subjected to sexual harassment. In this situation, you should attempt to resolve the matter. Refer to Chapter 11 for an in-depth discussion of your conflict-resolution options.

Part V
A Healthy Workplace Is a Happy Workplace

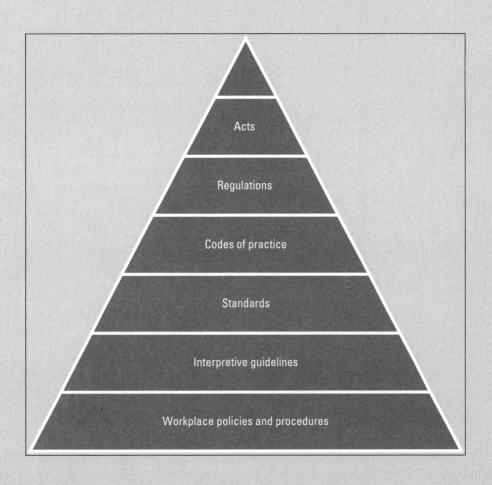

Learn more about the health and safety responsibilities your small business must adhere to by visiting www.dummies.com/extras/hrsmallbusinessau.

In this part ...

- ✔ Health and safety at work means you're responsible for making it happen. Learn risk management methods that you must apply to fulfil the general duty of care, and how to consult with staff to make health and safety everybody's responsibility.

- ✔ Understand who is eligible for workers compensation and what is or isn't a workplace injury, and learn how to navigate your way with medical practitioners and others when rehabilitating injured workers or transitioning them to another employer or career.

Chapter 14

Safety at Work Is Everyone's Responsibility

In This Chapter

▶ Understanding your duty of care as an employer

▶ Working out the duty of care required from employees and others

▶ Realising that preventing injury is better than curing injury

▶ Identifying, evaluating and controlling risks

▶ Consulting with the people you're protecting

▶ Applying a hierarchy of laws, regulations standards, codes and guides

How do I injure thee at work? Let me count the ways.

Anonymous

*W*ith apologies to the poet Elizabeth Barrett Browning for distorting the opening line to her beautiful poem written to her husband Robert Browning in 1845, people can injure themselves in countless ways in the workplace. And, no matter how careful or careless the injured person, you're held responsible for every trip, fall and falter. You may not be personally responsible for every incident that triggers workplace injuries but you are responsible for each and every rehabilitation program, compensation payment and penalty imposed on your business, not to mention rising insurance premiums.

In this chapter, I explain your duty of care to staff, contractors and other persons who may be affected by the conduct of your small business. I describe how you can fulfil the duty of care through education and training, and explain the simple four steps of health and safety risk management.

I provide tips on how communication with staff and others in your small business can form an essential element of your workplace health and safety strategy. And I outline the national scheme of workplace health and safety regulation, describing the hierarchy of laws, regulations, standards, codes of practice and guidelines — some of which you must obey and others which you can use to guide you through this very sizeable responsibility.

Fulfilling Your Duty of Care

Health and safety laws are administered by Australian states and territories. However, a national body — Safe Work Australia — is entrusted with the task of harmonising the various state and territory laws to achieve consistency across jurisdictional borders. And some states and territories have adopted the model Workplace Health and Safety Act, also designed to harmonise the various laws within one national system (Victoria and Western Australia have chosen to remain outside the nationally harmonised system).

Consequently, terminology may differ depending on which state or territory your small business premises are located in. Nevertheless, one basic principle remains the same — as the person who controls the workplace, you're primarily responsible for all health and safety.

Victoria and Western Australia

Health and safety laws regulated by the states of Western Australia and Victoria impose a *duty of care* for employees engaged in your small business. The duty of care is defined in each state's health and safety laws as follows:

> *An employer must, so far as is reasonably practicable, provide and maintain for employees of the employer a working environment that is safe and without risks to health.*

The duty of care is fulfilled by undertaking a range of practical measures, such as consultation with staff, recording hazards and measures to address health and safety, education and application of risk-management strategies to control risks. These measures are covered throughout this chapter.

Other states and territories

The model Workplace Health and Safety Act applicable in Queensland, New South Wales, South Australia, Tasmania, ACT and NT imposes a *primary duty*, as follows:

> *A person conducting a business or undertaking (PCBU) has a duty to ensure, so far as is reasonably practicable, the health and safety of:*
>
> *workers engaged, or caused to be engaged by the person, and*
>
> *workers whose activities in carrying out work are influenced or directed by the person, while the workers are at work in the business or undertaking.*

The PCBU also has a duty to ensure, so far as is reasonably practicable, that the health and safety of other persons isn't put at risk from work carried out as part of the conduct of the business or undertaking.

Acting on health and safety

In general, you fulfil your duty of care and primary duty when you, insofar as is reasonably practicable, ensure the

- ✔ Health of workers and the conditions at the workplace are monitored for the purpose of preventing work-related illness or injury
- ✔ Provision and maintenance of a work environment that's without risks to health or safety
- ✔ Provision and maintenance of safe plant, structures and safe systems of work
- ✔ Provision of any information, training, instruction or supervision necessary to protect all persons from risks to their health and safety arising from work carried out as part of the conduct of the business or undertaking
- ✔ Provision of, and access to, adequate facilities for the welfare of workers at the workplace
- ✔ Safe use, handling (including transport) and storage of plant, structures and substances

Reasonably practicable action

Reasonably practicable refers to action that can reasonably be done in the circumstances of each particular business. This means that you must satisfy the duties included in the preceding list as far as you are reasonably able to, taking into account and weighing up all relevant matters, such as:

✔ The availability and suitability of ways to eliminate or minimise the risk

✔ The degree of harm that might result from the hazard or risk

✔ The likelihood of the relevant hazard or risk occurring

✔ What you know, or ought reasonably to know, about the hazard or risk and the ways of eliminating or minimising the risk

The cost of eliminating or minimising the risk may be taken into account, but only where the relevant matters included in the preceding list have been taken into account. For example, you may have many ways to minimise or eliminate the risk to health and safety from an identified hazard such as lifting and loading of goods onto transport vehicles. You could purchase specialised equipment to load the goods. You might outsource the task to another specialist service. Or you could limit the weight and size of the packaging of the goods.

After evaluating the risk, the costs of some of these methods of eliminating the risk may greatly outweigh the actual possibility or consequences of the risk to health and safety. Therefore, you would choose the most cost-effective method that minimises the risk of injury to your staff, in line with the nature of the risk.

Exercising due diligence

You must exercise *due diligence* to ensure that your small business complies with your duty of care.

This means that you're expected to take reasonable steps to

✔ Acquire and keep up-to-date knowledge of work health and safety matters

✔ Ensure that the business has appropriate processes for receiving and considering information about incidents, hazards and risks and responding in a timely way

✔ Ensure that the business has appropriate resources and processes to enable risks to health and safety arising from work carried out as part of the business to be eliminated or minimised

✔ Ensure that the business implements processes for complying with its duties and obligations

✔ Gain an understanding of the hazards and risks associated with the nature of the operations

Due diligence means establishing systems to ensure that your business continues to comply with the relevant duties and obligations imposed by the law, not just once a year or whenever a problem arises. Due diligence also means not leaving the responsibility to a manager that you employ to operate your business.

Office holders' duty

The model Workplace Health and Safety Act extends the primary duty (duty of care) to *office holders*. This includes business owners and company directors, whether they work in the business or not. The scope of the officers' duty directly relate to their role in the business. In other words, as both an owner of the business and someone who normally controls most of the main decisions, you're wearing both hats (owner and manager). You need to be diligent in examining and taking care that your business resources and systems comply with the duty of care as required by the law.

Where you as owner of the business rely on the expertise of a manager or other person for your health and safety, that expertise must be verified and the reliance on that person must be reasonable.

See the section 'Risk Management Is the Key to a Healthy Workplace', later in this chapter, for more on risk-management methods, and how to implement a system that enables continuous examination and adjustment to ensure compliance and a healthy workplace.

Health and Safety Duties of Staff and Others

The duty of care is not all one-sided. Staff and others must take reasonable care for their own health and safety while at work or visiting your workplace, and take reasonable care that their acts or omissions do not adversely affect the health and safety of other persons that may be affected by their conduct.

Staff duty of care

As well as taking reasonable care of their own health and safety, staff must also

✔ Comply, so far as they're reasonably able, with any reasonable instruction given by you that complies with the law

✔ Cooperate with any reasonable business policy or procedure that relates to work health or safety, about which they have been notified

Staff duty of care is subject to a consideration of what is not only reasonable but also proportionate to the control your staff are able to exercise over their work activities and work environment. Whether an instruction, policy or procedure is 'reasonable' depends on all relevant factors, including whether the instruction, policy or procedure is lawful, whether it is clear and whether affected staff are able to cooperate.

Duties of other persons in the workplace

Other persons who are in your business premises— for example, visitors, customers or contractors — must take reasonable care both for their own health and safety, and that their acts or omissions don't adversely affect the health and safety of others. They must comply with any reasonable instruction given by you or your managers that allows the business to comply with the law.

For example, you would not allow visitors to enter parts of the business that require hard hats and other safety equipment or enter premises unaccompanied and unsupervised, and visitors must comply with your instructions in these areas.

Prevention Is Better than the Cure

Any system to manage the health and safety of employees, even in office-based environments, requires adequate training and staff induction. Consequently, you need to ensure training and inductions are performed when employees start their employment (normally prior to them performing duties) and during the course of employment to ensure that their knowledge is current and front of mind.

Generally the need for training staff works on three levels:

✔ Employees are trained and accredited to perform health and safety tasks in accordance with prescribed regulations or codes of practice, such as first aid.

✔ Employee representatives (if this form of consultation is adopted) are suitably trained and accredited to understand and perform health and safety tasks, such as risk assessments.

✔ Management-level employees are suitably trained and accredited to understand and perform health and safety tasks, such as risk assessments, conduct inductions for new staff, ensure premises, plant and equipment are compliant with appropriate codes or standards, and oversee the implementation, management and/or monitoring of building safety and evacuation procedures where relevant.

According to Victoria's *Occupational Health and Safety Act 2004*, the need for training and induction arises from the general duty to

> *. . . provide such information, instruction, training or supervision to employees of the employer as is necessary to enable those persons to perform their work in a way that is safe and without risks to health.*

This is similar to requirements in the other states and territories.

Depending upon the nature of your business, you may conduct training yourself, delegate to a competent and trusted manager, or engage expert advice to guide you on the elements of an effective induction and training program. Where specific accreditation or qualifications are required, you can send your staff to a professional, occupational or industry specialist in the relevant field.

If your small business operates in the construction and building industry, you can't start employees until they have undertaken a structured induction on health and safety and obtained a general construction training induction card or certificate. Consult your applicable state or territory health and safety authority for further information on the training and induction requirements and how employees can achieve them.

Risk Management Is the Key to a Healthy Workplace

Risk management underpins each and every state and territory workplace health and safety regulatory system. It underpins the duty of care, primary duty (refer to the section 'Fulfilling Your Duty of Care', earlier in this chapter), and the form and nature of the applicable codes and standards.

Risk management is a systematic examination of any activity, premises or operational system to

- ✔ Identify risks
- ✔ Evaluate the likelihood and potential consequences of the risks
- ✔ Act to eliminate or control the risk
- ✔ Review and monitor health and safety outcomes

The risk-management system outlined in the preceding bullets is internationally recognised and applied under Australian and New Zealand standards — specifically, AS/NZS ISO 31000: 2009 Risk management — Principles and guidelines (as updated from time to time) and also AS/NZS 4801: 2001 Occupational health and safety management systems — Specification with guidance for use. If you're not familiar with the international and Australian standards, they establish specific procedures to manage particular financial, legal, health, technical, scientific and other situations to a nationally recognised and acceptable standard. In this case, the standards describe how to implement a procedure to eliminate or reduce risks to health and safety at work. You can get further information on the specific standards from Standards Australia (www.standards.org.au).

Identifying risk

Identifying risks to health and safety means looking at your business premises, work methods and other work activities to identify the hazards that may cause or contribute to the possibility of illness or injury to you and your work colleagues. At this stage of the process, the fundamental task is to inspect your business premises, work methods and activities with a pen and paper, noting every hazard that may cause risk to health and safety.

You just identify risk at this first stage — you don't evaluate the risk from the hazard yet. If you start filtering out the potential risks to health and safety at this stage, you will fail to satisfy your obligation to ensure a safe and healthy workplace. The evaluation comes in the next stage (see following section).

Evaluating risk

Evaluating risk is a simple three-step procedure that enables you to understand the nature of the risk to health and safety from the hazard. Once you have evaluated and rated the risk, then you can treat the risk.

Firstly, Table 14-1 shows how you can organise the list of risks or hazards that you have identified. Use Tables 14-2 and 14-3 to rate the *consequences* if the risk to health and safety was realised and the *probability* of the risk from the hazard occurring. Finally, use Table 14-4 to match the numerical and alpha ratings you allocated to the hazard (in columns two and three of Table 14-1) to the overall risk rating. Place the alpha risk rating in the final column of Table 14-1.

Table 14-1	Organising Identified Risks and Hazards		
Hazard or Risk	*Potential Consequences of Risk (1–5)*	*Probability of Risk (A, B, C, D, E)*	*Analysis Rating*

Table 14-2		Consequences if Hazard or Risk Realised
Level	*Descriptor*	*Description*
1	Insignificant	No injuries, low financial loss
2	Minor	First aid treatment, on-site hazard immediately contained
3	Moderate	Medical treatment required, on-site hazard contained with outside assistance
4	Major	Extensive injuries, loss of production capability, off-site exposure to hazard with no detrimental effects
5	Catastrophic	Death, toxic release off-site with detrimental effect

Table 14-3	Probability of Hazard or Risk Occurring	
Level	Descriptor	Description
A	Almost certain	The event is expected to occur in most circumstances
B	Likely	The event will probably occur in most circumstances
C	Moderate	The event should occur at some time
D	Unlikely	The event could occur at some time but unlikely
E	Rare	The event may occur only in exceptional circumstances

Table 14-4	Qualitative Risk Analysis Matrix				
Likelihood	Consequence				
	Insignificant (1)	Minor (2)	Moderate (3)	Major (4)	Catastrophic (5)
A (Almost certain)	S	S	H	H	H
B (Likely)	M	S	S	H	H
C (Moderate)	L	M	S	H	H
D (Unlikely)	L	L	M	S	H
E (Rare)	L	L	M	S	S

Once you have completed Table 14-1 for all identified risks in your business, you can use Table 14-5 to evaluate the level of risk, and thus understand the dimensions of the risk and be guided in the action that you should take to treat the risk.

Table 14-5	Analysis Rating and Action
Analysis Rating	*Action Required*
H High risk	Unacceptable risk. Detailed research and emergency management planning required. Inform all staff and consider measures to eliminate risk. Design and implement strategy for induction of staff in response to occurrence of hazard or risk.
S Significant risk	Unacceptable risk. Research and consider measures to eliminate or minimise risk. Inform all staff. Design and implement strategy for induction of staff in response to occurrence of hazard or risk.
M Moderate risk	Review or design safety measures of plant and equipment. Consider alternative work methods and procedures. Inform relevant staff. Conduct awareness education. Monitor level of risk.
L Low risk	Manage by routine procedures. Conduct awareness education. Monitor level of risk

Treating risk

Treatment of risks to health and safety always aims firstly to eliminate the risk. If elimination isn't possible or reasonably practicable, you should then aim to minimise the likelihood of the risk of injury by controlling the hazard.

Treatment measures should be adopted according to the following hierarchy of hazard control measures:

✔ The primary level response eliminates risk in the workplace at the source — this is generally considered the most effective intervention.

✔ The secondary level of intervention controls exposure to the risk and aims to minimise the risk to employees.

✔ Tertiary intervention aims to provide treatment to employees who have experienced a work-related injury.

For example, the risks to staff health from exposure to toxic materials could be eliminated simply by substituting the substances with less toxic or hazardous materials. If that's not possible, handling procedures and protective clothing may be used to limit exposure. Thirdly, you may have monitoring, contingency or emergency procedures in place to enable swift and effective action to treat people injured or exposed to the risk. Sometimes you might apply all three levels of treatment to an identified risk.

The risk to health and safety from fire hazards is a classic example of where all three levels of treatment are deployed. Firstly, construction and maintenance of commercial business premises must comply with strict building design codes. This addresses the risk at the source. (You don't get approval to build a factory using timber when that factory includes a blast furnace.) Secondly, emergency evacuation procedures should be in place with trained 'safety officers' responsible for directing staff and other people out of premises under threat of fire hazard, and fire retardant and sprinkler systems designed to operate if smoke or fire is evident. You should also rehearse the evacuation procedure. This educates staff to the hazards of workplace fire events and minimises the risk of casualties in the event of an actual fire. Thirdly, emergency fire and medical services can attend to treat people affected by incidents of fire and related risks to health and safety.

If your small business operates from leased premises, get to know the landlord and make sure that the building is maintained in a safe manner, and that an adequate emergency evacuation procedure and compliant fire sprinkler systems are in place.

You need to have a well-established procedure in place for notification of injuries, and first aid and emergency responses to ensure injured workers are treated promptly and further risk to health is eliminated, and that these injuries and treatments are recorded.

Monitoring and reviewing

To complete the risk-management cycle, you should monitor the effectiveness of the measures that you have implemented to treat the risks to health and safety. Adjustment to the treatment depends upon how successful the measure has been in either eliminating or controlling the risk.

Make sure you retain records of all of the measures that you have undertaken and the periodic risk assessments that you conduct for your small business.

Go to www.dummies.com/go/hrsmallbusinessau for a risk management flow chart and model risk assessment and control workbook to guide you in this procedure.

Consulting with Employees and Others

You must, so far as is reasonably practicable, consult with workers who carry out work for your business or undertaking who are, or are likely to be, directly affected by risks to health and safety. The duty is not limited to consulting with employees but also includes

- ✔ Contractors
- ✔ Labour hire workers
- ✔ Subcontractors
- ✔ Volunteers
- ✔ Any other people working in your business or undertaking who are, or could be, affected by your business.

Note: The duty is qualified by the phrase 'so far as is reasonably practicable', which means that the circumstances in each case, including the urgency of the health and safety issue and the seriousness of the risk, are relevant when determining the level of consultation required.

You and your staff can agree to procedures for consultation that best suit your circumstances. However, if procedures for consultation have been agreed to, you must comply with them.

In most small businesses, speaking directly to staff or using the usual methods to communicate business matters should be adequate. You're not obliged to appoint or elect health and safety representatives or establish committees to oversee your health and safety activities — although nominating at least one employee to take on the task (normally an administrator or payroll officer) of maintaining your health and safety policy, records and literature is a good idea.

Consulting with staff at the right time

You must consult with staff when

- ✔ Identifying hazards and assessing risks arising from work and making decisions about ways to eliminate or minimise those risks

- ✔ Making decisions about the adequacy of facilities for the welfare of workers

- ✔ Making decisions about the procedures, including those for

  - Monitoring the health and safety of workers

  - Monitoring workplace conditions

  - Proposing changes that may affect the health or safety of workers

  - Providing information and training to workers

  - Resolving work health or safety issues

- ✔ Carrying out any other activity prescribed by the regulations

Of course, you may choose to consult with staff about health and safety matters in other instances as well — for example, when conducting investigations into incidents or 'near misses'.

The obligation to consult means

- ✔ Relevant information about the work health and safety issue is shared with staff.

- ✔ Staff are given a reasonable opportunity to express their views, raise issues and contribute to the decision-making process on how to deal with work health and safety issues.

- ✔ The views of staff are taken into account.

- ✔ Staff are advised of the outcome of the consultation in a timely manner.

Consultation doesn't require consensus or agreement, but it does entitle your staff to contribute to any decisions made.

Duty holders consulting with each other

If more than one person has a duty in relation to the same issue or activity, each of those persons must consult, cooperate and coordinate activities with each other, so far as is reasonably practicable. A number of different duty holders may be involved in an activity — for example, they could be

> ✔ Contractors
>
> ✔ Officers (company directors)
>
> ✔ Owners of the building where the work is carried out
>
> ✔ Staff members
>
> ✔ Suppliers

Each duty holder can have an effect on work health and safety in relation to the activity and, therefore, must share information and cooperate with each other to ensure that each person can meet health and safety duties effectively without gaps or inconsistencies.

Don't take No for an answer when dealing with landlords and others who contribute to a safe working environment. Everyone is individually and collectively responsible.

Applying Standards, Codes and Regulations

Beyond the general duty of care, and obligations to consult, educate and apply good systems for controlling hazards in the workplace, myriad regulations, standards and codes of practice have been developed to regulate how you control risks to the health and safety of employees and others in your small businesses.

Such regulation operates in a hierarchy of importance. The framework of regulation in workplace health and safety can be best illustrated by means of a pyramid, as shown in Figure 14-1.

Figure 14-1:
Pyramid of workplace health and safety regulation.

Acts

Regulations

Codes of practice

Standards

Interpretive guidelines

Workplace policies and procedures

At the top of the pyramid are various health and safety laws enacted by state and territory parliaments (including the model Health and Safety Act). The Acts of parliament set the duty of care and related obligations while the regulations provide specific requirements to give effect to the general responsibilities enacted under the legislation — for example, requiring licences for specific activities and the keeping of particular records.

Codes of practice provide practical guidance on how to meet the standards set out in the Act and the regulations. Codes of practice are admissible in proceedings as evidence of whether or not a duty under the laws has been met. They can also be referred to by an inspector when issuing an improvement or prohibition notice.

Governments recognise that equivalent or better ways of achieving the required work health and safety outcomes may be possible. For that reason, compliance with codes of practice isn't mandatory — providing that any other method used provides an equivalent or higher standard of work health and safety than suggested by the code of practice.

Standards are generally non-enforceable guides to assist businesses in complying with the legislative requirements. Some standards may be prescribed by an industry association as integral to quality assurance and can often be used to accredit an employer as having fulfilled particular quality standards. If you contract with governments to deliver goods or services, you're normally expected to comply with, or be accredited to, approved standards.

Interpretive guidelines are a formal statement on how Safe Work Australia regulators believe key concepts in the model Health and Safety Act operate and, in doing so, provide an indication of how the laws are likely to be enforced.

I have added workplace policies and procedures to Figure 14-1 because these describe how you as the small-business owner and employer intend to address the duty of care and the various elements of the system to ensure the health, safety and welfare of the people employed in your business. The codes and standards are important resources for the formulation of the workplace systems and procedures.

Chapter 15

Workers Compensation and Rehabilitation

In This Chapter

▶ Understanding your workplace injury responsibilities

▶ Managing employees' return to work plan

▶ Working within doctor requirements

▶ Fighting an injury claim

▶ Finding solutions for permanently incapacitated staff

Advice after injury is like medicine after death.

Proverb

Compensation and rehabilitation for personal injuries suffered while at work are two keystones in the three-part foundations of Australian workplace health and safety. (The statutory duty of care owed to your employees and the practical measures you can take to ensure the health, safety and welfare of all people employed or directly affected by the conduct of your small business is the other keystone — refer to Chapter 14 for more on this.)

In this chapter, I explain your responsibilities under the various state and territory laws regulating workers compensation. I explain who is covered by the law and the meaning of workplace-related injury. I outline your obligation to rehabilitate injured employees, and attempt to demystify return to work programs, including how to talk with medical practitioners and other health professionals involved with the treatment of injured employees. I cover disputing a workplace injury claim, and also explain how to manage permanently incapacitated employees.

Knowing Your Responsibilities

The origin of Australian workers compensation lies in 19th-century British law. Prior to the implementation of workers compensation laws, an injured worker's only means of receiving compensation was to sue the employer for negligence at common law. Over many years, governments have curtailed the rights to damages for personal injury at work under common law as statutory compensation payments and access to rehabilitation became the primary means of ensuring injured workers were adequately supported.

You can find many similarities in the eight Australian state and territory workers compensation schemes; however, you need to be careful to also note the differences, because you're obligated to comply with the insurance arrangements, compensation and rehabilitation schemes applicable in the state or territory in which your small business is based and in which your staff work.

The first similarity between all state and territory legislation is that, as the employer, you're responsible for insuring your workforce against the possibility of injury suffered while performing work in your small business. The second similarity is that you're responsible for administering weekly compensation payments to workers who are injured while performing work at your small business.

However, whether a person you employ is entitled to compensation for an injury suffered while at work depends on how the following key terms are defined by the state and territory law in which your small business operates:

- ✔ Workers
- ✔ Deemed Workers
- ✔ Injury
- ✔ Workplace

Generally, if a person working in your small business fits the definition of 'worker' or is otherwise deemed to be a worker by the law, and that person suffers an injury at your workplace, she is entitled to compensation and you're responsible for her rehabilitation. However, defining 'worker' isn't always that simple. The following sections cover the meaning of terms as they're applied in each Australian state and territory.

Defining workers

A *worker* is generally defined as a person employed by you under a contract for service — that is, someone you would normally classify as an employee. However, the term also covers persons who fall within the grey areas of employment regulation, such as some independent contractors and labour-hire employees.

Table 15-1 summarises the definitions of 'worker' applied in each state and territory. Use it to determine who may be covered in your small business. Your local workers compensation insurer or state or territory Workcover authority will also be able to confirm the coverage.

Table 15-1	Defining Workers
State or Territory	*Definition of 'Worker'*
Australian Capital Territory	An individual who has entered into or works under a contract of service with an employer, whether the contract is expressed or implied, oral or written, works for labour only or substantially labour only, or works for another person under contract unless the person is paid to achieve a stated outcome, and has to supply plant and equipment, and is liable for the cost of rectifying any defective work or has a personal services business determination.
New South Wales	A person who has entered into or works under a contract of service or a training contract with an employer (whether by way of manual labour, clerical work or otherwise, and whether the contract is expressed or implied, and whether the contract is oral or in writing) including labour hire employees and outworkers.
Northern Territory	A person with a contract or agreement of any kind to perform work or a service. Exclusions apply for people who supply an ABN.
Queensland	An individual who works under a contract of service; a person who works under a contract, or at piecework rates, for labour only or substantially for labour only. In particular, any person who works for another person under a contract (regardless of whether the contract is a contract of service), unless the person can satisfy all three elements of a results test*, or it can be shown that a personal services business determination is in effect for the person under the *Income Tax Assessment Act 1997* (Cth).
South Australia	A person by whom work is done under a contract of service (whether or not as an employee), a person who is a worker deemed by virtue of the law, a self-employed worker; this includes a former worker and the legal personal representative of a deceased worker.

(continued)

Table 15-1 *(continued)*

State or Territory	Definition of 'Worker'
Tasmania	Any person who has entered into, or works under, a contract of service or training agreement with an employer, whether by way of manual labour, clerical work or otherwise, and whether the contract is express or implied, or is oral or in writing, and any person or class taken to be a worker (deemed) for the purposes of the law.
Victoria	An individual who performs work for an employer or agrees with an employer to perform work at the employer's direction, instruction or request, whether under a contract of employment (whether express, implied, oral or in writing) or otherwise; or someone who is deemed to be a worker.
Western Australia	Any person who has entered into or works under a contract of service or apprenticeship with an employer, whether by way of manual labour, clerical work or otherwise, and whether the contract is expressed or implied, is oral or in writing.

*The three elements of the Queensland results test to be satisfied are that the person performing the work is paid to achieve a specified result or outcome, the person performing the work has to supply the plant and equipment or tools of trade needed to perform the work, and the person is, or would be, liable for the cost of rectifying any defect in the work performed.
Source: Safe Work Australia © Commonwealth of Australia 2012.

Understanding deemed workers

Many occupations have not traditionally been viewed as falling within the definition of employment or operating as contracts for service but, nevertheless, workers in these occupations are protected if they suffer an injury in the course of performing their chosen occupation, vocation, profession or endeavour. This protection has been achieved by *deeming* such people to be workers for workers compensation purposes even if they're not considered workers under other forms of employment regulation.

Table 15-2 lists the types of employment or working arrangements outside of the traditional forms that are deemed workers for the purpose of workers compensation, by state and territory.

Table 15-2 provides a useful reference point to determine whether other people who work with or for your small business (not employees) are covered by workers compensation while working with or for your business.

Table 15-2	Defining Deemed Workers
State or Territory	*Definition of 'Deemed Workers'*
Australian Capital Territory	Regular contractors, subcontractors, trainees, outworkers, timber contractors, family day care carers, religious workers, volunteers, public-interest voluntary workers
New South Wales	Workers lent or on hire; outworkers; other contractors; contractors under labour-hire services arrangements; rural workers; timber-getters; salespersons, canvassers, collectors and others; tributers; mine employees; mines rescue personnel; jockeys and harness racing drivers; drivers of hire-vehicles or hire-vessels (covered by contract of bailment); caddies and others employed through club; shearers' cooks and others; fire fighters in fire district; workers at place of pick-up; boxers, wrestlers, referees and entertainers; voluntary ambulance workers; ministers of religion; ministers of religion covered by policies; participants in training programs
Northern Territory	Workers of householders, working directors, jockeys, taxi drivers, community workers and volunteers, family members, emergency service volunteers
Queensland	Workers lent or on hire (including through labour-hire firms and holding companies), share farmers, salespersons, labour workers, contractors and workers of contractors
South Australia	A person covered by a contract, arrangement or understanding under which the worker works for another in prescribed work or work of a prescribed class, including building work (other than wall or floor-tilers), cleaning work, council driving, taxi and hire car driving, transport driving, work as an entertainer, work as an outworker, work as a licensed jockey, work as a minister, priest or member of another religious order (except Anglican, Catholic, Lutheran and Uniting churches or the Salvation Army)
Tasmania	Contractors where the work exceeds $100 and is not incidental to a trade or business regularly carried on by the contractor; services of workers lent or on hire; police volunteers; volunteers performing fire-fighting operations, fire prevention operations and ambulance services; port and harbour persons engaged at places of pickup; salespersons, canvassers and collectors; luxury hire-car drivers and taxi drivers; jockeys; specified clergymen; participants in training programs

(continued)

Table 15-2 *(continued)*

State or Territory	Definition of 'Deemed Workers'
Victoria	Students under work experience and practical placement arrangements, apprentices, persons participating in declared training programs; secretaries of co-operative societies; door-to-door sellers; timber contractors; drivers of passenger vehicles; owner-drivers carrying goods for reward; contractors; share farmers; declared workers of religious bodies and organisations; Crown employees, ministers, government members, judicial officers, bail justices, public corporation members, retired police reserve members; municipal councillors; persons engaged at places of pick-up for the purposes of being selected for work (for example, fruit pickers); jockeys and track riders, riders and drivers in mixed sports gatherings; outworkers; sailors
Western Australia	Workers lent or let on hire, workers under a contract in substance for personal manual labour or service, workers under an industrial award or agreement, deceased workers, police officers (who suffer an injury and die as a result of that injury), clergy, tributers, jockeys, Crown workers, certain persons deemed workers, working directors

Source: Safe Work Australia © Commonwealth of Australia 2012.

Defining workplace injuries

Whether a person (*worker*) is entitled to workers compensation is dependent on the relationship of the injury to the person's work. Although the ordinary meaning of injury includes harm caused to a person's body as a result of trauma, determining whether a particular event, incident or series of incidents causing harm or damage to a person constitutes a workplace injury involves considering several factors, as follows:

- ✔ **Relationship to employment and contribution of employment:** A relationship or link between the injury and employment needs to exist before the worker can claim workers compensation. In addition, a worker's employment has to be a significant or substantial contributor to the injury.

- ✔ **Aggravation and acceleration:** Sometimes employment isn't the cause of an original injury, but the employee's work may have aggravated or accelerated an existing injury, leading to a right to compensation.

Employment forms often ask prospective employees whether they have a pre-existing illness or injury that may affect their ability to perform the work. This is an area of employment regulation that is quite complex and is a source of some risks for your small business if you manage it incorrectly. The right to ask the question must be viewed in the context of your other obligations under anti-discrimination and workplace rights laws. Refer to Chapter 12 for an explanation of the issues impacting on this area, and what you can ask prospective employees.

✔ **Diseases:** Diseases are classed differently from physical injuries, and include any physical or mental impairment, disorder, defect or morbid condition, whether of sudden or gradual development.

Because the term 'disease' is interpreted differently in each state and territory, all jurisdictions except Queensland have in their regulations tables of diseases that are deemed to be caused by work. Seek advice from your state or territory Workcover authority for more information on the most current table of diseases.

✔ **Industrial deafness:** Industrial deafness is generally judged separately from other forms of injuries. All states and territories have an impairment threshold in place for industrial deafness, which means that injured workers aren't entitled to lump sum compensation until they reach the threshold level. Seek advice from your state or territory Workcover authority for more information on the threshold level.

Injuries must occur in the workplace

Being injured is of itself not sufficient to entitle the worker to compensation. The injury must arise out of or in the course of employment. So, which part of the daily grind constitutes your workplace and what is excluded?

Physical injuries occurring on work premises during the course of performing a job are considered as arising in the course of employment. However, determining whether or not a person was at work when injured isn't always simple. For example, do injuries that occur in the following circumstances satisfy the definition of a workplace injury:

✔ Breaks spent at the work premises?

✔ Breaks spent outside the work premises?

✔ Journeys to and from work?

✔ Work-related travel?

The good news for employees is that work-related travel (that is, travel on official working business) and authorised breaks at work premises are at the time of writing considered to be in the course of employment in each state and territory. However, journeys to and from work (that is, travelling from home to work and back) are only covered in NSW, Queensland, Northern Territory and the ACT.

Authorised breaks spent outside of the work premises are equally problematic. If workers suffer an injury during a lunch break while off normal work premises, for example, they're covered for compensation everywhere in Australia except in South Australia and Tasmania (in which case they're not covered).

Excluding reckless and wilful behaviour

In most states and territories, workers compensation laws prescribe certain circumstances in which workers compensation will be denied even though the worker has suffered an injury. Workers who suffer an injury but were reckless or wilfully misbehaving when they suffered the injury are excluded from receiving workers compensation benefits. However, an injury caused by the serious and wilful misconduct of a worker that results in death or serious and permanent impairment will usually mean workers compensation is payable. For example, a worker will have been reckless or wilfully misbehaving by driving drunk or at prohibited speeds or in contravention of clear directions and signage at worksite. Anyone hurt by their actions will be covered, but the worker at fault won't be covered.

Mental stress, anxiety and other psychological injuries

To be eligible for compensation, workers who claim to have suffered a psychological injury must be able to demonstrate that the injury wasn't related to any reasonable action taken by their employer in relation to a dismissal, retrenchment, transfer, performance appraisal, demotion or disciplinary action. In general, any management action taken on reasonable grounds and in a reasonable manner doesn't expose your small business to successful claims for workers compensation.

One of the most frustrating experiences for any employer occurs when employees avoid a job performance warning by absenting themselves from work, claiming to be ill because of an action of their employer. In this situation, you may be tempted either to not provide notice to the employee that you intend to warn or counsel them or do nothing at all. However, continuing to address the unsatisfactory performance in the correct manner is vital, because failure to do so only adds to your frustration. Don't issue a warning or dismiss an employee while he's on personal leave or workers compensation. You will only expose yourself to a claim that you have unlawfully and adversely acted against the person because he's ill. Wait until the employee returns to work or when it becomes apparent that he's not going to be able to return to work. See the section 'Managing Permanently Incapacitated Staff', later in this chapter, for more on this.

Planning the Return to Work

As important as compensation is to employees who suffer a workplace injury, rehabilitating workers and helping them return to work as soon as possible is also important. The importance of this objective is reflected in every state and territory law regulating workers compensation. Whenever a worker is absent from work due to a workplace injury, you have an obligation to support the worker to recover and return to work.

Rehabilitation starts right away

Most of the injuries that occur at your work and that lead to claims for compensation shouldn't be a surprise to you. (Notification of injuries should be part of your health and safety procedures — refer to Chapter 14 for more on this.)

Nevertheless, sometimes the first that you know about a workplace injury is when you're notified of the employee's absence and receive a medical certificate indicating that the person is unfit for work. The natural inclination of most employers is to leave such workers alone, not contact them and wait patiently for their return to work. The last thing that you want is to be accused of harassing injured workers when they're at their most vulnerable. However, news flash folks — rehabilitation starts now. The obligation to support workers to return to their pre-injury health commences as soon as you become aware of the injury and usually extends for at least 12 months.

Implementing a return to work policy

Throughout Australia, small-business owners are expected to have a return to work policy or program in place, covering all of the workers in the business. This policy or program doesn't have to be in writing, but doing so is worthwhile.

I'm a great fan of employment policies because they provide a convenient guide or checklist that you can follow when a situation arises, which enables you to act swiftly and confidently. Refer to Chapter 8 for more on employment policies.

Go to www.dummies.com/go/hrsmallbusinessau for a model workplace injuries return to work policy.

Designing an individualised return to work plan

The real rehabilitation work occurs when you create an individual return to work plan for an injured worker. This plan provides a map for the injured worker, the treating medical practitioner, occupational rehabilitation providers, insurer and yourself (as well as anyone else who contributes to the rehabilitation), guiding the return to work to a successful conclusion.

The individual return to work plan is a form of injury management planning, and should outline the medical and other health services required to return the injured worker to the workplace. Importantly, you should include information on the worker's physical or mental capacity for work, the rehabilitation goal (such as return to full physical capacity), and the actions required by the worker, employer, nominated treating doctor, rehabilitation provider and insurance agent.

Follow these steps to create and implement an individual return to work plan:

1. **Appoint a return to work (RTW) coordinator.**

   Appoint yourself to this role, because the coordinator needs to be a person in the business who has the authority to make decisions.

2. **Collect and share information on the injured workers capacity.**

   See the section 'Communicating well with doctors', later in this chapter, for more.

3. **Develop the RTW plan.**

   This plan should include information on the capacity of the injured worker, rehabilitation goals, health aids and workplace adjustments, hours of work, list of duties (and prohibited duties), timetable and the names of all parties that contribute to the RTW plan.

4. **Consult with the injured worker and other parties on the RTW plan.**

   This could include the treating medical practitioner, your insurer and any rehabilitation providers that may be contributing to the return to work.

5. **Get agreement to the RTW plan from all parties.**

6. **Implement the RTW plan.**

   This means the injured worker commences work in accordance with the RTW plan.

7. **Monitor and review progress.**

   Progress must be monitored as required under the RTW plan. If appropriate, you can adjust the plan if the recovery is slower than expected, or accelerate it if the injured worker's recovery is more rapid.

8. **Return the worker to pre-injury job, or provide with permanently modified duties or an alternative job.**

   The goal is to return workers to full capacity so that they can resume the work that they performed for you before the injury occurred. However, that may not always be achievable and, therefore, you need to give consideration to a worker resuming work permanently in an alternative job or with modified duties, hours of work or similar.

Dealing with Doctors (and Not Getting a Headache)

The first useful task you can undertake in the return to work planning phase is to better understand the nature of the injury and the impact it has on the worker's capacity to perform the job.

You can't rely on the worker alone for information and to guide the return to work plan. You must make an attempt to involve the health professional who is treating the worker and others if necessary who have the professional capability to support the worker's rehabilitation and return them to work.

The doctor and patient relationship is clearly confidential and the worker's medical records are sensitive personal information. Therefore ask the worker for authority to speak directly to their treating medical practitioner and in turn they should permit the doctor to speak to you. You don't need a written authority but I would recommend that you ask the worker to either sign a note or send you an email permitting you and their doctor to speak about the injury. State and territory Workcover authorities sometimes publish template forms that you can download and use for these purposes. I recommend you go to their websites and search for them as they can save a lot of time creating your own.

Communicating well with doctors

Make a list of the information that you need from the worker's doctor and the information that you want to provide to the doctor about the work and the workplace.

Questions you could have for the doctor may include the following:

- ✔ What is the nature of the injury?
- ✔ How does the injury affect the worker's physical or mental capacity? For example, does the injury restrict the worker's capacity to walk, grip objects, use a computer, or drive a car or forklift?
- ✔ What is the prognosis for recovery?
- ✔ How long does the doctor predict a full recovery is likely to take?
- ✔ What is the worker capable of performing now?
- ✔ Could medical or other aids be used to assist in recovery?

Here is some information you may need to share with the doctor:

- ✔ The primary purpose of the job and the tasks that the worker performs to successfully do the job.
- ✔ The working environment — for example, factory, retail, warehouse, driving, public relations, office or dental clinic.
- ✔ The current environmental and operational impediments (if any) to the worker returning to work — for example, minimum licensing standards or certificates that attest to the worker's fitness to perform the work.
- ✔ The potential adjustments that you can make to the work and workplace to assist in recovery and the return to work.

Talking with the treating doctor is a two-way conversation, and you should take the opportunity to share as much information as is necessary to manage the return to work plan.

Confirming incapacity and suitable duties

Medical practitioners throughout Australia usually certify the fitness of their patients to attend work and perform duties (in other words, their capacity for work) along one of the following lines:

- ✔ **Suitable duties only.** This means work suited to the worker's current abilities, taking into account his current capacity for work and medical condition, age, skills, work experience, place of residence and pre-injury employment.

- ✔ **Fit for restricted or light duties.** This is similar to suitable duties and is a term usually applied to manual or physical work.

- ✔ **Unfit for any duties.**

The certificate may also nominate a limited number of days per week or hours each day that the worker would be fit to work or perform some suitable duties.

Having workers return to work isn't unusual, and is often beneficial to the rehabilitation, allowing employees to build confidence gradually while recovering from the injury. However, this measure should be temporary on the way to a return to full capacity and to the pre-injury work.

Certificates that nominate suitable, restricted or light duties usually stem from one-way conversations with doctors and their patients, the injured workers. The treating doctor can't truly understand the worker's capacity for work unless you explain the work to them and the environment in which it is performed. So be prepared to challenge medical practitioners to consider all of the information in certifying whether or not the worker is fit for suitable or restricted duties.

Disputing Claims of Workplace Injury

If you don't dispute the claim that a worker has suffered a workplace injury, the procedure to manage injured workers is fairly straightforward. Your insurer investigates the matter, seeking your response to the claim and weighing the medical evidence it collects independently of the treating medical practitioner, and then decides the claim. Rehabilitation providers are appointed to assist in the return to work and the other steps then follow (refer to the section 'Planning the Return to Work', earlier in this chapter, for more).

If you dispute the claim, however, you need to inform the insurer's investigator, providing as much factual material on the circumstances of the worker's health and the events surrounding the alleged causes of the injury. Ultimately, whether the claim for compensation is accepted is up to the insurer, not you. It may be frustrating, but you cannot control the outcome. The only element that you can control is the arrangement for return to work.

Whether you dispute or accept the claim for workers compensation, your task is the same. You must implement a return to work plan.

If the treating doctor has certified the worker can only return to suitable or restricted duties (refer to the preceding section), the question still remains as to whether providing these duties short of a full recovery and return to the pre-injury work is reasonable.

You don't have to accept injured workers back to work purely on the authority of the medical certificate if doing so isn't reasonable or practicable. Your small business is likely to be less able than larger businesses to provide suitable duties. For example, if the worker's pre-injury job was maintenance work and the doctor certifies that the worker is currently unfit to lift or bend over, allowing her to return to work may be unreasonable because she can't practically perform any useful duties. If you do intend to dispute a claim and providing suitable duties isn't reasonable, you should document the reasons for such a decision.

The objective of the return to work plan is to assist the worker to recover and return to work. At some stages of the plan, providing suitable duties may be reasonable and practical, and not so at other times. Even where the employee isn't at work, you should continue the return to work plan, including regular consultation with the worker's medical practitioner and rehabilitation providers.

Managing Permanently Incapacitated Staff

In some cases of workplace injury, you need to decide whether the injured worker is capable of resuming pre-injury employment or instead requires permanently modified duties or alternative employment in order to return to work. This is an incredibly tough decision, especially when the injured worker is permanently incapacitated and unable to return to their pre-injury job.

Note: In this section, I concentrate on injured employees because other injured workers (deemed or otherwise — refer to the section 'Knowing Your Responsibilities', earlier in this chapter) not directly employed by you are more likely to move on to alternative employment with other employers or businesses.

When deciding the future employment of the injured person and, in particular, whether he can continue to be employed in your small business, consider the following:

- ✔ **Whether or not you've satisfied all of the legal requirements.** This includes providing a return to work plan and supporting the rehabilitation program for at least 12 months.

- ✔ **Whether you've made a thorough and objective assessment of the work capacity of the injured employee.** You can't make a decision about future employment unless you have sufficient medical information you can use to objectively determine the capacity of the person to perform the inherent requirements of their pre-injury position. *Inherent requirements* of the job are the fundamental aspects of the job that a person must be able to perform in order to meet the essential elements of the job — see Chapter 12 for a more extensive explanation and the exemptions for employers where the return to work would impose unreasonable hardship on the employer.

The medical information for the injured worker should provide a prognosis of the person's capacity for work into the future and, if she hasn't resumed any work at all, the likelihood of the person being capable of returning to work to perform the job in which they had been employed.

Armed with the medical information for the injured worker, you need to adopt one of the following courses of action:

- ✔ Return the worker to pre-injury employment

- ✔ Provide alternative employment or permanently modified duties

- ✔ Terminate worker's employment

The first two actions in the preceding list will primarily be based on the medical information, and your ability to make reasonable adjustments to the job duties and workplace to accommodate the permanent impairment of the injured employee. Termination of employment also depends upon the medical information but includes consideration of whether termination of employment would be discriminatory or unfair. See Figure 15-1 for a decision-making flow chart.

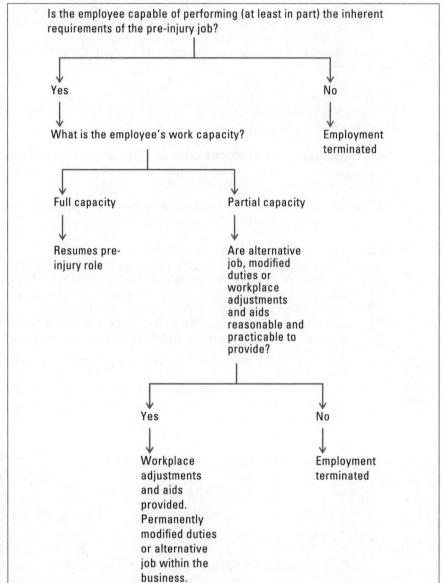

Figure 15-1:
Return
to work
decision-
making flow
chart.

Terminating the employment of an employee who's not capable of performing the inherent requirements of the job isn't unlawful discrimination. This means the only other consideration is whether termination would be unfair. The Fair Work Commission will take into account all of the circumstances of the decision to dismiss the employee including:

- ✔ Validity of the decision in relation to the employee's conduct and capacity
- ✔ Whether the employee had an opportunity to respond
- ✔ The opportunity to have a support person
- ✔ Any other matters the Commission considers relevant

If you follow the steps outlined in this section and act on the advice provided in this chapter, you will significantly reduce the risk of the termination being treated as unlawful or unfair.

Part VI

The End of the Employment Relationship

Five Steps to Avoiding Unfair Dismissal Claims

- **Be clear and consistent in your expectation of staff:** Employees can rightly be held accountable for unsatisfactory performance as long as they know you will consistently apply clearly articulated and reasonable standards of performance.

- **Make sure you give staff an opportunity to improve:** Unless the conduct is so serious that it wouldn't be reasonable to continue employment, you must provide staff with a reasonable opportunity to reach your expected standard of performance and conduct.

- **Be honest and act decisively:** Everyone should be able to find a job that suits, but sometimes that job won't be in your business. If someone isn't working out, act decisively to end the employment within the first six months, clearly explaining the reason.

- **Record good and not so good work performance as it happens:** You need to show evidence of the reasons for dismissal — and you can't make it up later on. Regular performance reviews, and written warnings and directives are essential records that you need to be able to access if you have to go to the Fair Work Commission.

- **Ensure staff are supported appropriately when their job is in jeopardy:** Employees are entitled to have another person present to assist them in any circumstances where dismissal is possible (that person can't be a lawyer acting in a professional capacity).

Check out www.dummies.com/extras/hrsmallbusinessau to discover more about handling the end of an employee's relationship with your small business.

In this part ...

- Understand your obligations and those of employees to provide notice of termination of employment. Learn what termination payments you must pay and the tax withheld. Use the checklist to ensure that superannuation and other entitlements are correctly paid.

- Understand what may be an unfair dismissal, and use the checklist and other resources to minimise the risk to your small business of a successful claim for compensation against you.

- Learn the difference between regular dismissal and genuine redundancy and what you must do to stay on the right side of the law, including when selecting who stays and who goes.

Chapter 16

Resignation of Employment

· ·

In This Chapter

▶ Providing notice of resignation

▶ Understanding notice period obligations

▶ Calculating payments, tax and superannuation

▶ Finding out why employees are leaving

· ·

Please accept my resignation. I don't care to belong to any club that would accept me as a member.

Groucho Marx

*Y*ou would think ending the employment relationship would be a simple matter. An employee tells you she's leaving. She works through the notice period, you agree to let her go immediately or you pay her in lieu of the notice period. Whatever option is chosen, the employment ends and everyone gets on with their working lives. Mostly, the reality does work that way, but you need to be aware of some important rules even within these best-case scenarios — because these rules could cost you money if you don't observe them.

For example, you need to keep in mind taxation and superannuation considerations when preparing the final payments, and observe various niceties over the remaining period of employment. In this chapter, I explain the requirements and obligations of employees when they resign, and your obligations to pay them correctly, including the taxation and superannuation implications.

Finding out the reasons behind an employee's resignation, and learning from people as they go on their way, can be really helpful for your small business. So I also explain how you can find out these aspects through a well-structured exit interview procedure.

Understanding Notice of Resignation Requirements

Employees are usually expected to provide notice to you that they intend to resign their employment and move on to other things, right? Well, yes and no.

The National Employment Standards (NES) prescribe the period of notice that you as the employer must provide to employees to terminate their employment, but they don't impose a mutual obligation on employees. The requirement for employees to provide notice of resignation appears in an applicable modern award or is provided in the contract of employment. Unless an award or contractual obligation to do so exists, your employee can walk straight out the door never to be seen again with no notice at all.

Providing notice under a modern award

Modern awards generally impose an obligation on employees to provide notice of resignation in similar or identical terms to the employer under the NES. Here is an example of a typical provision extracted from the General Retail Industry Award 2010:

> **14. Termination of employment**
>
> *Notice of termination is provided for in the NES.*
>
> **14.1. Notice of termination by an employee**
>
> *The notice of termination required to be given by an employee is the same as that required of an employer except that there is no requirement on the employee to give additional notice based on the age of the employee concerned. If an employee fails to give the required notice the employer may withhold from any monies due to the employee on termination under this award or the NES, an amount not exceeding the amount the employee would have been paid under this award in respect of the period of notice required by this clause less any period of notice actually given by the employee.*

Note: Although most modern awards provide similar provisions to the preceding award, differences do exist across awards. Check the specific modern award whenever the situation arises.

Including resignation notice in employment contracts

Generally, including a provision in an employment contract that makes clear the period of notice required from an employee when resigning employment is wise. This provides you with sufficient notice, during which you can recruit another person to replace the person leaving, or otherwise adjust the work to minimise the disruption to the efficient operation of your business.

Where a modern award applies to your employees, reference in the contract to the modern award provision is usually sufficient to cover the issue and avoid any dispute when an employee resigns.

Go to www.dummies.com/go/hrsmallbusinessau for a model employment contract that provides an example of how you would include a resignation notice obligation in the contract.

If a modern award doesn't apply to the employee and you don't provide an express term of employment imposing notice of resignation, the employee may just walk away from your business with no notice and still be entitled to payment for wages owing, overtime and the balance of accrued leave payments.

In some rare circumstances (perhaps where the employee is a highly paid chief executive), the issue could land in front of a judge in an Australian court. In these rare circumstances, the courts normally expect the employee (and for that matter, employers) to provide *reasonable notice* of the intention to terminate the employment relationship. This may be a period equivalent to that provided under a modern award through to several months, depending upon the nature of the employment relationship. However, such a dispute is unlikely to ever end up in court in relation to an Australian small business because the cost of litigation would far outweigh the amount of damages that could be recovered for failure to provide notice. Therefore, I strongly recommend that you expressly provide for a period of notice in the employment contract. (Refer to Chapter 7 for more on employment contracts.)

When notice isn't needed from employees

The obligation to provide notice of resignation doesn't apply to

- **Casual employees:** These employees are in intermittent or irregular employment, where the hours of employment are not predictable. Employers aren't normally obligated to offer continuing employment to casual employees beyond the period of employment in which they have accepted work, and casual employees aren't obligated to return after completing the agreed period of work.

- **Employees engaged for a specified period, task or season:** Employees employed under a fixed-term can't be terminated unless a serious breach of a term of employment has occurred. Under these forms of employment, employers and employees don't need to provide notice of the end of employment because the end is already specified by the nature of the arrangement. *Seasonal* employment is the same — when the season ends the employment ends.

- **Trainees:** This covers employees who have been employed to undertake work in conjunction with a formal training arrangement approved by a registered training provider. The employee's employment is usually limited to the period of the training arrangement. For example, a young person may be employed in a restaurant for the period that it takes to obtain a vocational qualification in hospitality.

Working or Not Working the Notice Period

You can have your employee work right through the notice period or you can waive the obligation. When a trusted employee who has provided loyal service to you decides to resign, the ideal situation is for them to continue to work during the period of notice, because this allows you sufficient time to recruit a replacement and ensure minimal interruption to your business.

However, where the resignation occurs due to an unhappy period of employment, retaining the person during the notice period may create more problems for you and ending the employment on the spot may be the better option.

When working out whether to retain someone during the notice period, consider how productive the person is likely to be and whether the risks to your business outweigh the benefits if he continues to work.

You can choose to waive the obligation to have the employee work through the notice period in either of two ways:

✔ Agree to have the employee leave immediately or on a date prior to the full period of notice.

✔ Pay the employee for the entire period that she would have worked over the notice period and end the employment immediately — in other words, provide payment in lieu of notice.

The following sections address these two options.

Ending employment by agreement

An agreement to cease employment on a date other than the date on which the notice would have ended means you're not obliged to pay the employee any wages in lieu of notice. You forgo the right to withhold monies owing for any period of the notice that the resigning employee won't be working. The employee forgoes the right to claim any further wages or entitlements from you effective from the date on which you have agreed to end his employment. All leave and superannuation entitlements cease to accrue from that agreed date.

If you and your employee agree to end employment before the end of the notice period, confirm this agreement with the employee in writing. You don't want the employee returning in several months asking for payment of the balance of the notice period (which some dishonest people are inclined to do).

Payment in lieu of notice

If you choose to unilaterally end the employment on a date prior to the end of the notice period provided by the employee, you must pay the full rate of pay that the employee would have received had he worked the period of notice, including all of the following:

✔ Allowances

✔ Incentive-based payments and bonuses

✔ Overtime and penalty rates

✔ Shift and annual leave loadings

✔ Any other separately identifiable amounts that the employee would normally be paid

Termination Payments

When employees resign from employment in your small business you're required to pay all of the money owing to them as soon as practicable and provide them with a final pay slip detailing the payments. In summary, you must pay

✔ Accrued annual leave and annual leave loading entitlements

✔ Accrued or pro-rata long-service leave (if applicable)

✔ Outstanding wages, including penalty rates and allowances

Annual and long service leave

If an employee is entitled to annual leave and annual leave loading (pursuant to a modern award), they must be paid out for both entitlements when their employment ends. This applies even if the modern award expressly states that entitlement to annual leave loading is not payable. Strange but true!

This anomaly is due to the interpretation placed on the part of the NES that provides that a ' … terminated employee with a period of untaken annual leave must be paid what they would have been paid if they had taken that period of leave'. If employees are entitled to leave loading during annual leave while employed, they are entitled to payment of it on unused annual leave when their employment terminates.

The entitlement to take paid long service leave while employed occurs usually after ten years of continuous service in your small business. However, employees are entitled to pro rata payment of the long service leave when they resign (in limited circumstances) and when their employment otherwise terminates before the ten years' service.

The entitlement to payment of long service leave depends on the employee having worked in your business for at least the qualifying period prescribed by the relevant state or territory long service leave law, the state or territory in which she works and the reason for resignation satisfying specific criteria.

Table 16-1 contrasts the entitlement to pro rata long service leave when employees resign from employment and when they're dismissed.

Table 16-1		Entitlement to Pro Rata Long Service Leave Payment			
Full Entitlement			Pro Rata Leave Payment on Termination of Employment		
State or Territory	Qualifying Period	Period of Leave	Qualifying Period	Payable on Dismissal by the Employer Unless	Payable Only When Resignation Due to
NSW	10 years	2 months	5 years	Serious and wilful misconduct	Illness, incapacity, domestic or other pressing necessity
VIC	10 years	2 months	7 years	Payable for any reason	Payable for any reason
QLD	10 years	2 months	7 years	Employee's conduct, capacity or performance	Illness, incapacity, domestic or other pressing necessity
WA	10 years	2 months	7 years	Serious misconduct	Payable for any reason
SA	10 years	13 weeks	7 years	Serious and wilful misconduct	Payable for any reason
TAS	10 years	2 months	7 years	Serious and wilful misconduct	Illness, incapacity or domestic or other pressing necessity
NT	10 years	13 weeks	7 years	Serious misconduct	Illness, incapacity, domestic or other pressing necessity
ACT	7 years	6.0669 weeks	5 years	Serious and wilful misconduct	Illness, incapacity, domestic or other pressing necessity

An employee who resigns prior to the required pro-rata qualifying period isn't entitled to any payment of long service leave. Refer to Chapter 6 for more on long service leave entitlements.

Tax and superannuation

You need to take special care to understand the differing tax treatment of some termination payments and the obligation to pay superannuation contributions on any final termination payments made to an employee.

Taxation of eligible termination payments

Taxation of termination payments depends upon the nature of the payment made to the employee. You can agree to pay some termination payments in the form of a lump sum payment when employees finish employment, because the employees may be better off than if the payments were taxed according to their marginal rate of tax. This lump sum payment is known as an *eligible termination payment* (ETP).

According to the Australian Tax Office (ATO; www.ato.gov.au), an ETP is paid due to a termination of employment when

- ✔ You or your employee requests it
- ✔ A mutual agreement has been made (including retirement)
- ✔ Your employee becomes permanently disabled
- ✔ Your employee dies

Table 16-2 contrasts the type of payments that can be included with those that can't be treated as an ETP. Visit www.ato.gov.au for more information.

Table 16-2	Eligible Termination Payments
Payments Included in an ETP	*Payments Not Included in an ETP*
Unused rostered days off (RDOs)	Payments for unused annual leave and/or leave loading
Payment in lieu of notice	Payments for unused long service leave
Unused sick leave	Salary, wages, allowances, bonuses and incentives owing to the employee for work done or leave already taken
A gratuity or 'golden handshake'	Compensation for personal injury
Compensation for loss of job	Payment for restraint of trade
Compensation for wrongful dismissal, provided it is paid within 12 months of the actual termination of employment	Foreign termination payments
Payments for loss of future super payments	Employee share scheme payments
Payments arising from your employee's termination because of ill-health (invalidity), other than compensation for personal injury.	An advance or loan
Payments in respect of genuine redundancy or paid under an early retirement scheme that are within the tax-free limit.	Payments in respect of genuine redundancy or paid under an early retirement scheme that exceeds the tax-free limit
Lump sum payments paid on the death of an employee	

Generally, you must pay an ETP within 12 months of the employment ending for the employee to qualify for a reduced rate of withholding tax. You should treat payments made outside 12 months as ordinary income and, therefore, the employee's normal marginal income tax rate applies.

Payments for unused annual leave and long service leave can't be included in an ETP. Nevertheless, they are taxed differently on termination depending upon whether the payment is made as part of genuine redundancy, early retirement due to ill-health or resignation. The ATO provides a step-by-step guide on how to calculate these termination payments. Go to www.ato. gov.au for more information.

As shown in Table 16-2, a genuine redundancy payment is included in an ETP but is generally tax-free unless the amounts exceed the statutory limits. Although small businesses are exempt from obligations to pay redundancy, in some circumstances you may agree to pay some form of redundancy and, as such, the payment may be exempt from taxation. The tax-free limits are adjusted at the commencement of each financial year — check with the ATO to find out the current limits.

If your employee leaves due to ill-health, his ETP may contain a tax-free invalidity component. According to the ATO's ETP guide, an employee is eligible for this segment if

✔ Payment was made because the employee can no longer work due to physical or mental ill-health

✔ The employee stopped working early (that is, before their last retirement day)

✔ Two legally qualified medical practitioners have certified it is unlikely the employee can ever work again in a role that he is reasonably qualified for, either through training, experience or education

Finally, an ETP is taxed at a percentage of the amount paid depending on your employee's age and whether the payment is within the cap determined from time to time by the regulations. (Check with the ATO for the current caps — www.ato.gov.au.) Table 16-3 shows the withholding tax rate for employees under and over the age of 55 years and the rate applicable to amounts paid in excess of the ETP concessional cap.

Table 16-3	ETP Withholding Tax Calculation	
Employee's Age at End of Income Year	**Payment**	**Withholding Tax including Medicare Levy**
Under 55 years of age	Up to the ETP cap	31.5%
55 years of age or older	Up to the ETP cap	16.5%
All employees	Over the ETP cap	46.5%

As with most taxation issues, the calculation of the appropriate amount of tax to be withheld on ETP can be somewhat complex. Contact the Australian Tax Office for help with determining your obligations in each particular situation that occurs.

Superannuation

Superannuation contributions are payable on an employee's ordinary time earnings. Ordinary time earnings includes wages earned by the employee working through the notice period preceding the last day of employment. No drama there. However, superannuation contributions must also be made for payments in lieu of notice. Such payments are considered to be ordinary time earnings and so superannuation must be paid on the amount of payment in lieu of notice.

Refer to Chapter 6 for more on superannuation obligations.

Withholding monies owed

I receive a lot of enquiries from employers asking whether they can penalise employees who don't provide the period of notice required under their contract of employment or the modern award. I feel the pain of these employers, I really do. Nothing is more annoying than an employee resigning without notice and leaving you in the lurch. However, you can't lawfully impose a financial penalty on employees. The good news is you can withhold money owed to the employee on termination of employment. The specific circumstances and amount withheld must be in accordance with the modern award provision (refer to the section 'Providing notice under a modern award', earlier in this chapter, for the provision provided in the General Retail Industry Award 2010).

For example, say you have an employee who has been employed by you for more than five years. According to the relevant modern award, the employee is required to provide at least four weeks' notice of the date on which she intends to resign and leave your business. If the employee leaves without your agreement immediately, you may withhold the equivalent of four weeks wages from

- Allowances
- Annual leave and leave loading
- Incentive-based payments and bonuses
- Long service leave payments
- Overtime and penalty rates
- Wages owing
- Any other separately identifiable amounts that the employee would normally be paid

Note: You can't withhold superannuation contributions owing to the employee.

Exit Interviews: Finding Out the Reasons for Leaving

When an employee leaves your small business, you may be tempted to put the experience behind you, and look forward to the contribution of the next person who joins your business. Very few employers take the time to genuinely learn from the experience of an ex-employee. However, taking the time to listen and understand what someone else thinks about you and your business will ultimately improve your chances of business success. It may be hard and you may not even want to learn from some employees, but it is essential to your business.

Listening and learning

A fatal flaw for small business owners is a 'tin ear' — that is, failing to listen and learn from others. This flaw will inevitably lead to the same mistakes holding your business back from reaching its potential. Don't fall into that trap!

The *exit interview* is the technique of choice for employers who wish to learn from the experience of the employee leaving their business.

When a person is leaving your business, he's inclined to be more forthright in expressing his views. This is fine and dandy, and you can learn lots of great stuff from a person uninhibited and no longer feeling constrained. However, the person most likely to be forthright at an exit interview is the same person who has probably told you what she really thinks about the business throughout the entire period of her employment. So you need to find ways to get all exiting employees to open up.

You don't have to be the person who conducts the exit interview. Small-business owners are often independent-minded, confident and a little bit scary to employees. So get someone else to conduct the interview for you. It could be

✔ A business consultant

✔ An employee in your business

✔ A family member

✔ A trusted colleague

The purpose is to have the departing employee open up and make sure you ask a person who can do this to conduct the interview. If you can't find someone to personally interview the employee, at least provide the employee with a questionnaire to complete and return to you on departure.

Preparing exit questions

Prepare a list of questions covering all of the areas of the business where you want to learn from the employee's experience. You should include a mix of open-ended questions, multiple choice and ratings. Include questions about the following themes:

✔ Adequacy of instructions, supervision or support provided to the employee

✔ Adequacy of tools and equipment

✔ Aspects of the job the employee found enjoyable and not enjoyable

✔ Autonomy over work

✔ Conditions of employment

- Customer relationships

- Efficiency of work systems and operational procedures

- Health and safety measures

- Quality of communication between staff and business owner

- Training and personal development opportunities

- Workplace culture, including commitment to addressing bullying, harassment and discrimination

Conducting the exit interview

Once you have your questions (refer to preceding section), you can invite the employee to participate in the interview.

Employees aren't obliged to participate in the exit interview or complete a questionnaire. You can only encourage them to do so.

Go to www.dummies.com/go/hrsmallbusinessau for a sample exit interview questionnaire. All the interviewer has to do is read the questions to the employee and record the answers — easy! The questionnaire should take only 15 minutes to complete.

Use the same exit interview form for all of the employees who leave your business. The information collected will have cumulative as well as immediate value because you should be able to detect trends in the responses provided.

Don't just bask in the beautiful glow of positive feedback. Learn from every response. For example, if you consistently rate poor or very poor on particular questions, you need to consider strategies to improve in these areas. This is how you can improve your small business.

Chapter 17

Employee Dismissal: A Matter of Fairness

In This Chapter

▶ Understanding which employees are protected

▶ Finding out what unfair dismissal actually means

▶ Learning the details of the Small Business Fair Dismissal Code

▶ Working your way through dismissal disputes

▶ Dismissing employees in Western Australia

▶ Knowing how unlawful dismissal is different

What I don't like about office Christmas parties is looking for a job the next day.

Phyllis Diller

The preceding quote is a classic gag from one of the great American comedians. As well as the humour, I love the self-deprecating digs. Claims of unfair dismissal against your small business, however, aren't funny, and often finish up as bad jokes at your expense. In this chapter, I explain how to manage the end of the employment relationship in a manner that should not result in additional expense for your small business.

This chapter covers Australia's *fair dismissal system*, which was introduced with a whole raft of changes to Australian employment laws and regulation under the national system of workplace relations on 1 July 2009. The changes to the law opened up the fair dismissal system to employees of all businesses, although small businesses must comply with a slightly different set of rules — known as the *Small Business Fair Dismissal Code*. In this chapter, I explain in detail how the system works, who can make a claim against you, what constitutes unfair dismissal, and what you need to do to minimise the risks of a damaging claim against your small business. I explain how you can apply the Small Business Fair Dismissal Code to minimise the risks of aggrieved ex-employees successfully claiming unfair dismissal, outline Western Australia's particular system, and cover the differences between unfair and unlawful dismissal.

Working Out Who's Protected from Unfair Dismissal

Not every unhappy ex-employee can make a claim against you alleging unfair dismissal. Various categories of employees are ineligible and the rest must serve minimum periods of employment in order to make a claim if they're subsequently dismissed. Somewhat perversely, the law describes eligibility according to whether the person is *protected* or *not protected* from unfair dismissal.

Employees who are protected

Employees are protected from unfair dismissal if, at the time they are dismissed, they have completed at least the minimum employment period and one or more of the following applies to them:

- ✔ They're covered by a modern award
- ✔ An enterprise agreement applies in relation to the employment
- ✔ The sum of annual rate of earnings and such other amounts (if any) worked out in accordance with the regulations is less than the high income threshold

The high income threshold is determined under a convoluted formula prescribed in the Fair Work Regulations 2009 and is adjusted on 1 July each year. The high income threshold from 1 July 2013 was $129,300 per year.

The minimum employment period is 12 months continuous service ending at the earlier of the following times:

- ✔ The time when the employee is given notice of the dismissal
- ✔ Immediately before the dismissal

Your small business must employ fewer than 15 employees at the time dismissal took place for the 12 months qualifying period to apply. If you employ 15 or more people at the time of dismissal, the aggrieved ex-employee must have been employed for at least six months.

Employees who aren't protected

The following categories of employees aren't eligible to claim unfair dismissal against your small business:

- **Employees who haven't met the minimum employment period** (refer to preceding section).

- **Employees who are transferring to an employer under a transfer of business** (not between related entities) who have been informed by the new employer in writing that their prior service won't be recognised. These employees must serve the minimum employment period with the new employer to be eligible to make a claim for unfair dismissal.

- **Casual employees** employed on an irregular basis. Only those casual employees who have been engaged on a regular and systematic basis and who have a reasonable expectation that their employment would continue can make an unfair dismissal claim.

Defining Unfair Dismissal

Where ex-employees are eligible to make a claim (refer to preceding sections), they still have to overcome several hurdles to successfully argue that they had been unfairly dismissed.

The *Fair Work Act 2009* (the Act) provides that an employee has been unfairly dismissed if the Fair Work Commission is satisfied that the:

- Person has been dismissed

- Dismissal was harsh, unjust or unreasonable

- Dismissal was not consistent with the Small Business Fair Dismissal Code

- Dismissal wasn't a case of genuine redundancy

The following sections help you work through three of the four criteria to understand what an unfair dismissal actually means. These criteria are the key to understanding what is and isn't an unfair dismissal. (The Small Business Fair Dismissal Code is a little more complex, and is discussed in detail in the section 'Getting to Know the Small Business Fair Dismissal Code', later in this chapter.)

Dismissal comes first

A person has been dismissed if the person's employment with his employer has been terminated on the employer's initiative, or if the person has resigned from his employment but was forced to do so because of conduct, or a course of conduct, engaged in by his employer — that is, they had been constructively dismissed.

A person isn't deemed to have been dismissed when

✔ The person was employed under a contract of employment for a specified period of time, for a specified task or for the duration of a specified season, and the employment has terminated at the end of the period, on completion of the task or at the end of the season.

✔ The person was an employee to whom a training arrangement applied, and whose employment was for a specified period of time or was, for any reason, limited to the duration of the training arrangement, and the employment has then terminated at the end of the training arrangement.

✔ The person was demoted in employment but the demotion doesn't involve a significant reduction in her remuneration or duties, and she remains employed with the employer who effected the demotion.

When working out whether dismissal has occurred, the following points are critical:

✔ Termination of employment at the *initiative of the employer* means you must have ended the employment. It can't be by agreement or resignation.

✔ *Constructive dismissal* means the resignation occurred because of the action of the employer. The employee must show that he was forced to resign because of conduct, or a course of conduct engaged in by his employer to force the resignation.

✔ An employee dismissed with notice prior to the expiry of a contract for a specified period or task (that is, an employee in temporary employment) may make a claim against you. Many employers, not just small-business employers, make the fatal mistake of believing temporary employment provides blanket protection for an employer who dismisses an employee. Wrong!

✔ If you dismiss your trainee or apprentice before she completes her qualification, you must ensure that the dismissal is done in compliance with both the unfair dismissal regulations and the traineeship agreement. Otherwise, the employee's dismissal may result in problems from the training authorities and the Fair Work Commission.

✔ Demotion is a relatively uncommon practice in the modern workforce but nevertheless may still expose your small business to a claim of unfair dismissal if the reduction in duties or remuneration is significant. Unfortunately, no single indicator exists for what is 'significant'. If you do demote an employee who hasn't performed to your satisfaction, the best course of action is to ask the employee to sign an agreed variation to his employment contract, specifying the changes. If he refuses, dismissal or a final warning are your other options.

Harsh, unjust or unreasonable dismissal

If you ever find yourself in the unenviable situation of having to defend a claim of unfair dismissal against you, keep in mind that the tribunal can only assess the merit of the claim and your response on whether or not a dismissal has been harsh, unjust or unreasonable, according to the following:

✔ **The validity of the reason for dismissal based on the conduct or capacity of the person:** This means the reason for dismissal must be based on fact and relate to the person's work performance or behaviour. This is probably the most important factor in determining a claim (as it should be).

Aggrieved ex-employees can be really clever at reconstructing the past to make their work performance look better than it really was. You can't take the tribunal through a time travellers' tour of the past so the best defence is to keep individual performance records throughout the entire period of employment. Tedious, but necessary if you wish to protect yourself.

✔ **Whether the person was notified of the reason for dismissal:** You must provide the employees with a reason for dismissing them. Under no circumstances should you provide a reason to the employee that isn't true, because it will inevitably be exposed as untrue and, as a result, your personal integrity will be questioned. No surer method exists to losing an unfair dismissal claim against you than to mislead the dismissed employee and the tribunal who will arbitrate the claim.

✔ **Whether the person was warned about the performance or conduct:** You don't need three warnings to justify dismissal and satisfy this criterion, but you do need at least one warning that failure to meet a reasonable standard of work or adjust behaviour will lead to dismissal. Prior warnings aren't necessary where the employee is summarily dismissed for serious misconduct.

- ✔ **Whether the person was given an opportunity to respond to the allegations of unsatisfactory performance or conduct:** Employees must know in sufficient detail the basis on which you're considering dismissal. Employees can't fairly have an opportunity to defend themselves or attempt to rectify their performance or behaviour if they aren't told what the problems are with their work performance or behaviour. Providing a fair opportunity to respond includes a face-to-face meeting where the performance or behavioural issues are fairly and squarely put to an employee for a response before you decide the penalty. Convening a meeting to offer an opportunity to respond when you've already indicated employment is going to be terminated is pointless.

- ✔ **The size of your business and your access to expertise in human resource management:** The tribunal may be more lenient in its assessment of your performance if it's satisfied that you didn't have either the resources or access to expert advice to guide you. However, before you put this book down, hide it from your employees, and plead blissful ignorance, I have a word of warning: I wouldn't rely on this defence. In 20 years, I haven't read a case where a tribunal accepted ignorance as an excuse for failure to have a valid reason and a fair procedure before dismissal.

- ✔ **The access to and participation of a support person or representative for the dismissed employee:** In circumstances where dismissal is possible, employees are entitled to have another person present to support them personally or represent them. However, the other person can't be a lawyer acting in a professional capacity.

- ✔ **Any other matter that the Fair Work Commission considers relevant:** This is the real sting in the tail that makes unfair dismissal claims a lottery for many employers. Even where you have a valid reason and the procedure applied was fair, the tribunal may still decide the dismissal was harsh, unjust or unreasonable, resulting in either reinstatement or compensation. For example, tribunals have looked at the impact of the dismissal on employees in terms of their ability to find another job as a matter relevant to its findings. The length of an employee's employment is also a frequent reason cited by tribunals in determining a dismissal to be harsh. You can do very little to prevent the risk of such matters affecting the attitude of tribunals on the fairness of the dismissal. You're best to emphasise the fundamental performance or behavioural reasons for dismissal and argue on how the poor performance or behaviour impacted on your business. A little sympathy your way may neutralise the ex-employee's tale of woe!

Genuine redundancy

Employees who've been dismissed because of a business downturn or their position is no longer needed — that is, they've been made redundant — can't bring a claim for unfair dismissal. However, the redundancy needs to be genuine.

A person's dismissal is a case of *genuine redundancy* if you

- ✔ No longer require the person's job to be performed by anyone because of changes in the operational requirements of your small business
- ✔ Have complied with any obligation in a modern award or enterprise agreement that applied to the employment and redundancy

A job is redundant if it's significantly reorganised (even if some of the tasks are still performed), fewer jobs are required to do the same or similar work, or the job is no longer required in any respect.

If the employee's terms and conditions of employment are regulated by a modern award, you're obligated to consult with the employee before employment is terminated. Check the applicable modern award before you announce the redundancy.

A person's dismissal isn't a case of genuine redundancy if it would have been reasonable in all the circumstances for the person to be redeployed within the employer's enterprise or enterprise of an associated entity of the employer. This means that you're expected to consider alternative jobs for the employee displaced by redundancy before you terminate employment. See Chapter 18 for a full commentary on managing redundancy occurring through the introduction of changes in your business.

Getting to Know the Small Business Fair Dismissal Code

The Small Business Fair Dismissal Code applies to small-business employers with fewer than 15 employees. Small-business employees can't claim that they were unfairly dismissed if dismissed in the first 12 months of employment. However, if employees of a small business are dismissed after the 12-month qualifying period, they may apply for reinstatement or compensation for unfair dismissal. If you follow the code, you should be able to successfully defend a claim made against you.

Understanding the code

The terms of the Small Business Fair Dismissal Code have been declared by the responsible government minister; the Fair Work Commission then decides whether any particular dismissal of a protected small-business employee is consistent with the code. I explain the content of the Code in this section — for further information you can also download the code from www.fairwork.gov.au.

Small business may be smaller than you think

The first and most obvious issue that must be considered before applying the code is the question of whether the employee claiming to be unfairly dismissed was employed by a small business. This will affect the eligibility of the dismissed employee, because if employed by a small business, she must have been employed for at least 12 months (rather than the standard six months for other employees).

The definition of a small businesses with fewer than 15 employees is calculated on a simple headcount — if you have 14 (or fewer), congratulations, you're a small business. However, if you employ 20 part-time employees working less than 20 hours each, you're not classified as a small business. On the other hand, if you employ 14 full-time staff working 38 hours per week, you are a small business.

The headcount does not include *irregular* casual employees. This means casual employees who don't have a regular pattern of employment and would not have a reasonable expectation of ongoing employment are excluded. For example, a person employed occasionally to cover staff absences due to annual or personal leave would be an irregular casual employee. An employee paid a casual loading but who works every Tuesday for eight hours isn't an irregular casual and would be included in the headcount.

Dismissal consistent with the code

A protected small business employee's dismissal is consistent with the Small Business Fair Dismissal Code if:

- ✔ Immediately before the time of the dismissal or at the time the person was given notice of the dismissal (whichever happened first), the person's employer was a small-business employer (as defined in the preceding section).
- ✔ The employer complied with the Small Business Fair Dismissal Code in relation to the dismissal.

Except where summary dismissal is justified, you must let the employee know he is at risk of being dismissed and provide a reason. In particular, you need to comply with the following criteria before you decide to dismiss the person:

- ✔ Have a valid reason for the decision to dismiss based on the employee's conduct or capacity to do the job.

- ✔ Warn the employee (preferably in writing), that he risks being dismissed if work performance or conduct does not improve.

- ✔ Provide the employee with an opportunity to respond to the warning and give the employee a reasonable chance to rectify the problem. This might include you providing additional training and some revision of the job expectations.

In reality, the obligations are basically the same obligations that are imposed on all employers, large and small, and which are discussed earlier in this chapter. The lesson is: Make sure you provide evidence that you have complied with these criteria and demonstrate that your business fits the definition of a small business at the time the employee was dismissed. If you can do this, the dismissal will be consistent with the code and you shouldn't be paying the employee any more money.

Serious misconduct

According to the Small Business Fair Dismissal Code, a small business employer dismissing an employee without notice or warning is deemed fair when the employer believes, on reasonable grounds, that the employee's conduct is sufficiently serious to justify immediate dismissal.

The code describes serious misconduct as including theft, fraud, violence and serious breaches of occupational health and safety procedures. For a dismissal to be considered fair it is sufficient, though not essential, that an allegation of theft, fraud or violence be reported to the police. The proviso is that you must have reasonable grounds for making the report.

Serious misconduct has long been understood under common law as behaviour that is of such a serious nature that it is inconsistent with the continuation of the employment contract. This could include behaviour such as stealing from you, maligning your reputation to customers, deliberately disclosing confidential business information to competitors, failing to attend work without reasonable cause, or any other action that is so fundamentally contrary to the employment relationship that all trust and confidence in the employee will have disappeared. For more examples of serious misconduct, see the sidebar 'Serious misconduct and Fair Work Regulations 2009'.

Serious misconduct and Fair Work Regulations 2009

Over the years the Australian parliament, and the courts and tribunals entrusted with enforcing the law have refined the type of behaviour that would fit the definition of serious misconduct. The Small Business Fair Dismissal Code encapsulates some examples of the behaviour that warrants summary dismissal but it is not exhaustive, so you can also look to other legislation.

For example, the Fair Work Regulations codify the common law meaning of serious misconduct with some useful examples of conduct justifying immediate dismissal, as follows. (Visit www.fairwork.gov.au for more.)

REGULATION 1.07: MEANING OF SERIOUS MISCONDUCT

1.07(1) For the definition of serious misconduct in section 12 of the Act, serious misconduct has its ordinary meaning.

1.07(2) For subregulation (1), conduct that is serious misconduct includes both of the following:

(a) wilful or deliberate behaviour by an employee that is inconsistent with the continuation of the contract of employment

(b) conduct that causes serious and imminent risk to:

   (i) the health or safety of a person

   (ii) the reputation, viability or profitability of the employer's business

1.07(3) For subregulation (1), conduct that is serious misconduct includes each of the following:

(a) the employee in the course of the employee's employment, engaging in:

   (i) theft

   (ii) fraud

   (iii) assault

(b) the employee being intoxicated at work

(c) the employee refusing to carry out a lawful and reasonable instruction that is consistent with the employee's contract of employment

1.07(4) Subregulation (3) does not apply if the employee is able to show that, in the circumstances, the conduct engaged in by the employee was not conduct that made employment in the period of notice unreasonable.

1.07(5) For paragraph (3)(b), an employee is taken to be intoxicated if the employee's facilities are, by reason of the employee being under the influence of intoxicating liquor or a drug (except a drug administered by, or taken in accordance with the directions of, a person lawfully authorised to administer the drug), so impaired that the employee is unfit to be entrusted with the employee's duties or with any duty that the employee may be called upon to perform.

This regulation defining serious misconduct is much more useful than the Small Business Fair Dismissal Code to guide you on the type of behaviour that justifies immediate dismissal. You should reference this definition in your own employment policies so that your employees know and understand that behaviour of this nature will lead to immediate dismissal.

As a small-business employer you're required to provide evidence of compliance with the code if an employee makes a claim for unfair dismissal. You do have one advantage over larger employers in that you're only required to show that you had reasonable grounds to believe (in other words, believable in the circumstances of the particular case) the employee's conduct was sufficiently serious to justify immediate dismissal. Notwithstanding the fluffy words in the official government guides and the code itself, the evidence of misconduct should be as strong as you can possibly make it. For example, if you dismiss the employee for theft, you must have evidence sufficient to convince police that it has occurred, not just a belief that the employee stole something from you.

The Fair Work Ombudsman provides a Small Business Fair Dismissal Code Checklist, which may assist you further in this area — go to www. fairwork.gov.au/Templatesformschecklists/Small-Business-Fair-Dismissal-Code-2011.pdf to access the checklist.

Resolving Unfair Dismissal Disputes

If an ex-employee alleges that you unfairly dismissed her, the Fair Work Commission will notify you of the application for reinstatement or compensation, and of the date and time that has been scheduled for the initial conciliation conference (normally conducted as a telephone conference). The notice will include a copy of the ex-employee's formal application, including the reasons she believes she has been unfairly dismissed, and some general guides from the Commission.

You're expected to complete a written response to the Fair Work Commission, and this response will be shared with the ex-employee (and her representative) ahead of the conciliation conference. At this point, you should get advice from someone who knows what they're doing. Unfortunately, unless you have access to a professional association or industry body that provides the service free of charge, this advice will also cost you money.

Only a fool would represent themselves through this process so get smart and get representation. It will save you money in the long run. If you insist on representing yourself (sorry for the crack about being a fool!), follow the steps described in the following section. They can enable you to focus on the important issues and keep you on track during the conciliation conference.

Settling during conciliation

The objective of the conciliation conference is to encourage you and the ex-employee to agree on mutually beneficial terms to resolve the claim. Yes, that can include paying the ex-employee more money — but not necessarily.

With the objective of minimising the risk of paying out more money in mind, here is my six-step guide to resolving an unfair dismissal claim at conciliation:

1. **Write down in point form the reason that you dismissed the employee, and list the evidence underpinning your reason.**

   For example, you may have dismissed the employee for failing to achieve monthly sales budgets. Your evidence is the job description that states the primary objective of the job is to generate sales for the business, the key performance indicators set in advance and provided to the employee, and monthly budget and actual sales spreadsheets showing the persistent failure to achieve the sales budget. Provide this summary of evidence in the form you send back to the Fair Work Commission before the conference.

2. **Listen to the conciliator's opening statement at the conciliation conference.**

   The conciliator will explain how he intends to conduct the conference, the rules for when you can speak and the aim to reach a mutually agreeable settlement. This is also explained in the guides that the Fair Work Commission sent to you with the notice of the conference.

3. **Allow the ex-employee their chance to speak first.**

   Don't argue with the ex-employee. You will get your chance to speak and arguing won't assist the successful resolution. You don't want to lose focus, and want to keep an objective mindset. (Besides, I don't want you getting upset and having a heart attack because of an ex-employee. Who's going to buy my next book if you fall off the tree?)

4. **Explain your position during your turn to speak.**

   Explain the procedure that you applied to

   • Inform the employee of your dissatisfaction with the work

   • The opportunity or opportunities that you provided for the employee to respond

- The nature of the warning(s) issued to the employee, explaining how the employee was risking her employment

- The measures that you put in place to assist the employee to achieve the standard of performance that you expected

Tell the conciliator the points where you agree and disagree with what the ex-employee listed in her application as the reasons she believes she was unfairly dismissed. Employees are likely to include statements of events that they believe would be favourable to their case for compensation.

You don't have to agree with the employee's version of events, but the conciliator wants to know whether any common ground is available so he can facilitate an agreement. Inform the conciliator that you have evidence to back up each of the points made in your statement. Don't concede that you have unfairly dismissed the employee.

5. **Ask the ex-employee what she wants from you.**

The conciliator may do this as well but it is important that you force the issue. The employee will either want

- Reinstatement to the job

- Payment for the loss of the job

- Revenge

- All of the above

Forget about the desire for revenge — even the Fair Work Commission can't order an act of revenge against you. You should tell the conciliator what terms you're prepared to negotiate and the terms that you will definitely not accept. This provides the conciliator with a clear agenda that he can focus on with the ex-employee (usually in a private conversation).

6. **Negotiate a settlement of the claim (if desired).**

If you believe you have less than an 80 per cent chance of successfully defending the case at the next stage arbitration, negotiate for a settlement — the 20 per cent margin of doubt is sufficient reason. Treat this conciliation as you would any other business decision and calculate the cost and benefit of defending the claim.

You don't have to accept the first bid at an auction and so don't feel compelled to agree to a sum of money that you don't believe is warranted. Be realistic and make a firm offer and don't deviate from it unless the conciliator gives you a very good reason to improve it.

Table 17-1 provides some help with formulating an offer to settle the claim.

Table 17-1 Deciding on Terms of Settlement for Unfair Dismissal Claims

Terms of settlement	Reason
Accept the ex-employee's resignation in substitution for the dismissal.	No employer is going to employ a person who has been dismissed from previous employment. Explain that you don't wish the person to suffer unnecessarily and so accepting the resignation is a gesture of good-will to assist in more easily finding alternative employment.
Pay an amount of wages equivalent to the notice period the ex-employee would otherwise have received if not immediately dismissed.	This would only be applicable in cases of dismissal for serious misconduct.
Pay an amount of wages equivalent to the scale of redundancy pay provided in the NES for the years of service	Small businesses aren't obliged to pay redundancy but the scale is a convenient benchmark on which to base your commercial decision. **Note:** The maximum compensation is six months ordinary pay and that's only awarded in extreme cases.
Estimate the cost of engaging lawyers to represent you at arbitration and offer an amount substantially less than that figure but sufficient to entice the ex-employee to settle.	Quantifying legal costs to represent your business is difficult. You could probably estimate a minimum of one to two days in court plus the equivalent in preparation costs. Ask a lawyer about costs for this amount of time.
Make an offer without admitting liability for having 'unfairly dismissed' the employee.	A commercial settlement doesn't require you to admit that you unfairly dismissed the employee.
Include a requirement of confidentiality in the offer and no disparagement.	Including clauses that require you and the ex-employee not to disclose the agreed settlement provides some comfort to you that the ex-employee will not broadcast the fact that they obtained some additional payment from you. The requirement not to disparage is designed to protect your good reputation — disgruntled ex-employees can harm your business with angry words to key customers and suppliers.

The conciliator will work hard to facilitate an agreement for the two hours he's paid by the Fair Work Commission. Use this time wisely — it doesn't cost you anything except your time.

The conciliator who facilitates the conference can't determine who is right and who is wrong. You'll be wasting your time if you think this is an opportunity to win the argument that your ex-employee is nothing but a lowdown good for nothing who is just looking to make fast money at your expense — so save your breath. All of that may be true, but you don't get the opportunity to argue this unless the case is eventually arbitrated (see the following section).

Putting your fate in someone else's hands with arbitration

If you can't settle the unfair dismissal claim at conciliation, it proceeds to a formal hearing and arbitration of the claim. At this stage, formal evidence, usually in the form of witness statements, is tested and arguments for and against the claim are made. The tribunal decides the issue by weighing the evidence against the same criteria covered in the section 'Harsh, unjust or unreasonable dismissal', earlier in this chapter.

The members of the Fair Work Commission decide the case and, unless you have grounds to appeal, you must accept the decision. Hopefully, it will go your way. You can find a Fair Work Information Statement document relating to the following sections at http://www.fairwork.gov.au/FWISdocs/Fair-Work-Information-Statement.pdf.

Remedies

Reinstatement is the primary remedy the tribunal is likely to award for larger businesses, unless it believes reinstatement isn't appropriate. However, a Fair Work Commissioner ordering reinstatement to a small business is highly unlikely. Once the employment relationship has been severed in a small business, re-establishing the trust and confidence necessary for it to resume is almost impossible.

For small businesses, the tribunal normally awards compensation in lieu of reinstatement. The maximum compensation that can be awarded is 26 weeks' (6 months') pay.

Before the tribunal awards compensation to the aggrieved ex-employee, you (and, more particularly, your representative) have an opportunity to argue your case to minimise the amount. In deciding compensation, the following must be taken into account by the tribunal:

- The effect of the order on the viability of the employer's enterprise
- The length of the person's service with the employer

✔ The remuneration that the person would have received, or would have been likely to receive, if the person had not been dismissed

✔ The efforts of the person (if any) to mitigate the loss suffered by the person because of the dismissal

✔ The amount of any remuneration earned by the person from employment or other work during the period between the dismissal and the making of the order for compensation

✔ The amount of any income reasonably likely to be so earned by the person during the period between the making of the order for compensation and the actual compensation

✔ Any other matter that the tribunal considers relevant

One of the more peculiar provisions of the Fair Work Act (which ironically provides an insight into the inherent bias of the law against employers) is the provision that the tribunal must reduce the amount it would otherwise order where it is satisfied that the misconduct of a person contributed to the employer's decision to dismiss the person. In other words, the Fair Work Commission can find that an employee was guilty of misconduct and unfairly dismissed at the same time! Your only compensation in this situation is the tribunal must reduce the compensation . . . strange but unfortunately true!

Part of the Small Business Fair Dismissal Code suggests that when a small business employer has followed the code, the dismissal will be *deemed* to be fair. However, you will need to be careful to ensure you comply with all of the criteria regulating dismissals and in particular the criteria defining whether or not a dismissal has been 'harsh, unjust or unreasonable'. No provision in the law actually directs the tribunal to deem a dismissal to be fair. The inclusion in the code is completely misleading and you should ignore it — it won't assist you to defend your decision to dismiss an employee.

Appeals

An employer or dismissed employee may appeal a decision on the grounds that a serious error of fact has occurred and it is in the public interest for the appeal to proceed. You can't appeal just because you don't like the decision. If you get to this stage (meaning you lost the original hearing), an appeal will cost you more money. You should get advice from someone with expertise in the area before proceeding.

Western Australia Is a Different System

Employees of unincorporated small businesses operating in Western Australia aren't covered by the national workplace relations system, so disputes over the dismissal of an employee are addressed by the Western Australian Industrial Relations Commission, not the Fair Work Commission. The terminology in Western Australia is slightly different — for example, the law refers to dismissals being 'harsh, oppressive or unfair', rather than 'harsh, unjust or unreasonable'. Nevertheless, some similarities exist between the two systems.

Here's how the Western Australian system generally works for small-business employers:

- Employees can make a claim of unfair dismissal to the Western Australian Industrial Relations Commission (WAIRC) within 28 days from the date of their dismissal.

- Dismissed employees, or their representatives, must complete the official form, file it with the WAIRC and then provide a copy to the employer.

- Probationary employees are entitled to make a claim for unfair dismissal. However, the WAIRC is required to take the formal period of probation, of up to three months, into account when determining the claim.

- When the employer has filed a response (no later than 21 days after receiving the employee claim), the matter is listed for a conciliation conference. This is an informal meeting conducted by a commissioner or registrar of the WAIRC that attempts to resolve the matter by mediation between the parties.

- If the matter is not resolved, it is listed for a formal hearing after which a commissioner will make a decision about whether or not the dismissal was unfair.

Similar to the national system (refer to the section 'Getting to Know the Small Business Fair Dismissal Code', earlier in this chapter), you must have a valid reason for dismissing an employee in Western Australia in relation to the capacity or conduct of the employee, and the dismissal must have been done in a fair and reasonable manner.

Fair and reasonable dismissal

The principle criteria to determine whether a dismissal has been done in a fair and reasonable manner are basically the same as the national system. You're expected to:

✔ Advise the employee of any problems with performance or conduct

✔ Provide the employee with an opportunity to respond

✔ Assist the employee to rectify the problem by providing additional training or explaining what the expected work standards are

✔ Ensure the employee has a reasonable chance to rectify the problem

✔ If the poor performance or conduct persists, explain that the employee is at risk of being dismissed if no improvement is shown

✔ Provide a warning of potential dismissal in writing

✔ Give the employee an opportunity to respond to the warning and a reasonable chance to rectify the problem

✔ Allow the employee representation in meetings with you

You're required to provide evidence to show that the dismissal procedure was fair, so maintain a record of each part of the process to ensure you're able to reproduce the documented evidence when required.

Immediate or summary dismissal for serious misconduct is treated in the same manner as the national system. For example, conduct involving theft, fraud, violence or serious breaches of occupational health and safety procedures.

Remedies for Western Australians

If the dismissal is found to be unfair, the WAIRC can make an order that the employee be reinstated to the same job the employee held before the dismissal. If reinstatement isn't practical, an order can require the person to be re-employed in a suitable job. In addition to reinstatement or re-employment, the WAIRC may order you to pay remuneration that has been lost because of the dismissal and to maintain the employee's continuity of service.

If reinstatement and re-employment are both impractical, the WAIRC may make an order for compensation for loss or injury caused by the dismissal to a maximum of six months' remuneration.

Unlawful Dismissal Is Something Altogether Different

Understanding the difference between an *unfair* dismissal and an *unlawful* dismissal is really important. Unlawful dismissal refers to decisions to terminate employment that are discriminatory, in breach of workplace rights or otherwise prohibited by the law.

The Fair Work Act creates various workplace rights and protections for employees and prospective employees against discriminatory and prejudicial action such as termination of employment for reasons of a person's race, colour, sex, sexual preference, age, physical or mental disability, marital status, family or carer's responsibilities, pregnancy, religion, political opinion, national extraction or social origin. Termination of employment for a reason that included one or more of these grounds is treated as an unlawful termination of employment. Visit `www.fairwork.gov.au` for more information.

Workplace rights

The Fair Work Act continues and in some instances extends the anti-discrimination prohibitions under a set of workplace rights described as *general protections*. I provide an explanation of the general protections of employees and unlawful discrimination in Chapter 12.

When unlawful discrimination doesn't apply

The unlawful discrimination prohibition doesn't apply to action that is

- ✔ Not unlawful under any anti-discrimination law in force in the place where the action is taken (including state law)
- ✔ Taken because of the inherent requirements of the particular position concerned

If the action is taken against a staff member of an institution conducted in accordance with the doctrines, tenets, beliefs or teachings of a particular religion or creed, the unlawful discrimination prohibition doesn't apply if the action was taken

✔ In good faith

✔ To avoid injury to the religious susceptibilities of adherents of that religion or creed

Unlawful termination of employment

The Fair Work Act makes it *unlawful* to terminate the employment of an employee for one or more of the following reasons:

✔ Temporary absence from work because of illness or injury

✔ Trade union membership or participation in trade union activities outside working hours or, with the employer's consent, during working hours

✔ Non-membership of a trade union

✔ Seeking office as, or acting or having acted in the capacity of, a representative of employees

✔ The filing of a complaint, or the participation in proceedings, against an employer involving alleged violation of laws or regulations or recourse to competent administrative authorities

✔ Race, colour, sex, sexual preference, age, physical or mental disability, marital status, family or carer's responsibilities, pregnancy, religion, political opinion, national extraction or social origin

✔ Absence from work during maternity leave or other parental leave

✔ Temporary absence from work for the purpose of engaging in a voluntary emergency management activity, where the absence is reasonable having regard to all the circumstances

The general protections in the Fair Work Act and prohibitions on terminating an employee's employment described in this section apply from the first day of employment. In relation to the general protections, the law applies even before a person starts employment, when they are prospective employees. Unlike unfair dismissals, no qualifying period of employment must be served before an employee can make an application for compensation against your small business. Consequently, this is an area of employment regulation that creates high risk levels. Your best method of reducing the risk of successful claims against your business is to be ever vigilant in the way that you treat employees. Visit www.fairwork.gov.au for more information.

Chapter 18

Termination, Change and Redundancy

. . . .

In This Chapter

▶ Letting your employees know about change in your business

▶ Understanding when redundancy is genuine

▶ Keeping in mind small-business exemptions

▶ Working out who stays and who goes

▶ Transferring employees to other businesses

. . . .

It's a recession when your neighbor loses his job. It's a depression when you lose yours.

Harry S Truman

*T*he business environment is ever changing. 'Innovate or perish' is the motto that your small business must live by if it wishes to grow and prosper. You need to consider changes to product and services, work methods, and the number and nature of jobs.

In this chapter I guide you through the challenging task of managing staff on the road to changing your business to a better and more successful enterprise. Your small business may be exempt from redundancy pay but you still need to navigate plenty of other regulatory obstacles through this journey. I explain the rules under the Fair Work Act, and the principles governing selection procedures where redundancy may result in the termination of employment of one or more employees. I also provide a checklist for action to keep you on a straight path.

Introducing change into your business isn't always about redundancy, and may also include growth strategies such as acquisitions, amalgamations and taking on new business. Each of these forms of change affects how you recruit, pay and treat staff. I discuss the choices you have when taking on new staff and the obligations that underpin transfers of business — whether it be through taking on outsourced work from governments and larger businesses or acquiring another business.

Introducing Change into Your Business

Change in your business generally comes about in three basic ways:

- ✔ Gradual adjustments to accommodate movement in competition, consumer preferences, logistics, access to supplies, regulation, profitability and technology

- ✔ Strategic or bold measures to grow your business, such as acquiring new businesses, capital investments, launching new products and services, and moving into new markets

- ✔ Remedial action to save the business from financial shocks, product and market failure, regulatory risks, or general overreach

One of the golden rules of business is that you can't stand still. Your small business either adapts or it dies. Therefore, you need to choose to get on board the first two change dynamics in the preceding list, lest you find yourself having to apply the third and least palatable change to your business.

Of course, you don't have a free hand to change your business as you want. Lots and lots of government regulations tell you what you can and can't do, and not all of them are related to the employment of staff. Licensing and accreditation standards need to be complied with, as well as shop trading hours, consumer laws, property and leasing agreements, and local council permits. Getting you up to speed on those matters is beyond the scope of this book. However, in the remainder of this chapter I explain how to manage the employment regulations while you introduce the changes to your business that are necessary for its success.

Don't be discouraged by the breadth of employment regulation — you can navigate a safe path through it and reach your business goals. It just takes a bit of grit and determination to see it through to the end.

Working Out Genuine Redundancy

The obligations to your employees affected by redundancy are derived from the unfair dismissal provisions of the Fair Work Act, the National Employment Standards (NES), individual common law employment contracts and any modern award or enterprise agreement applicable to them. In particular, the rights and obligations may cover

- ✔ A duty to consult with employees and their representatives
- ✔ Notice of termination
- ✔ Redundancy payments
- ✔ Reporting responsibilities to government agencies

Although termination of employment doesn't always necessarily flow from the redundancy of a person's job, when termination does occur, you must be careful to comply with your statutory and contractual obligations to the employees affected. The main issues that are likely to affect your small business are the duties to consult and the notice of termination of employment. Redundancy pay is only applicable if you employ 15 or more staff at the time redundancy occurs. I explain all of these issues in the following sections.

It's the job that is redundant not the person!

The common definition of redundancy applied by courts and tribunals is as follows:

> *Redundancy occurs when you decide that you do not want a job performed by anyone and it is not due to the customary turnover of labour.*

Redundancy can occur due to the introduction of change to the way in which work is performed or to the structure of your business, or due to shifts in demand for your products and services. The decisions you make that directly flow from the introduction of change impact on the nature and number of jobs required to perform the work of the business, which may characterise a job as being redundant.

The *customary turnover of labour* refers to the circumstances where jobs are expected to cease due to the nature of the work or the context of the industry. For example, work that is casual in nature isn't generally considered redundant when it's not renewed. Nor would seasonal or temporary work during a harvest of agricultural crops or shearing of sheep. In emerging industries such as consulting, the completion of assignments and projects delivered to clients in agreed time frames would not be considered redundancies. Redundancy happens where the work changes — either due to a deliberate business strategy (for example, growth or diversification) or the business experiencing significant downturns in demand for its goods and services, impacting on the full-time and regular part-time employees.

Individual tasks associated with the performance of a job don't have to disappear, as such, for a job to be redundant. A redundancy may include breaking up the functions of a single job and distributing them among other jobs. For example, the duties of a full-time employee may be redistributed to several part-time employees, or part-time employment may be amalgamated under a full-time job. The job may be re-located interstate or the tasks re-distributed among other staff or managers. The critical factor is whether the nature of the position has, after the reorganisation, substantially altered or the position no longer exists.

You must not artificially construct a redundancy for the purposes of terminating an employee who has performed poorly or acted improperly. The Fair Work Commission will look for the substantive reason for the termination if an aggrieved employee makes a claim for reinstatement or compensation. If other performance issues are discovered as motivating the termination, you may have to defend a claim of unfair dismissal. Refer to Chapter 17 for an explanation of unfair dismissal regulation.

Consultation

Modern awards force you to consult with employees when the change that you introduce to your small business may result in redundancy of jobs and subsequently lead to termination of an employee's employment. This is often ignored. In Chapter 17, I explain how consultation with employees is necessary for a dismissal to be considered a genuine redundancy. This means you must make the effort to consult.

The best approach to consultation is to follow these very simple steps:

1. **Once you have made a definite decision, speak to all affected employees, describing the nature and purpose of the proposed change.**

   This discussion should be supplemented, wherever possible, with written information. In particular, explain how the change may affect jobs.

You can maintain confidentiality of important information while consulting with employees, but disclosure of your strategy isn't something to be shy about. People generally respond well if you can explain how the change is intended to strengthen your ability to compete for new business, grow your market share and benefit the long-term viability of the business and job security.

Convincing people of the need to change may be difficult, especially where the change adversely affects their lives, but you must sell the benefits (sometimes the necessity) to the people who you will rely upon to assist you in achieving your goals. If you can't or won't do this, you significantly reduce the chances of a successful transition.

2. **Where jobs are altered or no longer required, explain what the new jobs (if any) are and how you intend to select employees for each new or restructured job.**

   You must also be honest about the consequences for those employees who aren't selected. You do have choices. Not every redundancy has to lead to dismissal. As I explain in Chapter 17, you're obliged to consider redeployment to another job in the business or (where you own other businesses) related entities. This may not always be an option, especially when the change has been introduced to reduce employment costs, but you must be able to demonstrate that you considered the option to demonstrate that the redundancy is genuine. See the section 'The Selection Dilemma', later in this chapter, for more on the principles and choices available for ensuring that you both select the best people for the jobs and comply with statutory obligations.

3. **Prepare a timetable for each stage of the changes that you intend to introduce, and share this timetable with your staff.**

   Uncertainty kills commitment and breeds conflict. I understand that not everything is certain in life or business, but unless you set deadlines, events will overtake you and change for the better may become change for the worse. Your staff are likely to respond maturely if you act maturely and decisively.

4. **Ensure that employees are given the opportunity to comment on the proposed changes and suggest any alternatives.**

   These suggestions may avert or mitigate the adverse effects of changes. Make yourself available or appoint a key person to deal with any inquiries or comments from your staff.

I'm often asked how long employers should consult with staff about proposed changes to the business. The answer to that is the same as the answer to the question 'How long is a piece of string?' It depends. In the case of staff consultation, the time depends on whether you're introducing the change to save the business or grow the business. If you don't have the luxury of time, the deadlines are likely to be very short. If you intend to enter new markets by developing your staffing capability, this may involve longer term strategies as staff undertake training or your recruitment is targeted to attract people with specialist skills.

Avoid setting unrealistic timetables. Over the years, I have observed in amazement the amount of time that government agencies spend implementing changes to organisational staffing structures. As the months progress and nothing is actually completed, people drift off to other employment. As they do so, I've seen the motivation of the remaining staff dissipate and productivity evaporate. Talk to your friends and family who have worked in government agencies and listen to their experiences. Then do the opposite.

Redundancy Pay Exemptions for Small Business

The NES prescribes the period of notice or payment in lieu that must be provided to an employee who has been dismissed due to redundancy.

Notice or payment in lieu is provided in addition to any other entitlements on termination, such as redundancy pay or accrued annual and long service leave. You're not exempted from the obligation to provide notice of termination because you own a small business.

Table 18-1 outlines the notice you're required to provide when terminating employment, based on period of service.

Table 18-1	Required Notice of Termination of Employment
Period of Continuous Service	*Period of Notice Required*
Not more than 1 year	1 week
More than 1 but fewer than 3 years	2 weeks
More than 3 but fewer than 5 years	3 weeks
More than 5 years	4 weeks

The period of notice is increased by one week if the employee is over the age of 45 and has completed at least two years of continuous service with the employer.

Redundancy pay

Table 18-2 outlines the payments prescribed by the NES to employees who are dismissed due to redundancy. You will need to make the payment outlined in Table 18-2, and pay any other entitlements that the employee has on termination, including the notice of termination or payment in lieu.

Note: The entitlements outlined in Table 18-2 apply only to employees of employers who employ 15 or more people, excluding irregular casuals. If you employ fewer than 15 staff, according to the NES formula, you don't have to pay redundancy.

Table 18-2 Prescribed Redundancy Pay	
Period of Continuous Service	*Redundancy Pay Required*
Less than 1 year	Nil
More than 1 but fewer than 2 years	4 weeks' pay
More than 2 but fewer than 3 years	6 weeks' pay
More than 3 but fewer than 4 years	7 weeks' pay
More than 4 but fewer than 5 years	8 weeks' pay
More than 5 but fewer than 6 years	10 weeks' pay
More than 6 but fewer than 7 years	11 weeks' pay
More than 7 but fewer than 8 years	13 weeks' pay
More than 8 but fewer than 9 years	14 weeks' pay
More than 9 but fewer than 10 years	16 weeks' pay
More than 10 years	12 weeks' pay

A week's pay means the ordinary time earnings of the employee excluding overtime, penalty rates, allowances and bonuses. Refer to Chapter 4 for a detailed explanation of the entitlement under the NES.

Redundancy pay and employment contracts

Redundancy entitlements may in some circumstances be provided in the individual terms of a person's employment contract. These obligations are quite separate to the entitlements under the NES. For example, the period of notice required to terminate the employment may be greater, or a more generous formula of severance payments may apply. The contract might also prescribe additional entitlements such as access to professional counselling or re-location services. In some circumstances, an entitlement to redundancy payments may be implied into the employment contract by your previous conduct. For example, you may have previously paid redundancy to other employees under a business employment policy.

Be very careful that you don't agree to a redundancy arrangement that's beyond your obligations under the NES without good cause. If you do enter into such an arrangement, make sure that you can provide for it in your accounts.

Entitlements under a contract of employment may be set off against those arising under the NES, but make sure you ensure they're not prescribed in addition to the NES entitlements. Otherwise, you may be paying twice for the same redundancy.

The Selection Dilemma

The *selection dilemma* occurs when several employees occupy the same or similar jobs and you decide to make redundant some, but not all, of these jobs.

A selection dilemma may also arise where the employee who occupies the redundant position has skills that are transferable to a different job with minimal (or no) further training, and would be just as capable of performing jobs that aren't redundant as the incumbent employee. The fact that an employee occupies the job being made redundant doesn't necessarily mean that selecting that employee in all cases is fair or necessary.

How are you going to select one employee over another? The following sections highlight the issues and suggest some possible solutions to the dilemma.

Looking at past performance

Past performance of employees may be taken into account when deciding on who will be selected for continuing employment and who will not. You should address selection decisions with the following in mind:

✔ The performance issue must have a basis in fact.

✔ The performance issue must be relevant to the remaining positions. For example, taking into account an employee's failure to meet performance targets may be unfair if the remaining position doesn't involve the particular targets.

Separate the circumstances where the motivating factor for the termination is poor performance from circumstances where performance is only taken into account in selecting which employee will be made redundant. In the former case, the poor performance must of itself be sufficiently serious to justify termination. In the latter case, the performance issue may be marginal, but may operate to distinguish two employees who are otherwise equal.

Spill and fill

To promote a fair selection process, you might consider a *spill and fill* procedure. This involves declaring all affected jobs vacant, and then inviting employees to apply for the new or remaining jobs. This process doesn't necessarily preclude inviting applications from outside the business. Each employee is then assessed for each job on his or her merits.

The benefits of this procedure are that it enables employees to apply for the job of their choice and allows you to reassess the skill and expertise of each employee to fit the emerging business environment.

Voluntary redundancy

Offers of voluntary redundancy may allow you to avoid having to make a selection between competing employees. Employees who express an interest in a voluntary redundancy package are clearly less likely to be interested in continuing employment. Better to find that out now rather than later.

Don't make an unconditional offer of voluntary redundancy. Your most valuable employee may put her hand up to accept the offer of voluntary redundancy. Once accepted, you are bound by the agreement and must allow the employee to take the voluntary redundancy package. Instead, you should call for expressions of interest from employees prior to an offer. This allows you to assess the interest of employees against the genuine operational requirements of the future.

Watch out for hazards

You need to follow some rules to ensure the introduction of changes in your business that end in redundancy are hazard free. This means exploring the options of redeployment, consulting with staff on leave and avoiding discrimination.

Redeployment to alternative positions

Section 389 of the *Fair Work Act 2009* makes it clear that a dismissal due to redundancy is not genuine

> *... if it would have been reasonable in all the circumstances for the person to be redeployed within the employer's enterprise or enterprise of an associated entity of the employer.*

As I outline throughout this chapter and in Chapter 17, you must consider whether alternative positions are available in the business even after a selection procedure has been completed. These employees could be given preference for such jobs provided that they satisfy the job requirements. If necessary, you should consider training. This will involve weighing up the cost and disruption of retraining, against the impact of termination on the employees and the risk of an unfair dismissal claim against you.

Employees on leave

You can't avoid the selection dilemma by targeting employees who are temporarily absent from work. These employees must be considered equally with other employees. In fact, selecting an employee for redundancy simply because that employee is on maternity leave, performing light duties while on workers compensation (or otherwise temporarily absent from work due to injury or illness) will breach both state and federal anti-discrimination law.

If the position of an employee returning to work from parental leave no longer exists and the employee is qualified and able to work for you in another role, the employee is entitled to work in another job. When more than one appropriate job is available, the employee is entitled to the role nearest in status and remuneration to the former position.

You must inform employees on leave about the changes and opportunities for alternative positions in the same manner as those at work.

Discrimination

The criteria used for selection must not discriminate on unlawful grounds. These grounds include race, colour, sex, sexual preference, age, physical or mental disability, marital status, family or carer's responsibilities, pregnancy, religion, political opinion, national extraction or social origin as well as absence from work due to illness or injury, and union membership. You must also be careful not to indirectly discriminate against employees. Indirect discrimination can occur if an employer relies on a factor which, although on its face may not appear to discriminate unlawfully, when applied has a disproportionate impact on one class of persons over another.

For example, an employer may decide to retain all employees who have had the least amount of time off work for any reason. This may in practice disadvantage women who have had time off work for reasons such as maternity leave. The imposition of this condition may also be unreasonable and therefore discriminatory if the remaining positions can be performed successfully notwithstanding time off work for such purposes. That you did not intend to discriminate is not a defence.

Working through a Checklist of Action

When contemplating the introduction of changes that may result in redundancies, following a checklist like the one provided in Figure 18-1 is wise.

☑	Calculate the impact of the change on the nature and number of jobs when planning changes to the organisation of work in the business
☑	If the number and/or nature of jobs will vary from the current structure, calculate the jobs that will either be made redundant or affected by the change
☑	Review employment contracts, applicable awards and the NES to determine your rights and obligations if redundancies were to be implemented. Calculate the cost to the business
☑	Consider ways and means to minimise the adverse impact — that is, avoid redundancies and/or minimise costs through use of alternative positions and re-deployment of staff
☑	Decide on the course of action, including a timetable and the selection procedures if a number of similar jobs must be reduced or are significantly changed
☑	Communicate the changes to affected employees
☑	Implement the change and the redundancies
☑	Advise the affected employees that their employment is terminated and pay all entitlements

Figure 18-1:
Checklist of
action.

The relationship between termination of employment due to redundancy and the obligation not to dismiss an employee unfairly or unlawfully is complex and requires particular attention to ensure you don't inadvertently breach one or more of your responsibilities under the law. Refer to Chapter 17 for further guidance.

Contemplating Business to Business Transfers

If you're contemplating taking on new work that has been outsourced or acquiring an ongoing business, you must familiarise yourself with the rules regulating transfers of business — especially if such work means employing staff from the business that you acquire. Importantly, the trigger for a transfer of business is based on whether the work performed by the employee has transferred rather than the nature of the business changed in the hands of the new employer. This covers a very large range of transactions between businesses including any mergers and acquisitions, and even the movement of functions between related business entities and contracting out of services such as outsourcing work.

The following sections take you through the important considerations.

Defining a transfer of business

The Fair Work Act regulates the employee entitlements that transfer from one employer to another when a transfer of business occurs. A *transfer of business* from one employer (the old employer) to another employer (the new employer) occurs when:

- The employment of an employee of the old employer has terminated
- Within three months after the termination, the employee becomes employed by the new employer
- The transferring employee performs the same, or substantially the same, work (the transferring work) for the new employer as performed for the old employer
- A connection exists between the old employer and the new employer

A connection between the new and old employer

The key to understanding when a transfer of business occurs is essentially a matter of whether or not a *connection* exists between the old and new employers. A connection will exist between the old employer and the new employer if the new employer (that is, you) owns or has the beneficial use of some or all of the assets previously owned or beneficially used by the old employer, and these are used in connection with (or relate to) the work that has transferred. This, for example, covers the typical arrangements where one business is purchased and things such as premises, equipment, intellectual property, vehicles, cash reserves and goodwill continued to be used, and the purchaser employs staff from that business to continue working in the same or similar jobs that they did for the employer who has sold the business.

The situations become a little bit more complex when you add the following arrangements that fit the definition of *a connection*:

✓ **Outsourcing work:** A connection exists between the old employer and the new employer if the transferring work is performed by one or more transferring employees, as employees of the new employer, because the old employer, or an associated entity of the old employer, has outsourced the transferring work to the new employer or an associated entity of the new employer.

The most likely scenario in this regard for small-business owners is work that's outsourced from government or larger businesses. For example, cleaning, catering, ICT data, software and equipment management, and general property management services that were previously done in-house.

No connection exists between the old and new employer if the contractor (the larger business) is simply re-allocating the work from one provider to another and the new employer doesn't have the beneficial use of some or all of the assets of the previous provider.

✓ **New employer ceases to outsource work to old employer:** A connection exists between the old employer and the new employer if the transferring work has been performed by transferring employees, as employees of the old employer, under an outsourced contract between the old and new employer, and the new employer has taken the work back to be performed in-house by those transferring employees.

In other words, a connection exists if the larger business decides to bring back in-house the work that it previously outsourced. In this instance, your only issue is transferring the employment records and accrued leave entitlements of the transferring employees back to the contractor.

✔ **Associated entities:** A connection exists between the old employer and the new employer if the new employer is an associated entity of the old employer when the transferring employee becomes employed by the new employer.

This connection prevents businesses from shuffling employees between related business entities to avoid the obligation to pay accumulated leave and (if applicable) redundancy pay. So you can move employees to another business that you own but their leave entitlements and service for other purposes follows them, as long as the work that they do is substantially the same (see following section).

Same, or substantially the same work

The architects of the transferring business law intended that the requirement that transferring employees perform the same or substantially the same work shouldn't be construed in a technical way. In other words, in a transfer of business situation, some minor differences may well exist between the work performed for the respective employers. However, the requirement is satisfied where, overall, the work is the same or substantially the same — even if the precise duties of the employees, or the manner in which they are performed, have changed.

Although the law is framed in terms of the work undertaken by an individual employee, it may be possible to categorise the work more generally when a transfer of business occurs and a group of employees is employed. If, for example, the old employer operates a retail business and sells it to you, the work that a transferring employee does might be characterised generally as sales assistant. The fact that the employee may have ordered stock for the old employer but now works exclusively in sales for you would not stop the employee from being a transferring employee.

Enterprise agreements transfer with staff

The employment instruments that transfer with the employee may be

✔ An enterprise agreement that has been approved by the Fair Work Commission

✔ A workplace determination

✔ A named employer award

✔ An individual flexibility arrangement made under an enterprise agreement or named employer award applicable to a transferring employee

✔ A transitional instrument (pre–Fair Work Act awards and agreements)

The transferring employment instruments that you're most likely to encounter are enterprise agreements made under the current laws or pre–Fair Work Act collective agreements and Australian Workplace Agreements (AWA). Consequently, your task before taking on a new business or outsourced work is to conduct your own due diligence. This is not difficult because, firstly, the owner of the business or outsourced work that you are taking on must disclose this information to you. Secondly, you can search the Fair Work Commission website (www.fwc.gov.au) using a keyword search to find out whether any of these employment instruments exist for the business, and so would transfer with the employment of any current staff.

Transferring conditions apply indefinitely

The employment instrument that covers the transferring employee continues to apply to the transferring employee indefinitely, unless it's replaced with another enterprise agreement, or the employee moves to another job in your business substantially different to the one transferred on.

New employees performing the same work

New employees recruited after the transfer of business (that is, after you take over the new business or commence the outsourced work) who perform similar work aren't employed on the transferring conditions unless your small business isn't covered by a modern award that would apply to the new employees. If you are covered by a modern award for that part of the business, the modern award applies to new employees while working with transferring employees who are employed on conditions that transferred with them when you acquired the new business. Clearly not an ideal situation.

Employees doing similar work but employed under different conditions can also be a trap for your small business if your employees aren't covered by a modern award and the business that you take over has an enterprise agreement or AWA that regulates the transferring employee's terms and conditions of employment. You may have tendered for the work or acquired the business on the assumption that you will be able to perform the work better or more efficiently with a lower cost structure. If you take on an employee of the business that you have acquired, you're bound to pay the wages and conditions (usually higher) contained in that transferring employment instrument to everyone else you employ doing that work. Therefore, conducting a thorough due diligence before you acquire and hire is essential.

Fair Work Australia orders

If all else fails, or you are really well prepared before taking on new work, the Fair Work Commission may make certain orders that modify the general transfer of business rules. In particular, the Fair Work Commission is able to make orders regarding the coverage of certain employment instruments and their application to transferring and non-transferring employees.

In doing so, the Commission must consider:

✔ The views of the new employer or a person who is likely to be the new employer, and the employees who would be affected by the order

✔ Whether any employees would be disadvantaged by the order in relation to their terms and conditions of employment

✔ If the order relates to an enterprise agreement, the nominal expiry date of the agreement

✔ The financial position of the new employer

✔ The efficient operation of the new employer's enterprise and the degree of fit between any transferable instrument and arrangements that already exist in the new employer's enterprise

I wouldn't place too much confidence in obtaining a favourable outcome from the Fair Work Commission because experience generally shows the Commission won't order a reduction in the terms and conditions of employment of transferring employees. If you do need to go down this path, you should seriously reconsider the value of taking on any employees from the old employer.

Recognising prior service of transferring employee

As the new employer, you must recognise transferring employees' service with their old employer when calculating certain NES entitlements. These are

✔ Personal or carer's leave

✔ Parental leave

✔ The right to request flexible work arrangements

The accumulated leave entitlements and the periods of service of transferring employees must be disclosed to you before you take on the new business or outsourced work. In fact, the old employer is required to hand over all of the employment records of transferring employees.

In the case of annual leave and an employee's service toward an entitlement to redundancy pay (if you employ 15 or more employees), you have a choice whether to recognise the prior service of the transferring employee. If you don't agree to recognise the service, the old employer must pay out these entitlements.

If you employ the transferring employee on substantially similar terms and conditions of employment, the old employer doesn't have to pay redundancy to the transferring employee.

If you transfer an employee to a business that is a related entity — that is, you have a controlling interest in both businesses — the service with the previous employer is deemed to be continuous for the purposes of all service-related NES entitlements including annual leave and redundancy pay.

Transferring employees and qualifying periods

Placing any transferring employees on a six-month qualifying period (and therefore restricting their right to claim unfair dismissal) is a good way to see how well they fit into your way of working. However, you must inform the transferring employee in writing before the new employment starts that a period of service with the old employer would not be recognised for this purpose and they are required to undergo the 6 or 12 months qualifying period of employment with your business in order to be entitled to claim unfair dismissal.

If you don't put this requirement in writing before they commence and you decide to dismiss them in the first six months, they will be able to make a claim against you for unfair dismissal. Refer to Chapter 7 for more on employment contracts.

Part VII
The Part of Tens

Visit www.dummies.com/extras/hrsmallbusinessau for a free bonus Part of Tens chapter.

In this part . . .

✔ Learn from experience and apply one or more of the ten tips to building a successful employment relationship.

✔ Get the lowdown on what you definitely should not do to have a successful employment relationship with your staff.

Chapter 19

Ten Ways to Build a Successful Employment Relationship

In This Chapter

▶ Looking before you leap

▶ Opening your business to a new employee

▶ Outlining what you want from employees

▶ Understanding the importance of consistency

▶ Ensuring staff get a fair go

*N*o doubt, you're like everyone else and would love to know the secret formula to successful employment relationships, but I have bad news for you — a secret formula doesn't exist. The good news is that many tried and true methods that characterise successful employment relationships are available, and I share some of them with you in this chapter.

Do Your Homework before Employing

A job opportunity exists for everyone in Australian workplaces. Sometimes, however, that opportunity isn't in your small business. Doing your homework before you employ is vital to a successful employment relationship. Needing to get someone on board quickly is often the commercial reality, and this is all fine and good, but if you haven't identified the personal qualities of the individual suitable to your business, you may regret your decision.

Tick the following five 'boxes' before you employ:

- ✔ Employees must add value to the business. Analyse what you need in the same way you make any other investment decisions for your business.

- ✔ Sell the unique qualities of what your business is all about. If you can't explain the purpose of your business, you can't expect your staff to get on board and stay the journey.

- ✔ Be prepared to go out and find the right person for the job. The perfect candidate won't necessarily come to you.

- ✔ Have a clear vision of how this person is going to work with you and others in the business. Good employment occurs from a good cultural fit.

- ✔ Get yourself organised and write down your plan of action. Recruitment can sometimes be about the 'vibe' but it's usually about the homework.

Refer to Chapters 2 and 3 for more on recruitment strategies.

Welcome People into Your Business

Never underestimate the value of a really thorough orientation program to induct new staff into your small business. Getting to know each other, and beginning to understand personalities, abilities, confidence, competency and experience all affects how well the person works with and for you. This means the first three months of employment are critical to future performance.

Welcome new employees into your small business. By this I mean get to know them personally, professionally and sometimes socially. Make them feel that they're important to the success of your business. Find out what motivates them and engender confidence and trust. If they feel welcome and trust you, they're highly likely to work hard for you.

Refer to Chapter 8 for ideas on creating a strong orientation program for new staff.

Explain Your Expectations

Nothing kills an employment relationship quicker than a misunderstanding of the job and the environment in which it is performed. ('Oh gee, sorry — didn't I tell you that you would be expected to clean the toilets and buy my lunch every day?')

Employees aren't mind readers. Be very clear on the expectations that you have for the performance of the job. A well-structured job description at the time of recruitment, an employment contract detailing the important terms and conditions, and clearly defined performance criteria when an employee commences work are vital if you want to commence an employment relationship on a good footing.

Be Consistent

I'm reluctant to draw comparisons with parenting, but employment of its nature establishes an unequal relationship of authority and control. If this relationship is to work effectively, the person in authority (that's you) must be consistent in the manner in which they exercise that authority. For example, when I ask a staff member to adopt a particular manner when responding to customer enquiries, I can't then ask them to adopt a different approach simply because I changed my mind. Most employees will do what you ask them, even if they have reservations, as long as you explain your reasons and consistently apply the approach throughout the business and with other employees. When you arbitrarily change your direction, staff become confused. They become unhappy, and they lose respect for your judgement.

Nothing stands still and change is a motto for everything. Small business is no exception. What I am saying to you is: *walk the talk*. Don't change course without good reason and without bringing everyone else along with you.

Another area where consistency is important is in the way you treat each individual employee in their terms and conditions. People are likely to judge their personal worth and how well they're treated by comparison with other staff in your business, their peers in other businesses and the 'gap' between you, managers and themselves. For example, a staff member may not mind working extra hours of work to complete tasks as long as she's satisfied everyone else is expected to do the same. Staff may be paid very well compared to their peers employed in other businesses but are likely to become disgruntled if you pay other staff in the business a greater bonus unfairly.

You often need to walk a fine line but, nevertheless, that line is worth walking if you want to maintain staff loyalty, confidence and trust, which is characteristic of every successful employment relationship.

Give Your Employees a Fair Go

It's amazing what people can achieve if you just give them a fair go. Of course, not everyone will take the opportunities offered to them but reflecting on what motivates people in their work and life is worth doing.

Motivation comes from the following sources:

- ✔ Biological
- ✔ External
- ✔ Inherent

Thankfully, in Australia people are many years beyond the old world of subsistence farming and piecemeal wages that were barely sufficient to meet the need for food, water, clothing and shelter. Minimum wages and modern awards ensure the very basic biological needs are satisfied, whatever job you perform.

External sources are the traditional, industrial-age methods of motivation. For example, all the rules that employers impose on staff, such as 'clocking on and off' each day, wage payments, and managers supervising work, are all extrinsic forms of motivation — in other words, the carrot and the stick.

The question for you is whether such factors truly motivate people working in your small business in the modern Australian economy. Sometimes the answer is yes but often it is more complex, and also involves something else.

Inherent or intrinsic motivation is underpinned by three driving forces:

- ✔ **Autonomy:** The drive for independence and the desire to work out how to do the job well on your own. I reckon small-business owners are motivated to be autonomous so why wouldn't it work for your employees?
- ✔ **Mastery:** The drive to do the job well, and to master the task. Most people want to do a good job and, if left to their own devices (with a bit of encouragement and the right tools and instruction) can learn how to master the job. People who have mastered the job take pride in their work and want to do better.
- ✔ **Purpose:** The drive people feel to get out of bed each morning, determined to accomplish something useful. You can't teach this. It comes from within. What you can do is engender a sense of belonging to something worthwhile in your business, through reinforcing your

goals and providing a wider vision of the purpose beyond the daily hum drum of the everyday. For example, the job may be washing dishes in a restaurant but the bigger purpose is how that person is contributing to an enjoyable night out for the customers who may be celebrating a birthday, anniversary or simply sharing time with good friends. Your task is to draw the connection between the job and the bigger picture.

I do a lot of work with recruitment and employment agencies, and this gives me a unique opportunity to observe the dynamics of *job matching* in practice. I am always pleasantly amazed at how many successful employment relationships have been forged after an employer has been convinced to give an unlikely candidate a fair go. People overcoming serious barriers to participation in life, such as a physical disability, may be the type of people who will be an asset to your small business. I'm not sentimental when it comes to this issue. The personal attributes of the person who has had to overcome adversity are what create the qualities that will build a successful employment relationship: Resilience, determination, ingenuity, persistence, empathy and patience. I could go on but what makes a successful employment relationship is the ability to think beyond whether or not you're discriminating in favour or against someone. Think about the qualities the person can bring to your small business that will help it succeed.

Celebrate Success

Along the path to business success are lots of ups and downs. Celebrating the little victories and success along the way is important. Your employees appreciate these moments as well, so don't forget to include them in the celebration.

Try these simple acts:

- ✔ Hand out small gifts when you've landed that new contract to supply a client with your goods and services.
- ✔ Take everyone out for lunch or dinner at a really nice restaurant.
- ✔ Consider a Christmas bonus. It's not just a giveaway — it's a thank you for a job well done.
- ✔ Hand out movie ticket vouchers when staff have made that extra effort needed to deliver the goods on time.

No job is so small that it can't experience success. I'm reminded of the scene from the Australian movie *The Castle* where the father and lead character, Darryl Kerrigan, is congratulating his son for having dug another hole in the backyard (for no apparent reason). It's not the holes in the ground that matter — making his son feel good about himself and encouraging him to do even better work does. You too can apply a bit of Darryl Kerrigan management technique to each and every staff member in your small business. They might just appreciate it.

Be Decisive

You have a lot of decisions to make every day and sometimes have to deal with competing demands for your attention. If you're like most small business owners and don't like delegation, the burden is on you to actually make decisions that enable your small business to continue to function properly.

Your employees are on the front-line of the business and so are regularly having to respond to customer enquiries, complaints and demands. If you're the one who must make a decision in response to the customer, decide on a course of action promptly, empower your employees to respond and stick to the decision. Don't backtrack if the heat is turned up on you and make sure that you support your staff.

Equivocation is a great word to describe the failure to make a timely decision. It even sounds like it means ... wobbling jelly! No-one respects a spineless jellyfish so your decisions should be:

- Measured (proportionate to the issue at hand)
- Sensible (rational and based on common sense)
- Timely (made at the moment when the decision will have the most positive impact for your business)

Get to Know the Person Not Just the Employee

One of the few commercial advantages that you have over your larger business rivals is the capacity to develop real personal relationships with your staff. Odds are that you started out in business with family members or close friends and, as such, have already forged lifelong bonds that other businesses aren't able to compete with — loyalty and trust. Try extending the personal touch to the people who work for you who you didn't know when you employed them.

Of course, pitfalls can occur on the path to getting to know your staff. Some may just not be interested in sharing their lives outside of work, and getting too close and personal (in a physical way) can land you in trouble — for example, sexual harassment. However, I'm an optimist and believe that spending 38 hours, five days a week, 52 weeks of the year together with other people shouldn't be an impersonal experience.

Getting to know each other can be a really rewarding exercise, and can occur through the following:

- ✔ Knowing the names of your staff's partners, husbands, wives, children and special others
- ✔ Sending birthday cards to family members
- ✔ Celebrating births, marriages, engagements
- ✔ Sending flowers and get-well cards when staff and their family members are seriously ill
- ✔ Spending a bit of time during the lunch break to share stories from home

All of these efforts may be worthwhile for no other reason than taking the opportunity to know and understand another person, which is its own reward. If you want to put a price on it, count the times that your staff ask you about your life, your interests and, when you're feeling a bit low, how you're feeling. Add the times that staff have offered voluntarily to work additional hours to complete tasks or cover for you when difficult customers are unnecessarily demanding to see you. You can't put a price on loyalty.

Model Good Behaviour

Employers are judged by the standards of angels so start aspiring to be a model employer.

You can't get around the fact that Australian regulatory authorities and tribunals impose very high standards on business owners and employers when it comes to the treatment of staff. You can look at unfair dismissal laws, protection of workplace rights, anti-discrimination and measures to prevent workplace bullying for examples of how employers are expected to behave. So you should set some standards of behaviour for everyone in your business and then lead by example.

Modelling good behaviour simply means living up to the standards of behaviour that you set for others in your business. Easier said than done, perhaps, so I have a few suggestions.

Make sure that you have written policies describing obligations and responsibilities for

- ✔ Equal employment opportunity
- ✔ Prevention of harassment (including sexual harassment) and bullying
- ✔ Workplace health and safety
- ✔ Acceptable use of internet, email and social media

These documents should describe how you intend to uphold the standards of conduct espoused in the policy. This would include a range of education programs and procedures to investigate complaints and methods to resolve conflicts. A regulatory basis normally applies to each of these themes, which you can take your lead from as to the actual standards of behaviour.

For example, workplace rights and anti-discrimination laws prohibit actions that discriminate or prejudice a person's employment on the basis of personal attributes such as age, colour, physical features, gender, sexual orientation, sex, race, disability, marital status, parental status, family responsibilities, carer status, pregnancy, breastfeeding, trade union activity, political or religious belief and even personal association with anyone who possesses such characteristics. You can create more policies depending upon what is important to your small business.

Go to www.dummies.com/go/hrsmallbusinessau for employment policies that you can model your own on.

Of course, written policies aren't the only method of demonstrating model behaviour. The day when you have to have a written policy describing every aspect of behaviour at work would be a sad day indeed. Employees don't need to have a policy to know stealing from you is wrong or that punching a work colleague in the face is unacceptable. Some things are pretty obvious. Nevertheless, staff will follow your lead in so many subtle ways:

- ✔ **Sexually suggestive conversations and jokes.** Everyone likes a joke, and sometimes employees may be able to share a double entendre or two but don't initiate or share in the fun. I've seen working relationships fall apart and careers destroyed by accusations of harassment that commenced with a joke.

✔ **Management versus bullying.** Where is the line between a manager who forcefully delivers a message to improve work and one who engages in genuine bullying? Working that out can be difficult, so you have to stay away from the line completely. Ultimatums, shouting and abusive language are now all ancient history. You must adopt the quiet, polite but nevertheless assertive mode of management to ensure you're on the right side of what's acceptable behaviour.

Always Encourage and Reward Good Performance

Don't forget the fundamental reason you and your staff are all spending time together. The relationship is an economic one and a venture in which you're all working to succeed. That usually means financial success (but does not always need to be so). You have a reasonable chance at success if you encourage and reward the right performance and behaviour.

Good performance is reinforced by applying a five-step circular process of continuous improvement:

✔ Defining the results, means, quality, attributes and behaviour that you want employees to exhibit and pursue

✔ Removing the barriers that inhibit successful performance, such as training and equipment

✔ Encouraging good performance through motivation, communication and reward

✔ Measuring performance regularly to see how well you're progressing toward your goals

✔ Learning from the immediately experience and adjusting to create improved opportunities to succeed

If you integrate this performance management system with your business plan, everyone should be working toward the same goals.

Chapter 20

Ten Things You Should Never Do At Work

. . . .

In This Chapter

▶ Keeping in mind family and business problems don't mix

▶ Understanding blaming others won't cut it

▶ Realising sleeping with the boss is a recipe for disaster

▶ Understanding your behaviour sets the tone

▶ Making the tough decisions now

▶ Knowing that honesty is the best policy

. . . .

*Y*ou may have read about, or even encountered during your working career, the bad boss, the moody boss, the uninspiring boss, the psychopathic boss, and the boss who won't spend any money, except on themselves. A little self-reflection goes a long way if you wish to avoid becoming one of those bosses in your own small business. Buy yourself one of those really large mirrors and remember to have a good hard look at yourself occasionally. In this chapter, I describe the things that you most definitely should not do at work.

Bring Family Problems to Work

The prevailing attitude to work and family was once quite clear: Leave your family life behind you when you come to work. Now it's not so clear. An array of HR beliefs, supported by employment regulations, mitigate against this traditional division of work and family, such as:

✔ Compassionate leave

✔ Flexible work arrangements

✔ Parental leave

✔ Personal leave

✔ Workplace rights

Counselling services are available when work becomes too stressful, and workers compensation and return to work plans whenever an employee suffers psychological damage. All of this is fine and good for your staff, but for you as the boss, a line exists that you shouldn't cross when it comes to sharing your life's ups and downs at work.

When working out where the line is, you need to keep in mind that the intimate details of your personal and family life aren't anybody else's business. I appreciate that you can't separate yourself completely from the emotional highs and lows that family and other personal matters have on you, but you shouldn't deliberately share them with staff or use them as an excuse to treat staff badly.

If you bring your problems into work, don't be surprised when others do exactly the same.

Blame Others for Your Mistakes

It's your business, your decision, your money, your life. Do I have to say any more? If it doesn't work, the fault is yours, not the government's, not the union's, not the bank's and certainly not your staff's (however incompetent some of them may be — after all, you hired them). Success has many parents but failure is an orphan. If you see a mistake, fix it. If you see an opportunity, take it. If you don't see the risks, you will suffer the failures alone. This is as true in employment as it is for your other business investments.

Play Favourites

I know that some staff are really good and others aren't so wonderful and some are just a pain in the proverbial. However, playing favourites can get you into trouble when it comes to employment, promotion, wage negotiations, and dismissals. I don't mean you shouldn't reward the good workers and sanction those who do the wrong thing. But you do have to contextualise every decision around the specific employment obligations, the operational needs of the business, and the regulatory boundaries such as modern awards, minimum wages, the NES, unfair dismissal and anti-discrimination laws. This is not easy to do, so a bit of common sense and an old-fashioned, even-handed approach to staff is the best policy.

Sleep with Staff (Not a Good Look)

Picture any one of these scenarios: You're working late, you're travelling overnight for business, you've had a few too many drinks at the Christmas function and Judy, Kevin or Chris at work is really attractive and really understands what you are going through ... *stop, danger, don't go there!*

A few moments of pleasure may spell the end of your small business. Remember how you and your spouse are joint directors in the business? Remember that joint bank account? What about the other family employed in the business?

Getting involved personally, emotionally or physically with staff will complicate your life and business in many ways that you can't anticipate, and your business may no longer even be your business anymore. The Family Court may divide it up and the bank or ATO may end up closing it down.

Pay Yourself before Others

It's your business but your employees stand in front of you in the line when the wages are handed out. They don't risk their capital like you do but they don't reap the same reward either. Their stake in the business is their time, knowledge, skills and effort. Therefore, they get paid before you do. It's the law.

Act Inconsistently

If you can't stay on track, how can you expect staff to stay focused on the end game? Nothing confuses staff more than an unpredictable boss, and the surest way to lose good employees is to confuse them. Acting inconsistently is frustrating and will impact adversely on productivity, confidence and trust.

Put in place a clear performance plan for each and every employee. Each plan should have objectives that are SMART — that is, specific, measureable, ambitious but realistic and time-bound. Once these objectives are set, work with staff on how they're going to achieve them, and be consistent in how you encourage, cajole, support, reward and even growl at them to achieve these objectives. People will accept a hard boss who's also a fair boss. But they will walk out the door if you're an erratic boss.

Avoid Saying Good Morning

Greeting your staff cheerfully won't cost you anything, and your demeanour sets the tone for everyone. The culture of a workplace is established by the leader. Hello? That means you. If you want a happy and welcoming business environment, you need to set the standard.

I would love to have a dollar for all of the sweetly worded employment policies I've read that state a business's commitment to equality, respect, honesty and shared values — all while the bosses just go about doing whatever they want and treating staff anyway they please. Hypocrisy is the worst trait of any boss, so I will spell it out for you. Hypocrisy is the act of falsely claiming to possess characteristics (such as virtue, honesty and integrity) but living very differently. Live the values that you claim to hold by taking a genuine interest in the people you employ. Start by saying good morning — and really mean it.

Jump to Conclusions (and Over the Cliff)

When everything is falling apart and it seems clear to you that an employee has really stuffed up, stop and think before you act. Leaping to conclusions is usually the greatest mistake that employers facing unfair dismissal claims have made. You can warn or dismiss employees who have performed or acted badly, but you must give them an opportunity to tell you their side of the story before you act.

A fair procedure is not difficult:

1. **Find out the facts from those who know.**

2. **Invite the employee to explain the performance or conduct.**

3. **Be open and honest about the problem with the performance or conduct.**

4. **Unless it is serious misconduct, give the employee an opportunity to improve.**

5. **Support the employee to improve.**

6. **If no improvement is made, dismiss the employee.**

An entire industry is built around suing businesses that dismiss bad staff without a fair procedure. Make sure that you don't get caught in this very expensive industry, because you will be the one signing the cheque.

Put Off Important Decisions to another Day

Work performance may be unsatisfactory, arguments between staff annoying and conflict just bubbling below the surface but you really don't have time to deal with it now. Make time — otherwise, these issues will explode in your face and cost you more.

Intervention to prevent or resolve staff conflict and unsatisfactory performance is a bit like any other action necessary to build the success of your small business — timing is everything. If you miss the opportunity, events may just pass you by and any benefit that you could have reaped will disappear.

Forget Honesty Is Truly the Best Policy

Don't mislead the people you rely upon as to what is truly going on in your business, and don't blind yourself to the truth. Don't promise to do something for an employee that you can't or won't do.

I am often contacted by desperate small-business employers facing unfair dismissal claims, demands by government inspectors or conflicts with staff, and the issue is always the same. They have not told the truth and are desperately trying to dig themselves out of a big hole. You will always get into trouble if you're not open and transparent. Experts such as lawyers, judges and government officials are paid to expose dishonesty so just don't go there.

Index

• A •

Aboriginal and Torres Strait Islander cultural leave, and awards, 95
acceptable use of internet policy, 168
accommodating in conflict resolution, 212
accountability of job, describing, 39–40
accruing annual leave, 68–69
acknowledgement form in welcome pack, 157–158
additional hours of work (NES), 62–63
additional public holidays in states and territories, 77
adverse action, understanding, 224–226
Age Discrimination Act 2004, 205
allowances, types of, 101–103
annual leave
  and awards, 95
  entitlements to and costs of, 113–114
  NES provisions, 68–70
  payment for at termination, 290
  payments and superannuation, 130
  taking, 69
annual wage review, 99
Anti-Discrimination Act 1977 (NSW), 205
Anti-Discrimination Act 1991 (QLD), 206, 223
Anti-Discrimination Act 1998 (TAS), 206
anti-discrimination laws, relevance to interviews, 54–55
anti-discrimination in the workplace, introduction to, 17–18
Anti-Money Laundering and Counter-Terrorism Financing Act 2006 (AML/CTF Act), 150
anxiety and workers compensation, 272–273
appeals against unfair dismissal, 314
applicants for jobs, types of, 47–48
appraisal interviews, handling, 179
apprentices, terms and conditions of work for, 105–109
arbitration and conciliation in conflict resolution, 216–217

assessment tools for selection of staff, 52–53
associated entities, 332
attachments for employment contracts, 147–148
attribute performance scale, 177
Australian Capital Territory (ACT)
  agency administering portable long service leave scheme, 122
  definition of deemed workers in, 269
  definition of worker in, 267
  duty of care in, 251
  long service leave provision in, 120
  National Employment Standards (NES) in, 62
  payroll tax and thresholds in, 124
  pro rata long service leave payment in, 291
Australian Government Paid Parental Leave scheme
  details, 66–68, 112–113
  website, 66
Australian Human Rights Commission
  examples of bullying, 240–241
  examples of sexual harassment, 239
authority, consistency in exercising, 341
authority of job, describing, 39
autonomy in motivation, 342
averaging weekly hours of work (NES), 63–64
Award Flexibility provisions, 93–94
award minimum pay rates and progression, 186
award-free employees, 88
awards
  applicable, 88–89
  minimum wages in, 99–100
  understanding, 89–99

• B •

back-filling employees on personal/carer's leave, 115
bank account number for payroll form, staff to provide, 156

barriers to successful performance, 174–175

base wage, choosing, 194

behaviour policies in the workplace, 17–19

behaviour standards
  modelling, 345–347
  in staff handbook, 163–164

behavioural performance measurement, 177

behavioural standards and conflict, 202–203

bonuses
  individual and collective, 193–194
  paying, 191

Building and Construction industry,
    exceptions to long service leave, 121

Building and Construction On-site Award, 103

bullying
  definition, 18, 239
  preventing, 243–245
  reducing risks of, 242–243
  risk factors for, 241–242

bullying and harassment policy, using, 244–245

business context, describing in position
    description, 37

business plan or overview in welcome
    pack, 157

business structure, outlining, 9–10

business to business transfers, defining,
    330–332

business vehicles for private use,
    providing, 191

• C •

candidates for jobs
  criminal record checks, 57–58
  health issues, 56–57
  types of, 47–48

capacity to resolve conflict, 209

carer's leave
  avoiding back-filling employees on, 115
  and awards, 95
  cashing out, 114
  entitlement to and costs of, 114
  NES provisions, 70–72
  planning for emergencies, 115–116

cashing out
  annual leave, 69–70, 114
  long service leave, 121
  personal/carer's leave, 114

casual employees
  and resignation notices, 288
  rights of, 34–35

casual employment
  and awards, 90, 92
  definition, 29
  notice periods for, 80

casual loadings in modern awards, 104

changes in small business
  avoiding pitfalls in, 328–329
  consulting with staff about, 97
  introducing, 320

checklist of action during business changes,
    329–330

checklist and procedure for improving
    performance, 182–184

child, meaning under NES, 71

Children and Community Services Act 2004,
    effect in Western Australia, 85

Clerks — Private Sector Award
  flexibility provisions in, 93–94
  working hours for office-based work, 96

close supervision, definition, 39

coercion and workplace rights, 228–229

collaborative problem-solving, 210

common law, effect of statutory laws on, 141

community service leave
  and awards, 95
  costs of, 116–117
  NES provisions, 72–74

company dress code, 165

comparative performance measurement, 177

compassionate leave
  and awards, 95
  inability to plan for, 116
  NES provisions for, 71

compatibility, effect on staff performance, 176

competency assessment of job candidates, 53

compromising in conflict resolution, 212

conciliation and arbitration
  in conflict resolution, 216–217
  of unfair dismissal claims, 310–314

conclusions, jumping to, 352–353

conditions of employment, listing, 39

confidentiality of business information,
    using employment contract to protect,
    148–149

conflict, issues involved in, 207–208

conflict resolution
  legal constraints on, 208
  pre-conditions for, 208–209
  principles in Australian workplace laws, 206
  selecting best method, 210–216
conflict resolution, methods, 207–209
conflict in workplace
  signs of, 205
  sources of, 202–204
consistency in exercising authority, 341
constitutional corporation, definition, 83–84
constructive dismissal, 302
consultation and genuine redundancy, 322–324
consulting with employees and others about
      OH&S, 261–263
contesting in conflict resolution, 211–212
contingency planning for leave, 117
continuity of service and unpaid parental
      leave, 68
control test for determining whether
      independent contractor, 31
Copyright Act 1968, 170
copyright in work-created material, 169–170
cost of staff employment, ready reckoner for,
      134–136
costs of staff compared with revenue, 22–23
counselling of staff over poor performance, 182
criminal record checks and anti-
      discrimination law, 57–58

● *D* ●

decisions, postponing, 353
decisiveness, 344
deemed workers defined for compensation
      purposes, 268–270
default superannuation funds, using, 134
designs, rights of ownership of, 169
desirable selection criteria, 11
developmental performance management, 172
difficult, dirty or noxious work, allowances
      for, 102
direct discrimination of staff, 221–222
disabilities
  national minimum wage for employees
      with, 101
  and reasonable adjustments to workplace,
      55–56, 229–230
Disability Discrimination Act 1992, 205

disciplinary action in conflict resolution, 211
Discrimination Act 1991 (ACT), 223
discrimination in the workplace
  direct and indirect, 221–223
  during business change, 328–329
  educating staff about, 230–231
  introduction to, 17–18
diseases caused by work, 271
dismissal
  fair and reasonable in WA, 316
  point of occurrence, 302–303
disputes with staff, resolving, 98
dress codes for staff, 165
due diligence, exercising in health and safety,
      252–253
duty of care
  by staff and other persons, 254
  fulfilling, 250–253
duty holders, consulting with each other on
      OH&S, 262–263

● *E* ●

education of staff
  on bullying and harassment, 244
  on discrimination, 230–231
eligibility of employers for superannuation
      guarantee payments, 131–132
eligible termination payments (ETPs)
  taxation of, 291–294
  withholding tax calculation, 294
employees. *See also* staff
  assessment of suitability, 181
  getting to know as people, 344–345
  searching for, 12–13
  sources of, 12–13
employees with disabilities, national
      minimum wage for, 100
employees on leave during business
      change, 328
employer-nominated default superannuation
      funds, 134
employers, regulations in Western Australia,
      84–86
employing staff, reasons for, 8–10
employment
  checklist, 33
  ending by agreement, 289
  forms of, 28–33

employment contract checklist, 151
employment contract template
  creating, 143
  filling out, 143–147
employment contracts
  for apprentices and trainees, 108–109
  attachments to, 147–148
  elements of, 138
  importance of, 14
  protecting confidentiality of business
    information through, 148–149
  resignation notice in, 287
  signatories to, 148
  templates for, 143
  terms and conditions in, 142–143
employment disputes, resolving, 98
employment policies, 166–170
  in welcome pack, 157
employment records and privacy, 150
employment relationship
  as economic relationship, 12
  ending, 19–20
encouragement of staff, effect on
    performance, 175
engaging interviewer, 50–51
enterprise agreements, transferring with
    staff, 332–334
Equal Opportunity Act 1984 (SA), 206
Equal Opportunity Act 1984 (WA), 206
Equal Opportunity Act 2010 (VIC), 206
equity and fairness, effect on staff
    performance, 176
essential criteria for selection of staff,
    48–49
evaluation form for staff orientation, 162
evaluative performance management, 172
evidence and notice for personal/carer's
    leave, 71–72
example job responsibilities, 38
existing injury, aggravation and acceleration
    due to work, 270–271
exit interviews, 295–297
expectations, explaining to new staff,
    340–341
expense allowances, and superannuation, 130
expense-related allowances, 102
experience, learning from, 180
experience assessment of job candidates, 53
express terms of employment, 139

• F •

facilitation in conflict resolution, 213
factors of production, 9
'A fair go all round', in conflict resolution,
    214–215
'A fair go' for employees, 342–343
Fair Work Act 2009
  and bullying, 18, 239
  and constitutional corporations, 83–84
  employment termination provisions for
    apprentices and trainees, 108
  general protection of employees in, 224
  and National Employment Standards
    (NES), 62
  and unfair dismissal, 301
  and workplace conflict, 205
  and workplace rights, 223, 226
Fair Work Commission orders, 333–334
Fair Work Information Statement
  as part of employment contract, 147
  as part of welcome pack, 156
fairness and equity, effect on staff
    performance, 176
Family Law Act 1975, meaning of child under, 71
family problems at work, 349–350
Fast Food Industry Award, and part-time
    employees, 91
favourites, playing, 350–351
feedback
  to staff on performance, 178–180
  to unsuccessful job applicants, 50
filtering questions for short list, 49
financial returns from employees, estimating,
    22–23
fixed costs (FC), definition, 23
fixed-term employment
  and awards, 92
  definition, 31–32
flexibility arrangements in modern awards,
    92–95
flexible work arrangements (NES)
  applying, 64–65
  responding to written requests for, 65–66
forms of employment and awards, 90
fringe benefits, providing as reward, 189–191
fringe benefits tax
  on cars, 126–127
  defining, 125–126

recording and reporting, 127–128
reducing liability for, 128
full-time employment
and awards, 90
completing employment contract template
for, 143–147
definition, 28

• G •

General Retail Industry Award, junior rates of
pay in, 106
genuine occupational requirements,
having, 233
genuine redundancy
definition, 305
obligations, 321–324
goals of business in staff handbook, 163
good behaviour, modelling, 345–347
good performance, rewarding, 188–194, 347
government tribunals in conflict resolution,
215–217
greeting staff, 352

• H •

Hair and Beauty Industry Award, 102
harassment. *See also* sexual harassment
definition, 238
preventing, 243–245
reducing risks of, 242–243
risk factors for, 241–242
harmonious working relationships, strategies
for, 199
harsh dismissal, criteria for, 303–304
hazards. *See* risks
health issues of job candidates, 56–57
Health Professionals and Support Services
Award, 103
health and safety, acting on, 251–253
holidays and awards, 95
honesty being best policy, 353
Hospitality Industry Award, 104
hours of work, deciding on, 33–34
housekeeping in office, 165–166
*Human Rights and Equal Opportunity
Act 1986*, 205

• I •

ideal employee, describing, 11
implied terms of employment, 140
incapacity, confirming with doctor and
assigning suitable duties, 277
incentives
individual and collective, 193–194
paying, 191
inconsistent actions, 351–352
independent contractors
definition, 29–30
versus employees, 30–31
indirect discrimination of staff, 222–223
individual flexibility arrangements (IFAs)
as attachment to employment
contract, 148
content of, 92–95
industrial deafness caused by work, 271
Industrial Relations Act 1979, employee
coverage in Western Australia, 84–86
inequity and conflict, 203
inherent requirements of job
definition, 55
performing, 233–234
insurance premiums, for workers
compensation, 123
integration test for determining whether
independent contractor, 31
intellectual property rights, protecting,
168–170
internet, acceptable use policy, 167–168
interview questions and technique,
51–52
interviewing
techniques for, 50–56
topics to avoid, 54–56
inventions, rights of ownership, 169
investment in staff, calculating, 22–25
irrelevant criminal records and
discrimination, 57

• J •

job advertisement, example, 44
job analysis, conducting, 8–10, 26–28
Job Capacity Assessments, 101

job descriptions. *See also* position
    descriptions
  creating, 10, 36–40
  versus selection criteria, 42–44
job design to suit your business, 25–35
job matching, process of, 343
job title, in position description, 36–37
juniors, terms and conditions of work for,
    105–106
jury service, paying employees on, 116

• *K* •

key performance indicators (KPIs), for
    employees, 173–174
key selection criteria, listing, 40
knowledge assessment of job candidates, 53

• *L* •

*Labour Relations Legislation Amendment and
    Repeal Bill 2012*, effects within Western
    Australia, 85
law and workplace conflict, 205–206
leadership, effect on performance, 175
leave
  direct costs of paying, 112–122
  hidden costs of administering, 112–122
leave loading and awards, 95
limited direction, definition, 39
loadings, modern award transitional
    provisions for, 109
long service leave
  and awards, 95
  cashing out, 121
  costs of, 117–122
  exceptions to rules in Building and
    Construction Industry, 121
  making provision for, 118, 120
  NES provisions for, 74–76
  pro rata payment at termination, 290–291
  provision by State and Territory, 120

• *M* •

making up time, 95
managerial directives in conflict resolution,
    211

mandatory selection criteria, 11
marginal costs, definition, 22
marginal revenue, definition, 22
market rates of pay, competition in, 194–196
mastery in motivation, 342
maternity leave, special, 67
maximum hours of work (NES), 62–64
meal allowances and superannuation, 130
means-based performance measurement, 178
mediation in conflict resolution, 215–216
medical practice manager, example
    responsibilities, 38
medical practitioners, communicating with,
    275–276
member of a household, definition, 71
mental stress and workers compensation,
    272–273
Minimum Conditions of Employment Act 1993,
    application in Western Australia,
    84–86
minimum wages
  absorbing adjustments to, 187
  for juniors, 106
  in modern awards, 99–100
  paying above, 187–188
mistakes, blaming others for, 346
model Workplace Health and Safety Act, 250,
    251, 253
modern awards
  applicability, 88–89
  notice of resignation under, 286
  obligations to consult with staff about
    changes, 97
moral rights in copyright, 170
motivation of staff
  sources, 342–343
  using pay rates, 189

• *N* •

National Employment Standards (NES),
    basics of, 62–83
national minimum wage (NMW)
  by category (2013), 100
  for employees with disabilities, 101
  yearly ritual, 99
negotiations with unhappy staff on wages,
    196–197

New South Wales
  agency administering portable long
    service leave in, 122
  definition of deemed worker in, 269
  definition of worker in, 267
  duty of care in, 251
  long service leave provision, 120
  National Employment Standards (NES) in, 62
  payroll tax and thresholds in, 124
  pro rata long service leave payment in, 291
new staff, welcome pack for, 156–157
no safe job leave, 67
non-expense related allowances and
    superannuation, 130
Northern Territory
  agency administering portable long
    service leave scheme in, 122
  anti-discrimination laws in, 57–58
  definition of deemed worker in, 269
  definition of worker in, 267
  duty of care in, 251
  long service leave provision, 120
  National Employment Standards (NES) in, 62
  payroll tax and thresholds in, 124
  pro rata long service leave payment in, 291
notice of absence on community service
    leave, providing, 73–74
notice periods for employment termination,
    79–80
notice of resignation
  payment in lieu of, 289
  requirements, 286–288
notices and evidence for personal/carer's
    leave, providing, 71–72

• O •

Occupational Health and Safety Act 2004
    (VIC), 255
occupational health and safety (OH&S)
  applying standards, codes and regulations,
    263–264
  induction and training in, 255
office, general housekeeping in, 165–166
office holders' duty of care, 253
operating cost method for calculating car
    fringe benefits tax, 126
opportunity to resolve conflict, 208–209
ordinary earnings rule, exceptions and
    inclusions to, 130–131
ordinary hours of work and awards, 95–96
ordinary times earnings base for super
    guarantee contributions, 130
organisational structure
  outlining, 9–10
  and work flow design, 27–28
orientation (induction) of staff
  checklist for, 159–161
  process of, 156–162
orientation programs, benefits and
    drawbacks of, 15–16
other persons in the workplace, duty of care
    by, 254
outsourcing work, 331
overtime payments
  in modern awards, 104–105
  and superannuation, 131
ownership of inventions and designs, 169

P •

paid annual leave for full-time employees, 28
Paid Dad and Partner Leave (PDPL), costs of,
    112–113
Paid Parental Leave (PPL) scheme
  costs of, 112–113
  details of, 66–68
parental leave
  and awards, 95
  costs of, 112–113
  for full-time staff, 28
  NES provisions, 66–68
  obligations of employee, 68
part-time employment
  and awards, 90
  completing employment contract template
    for, 143–147
  definition, 29
past performance in redundancy
    selection, 327
pay, elements of ordinary rate of, 119
pay rises, expectations of, 186
payment in lieu of notice, 81, 289
  and superannuation, 131
payment for not working on public
    holidays, 78

payroll tax, costs of, 123–124
penalty rates
  modern award transitional provisions for, 109
  in modern awards, 103–104
performance
  checklist for improvement, 184
  encouraging, 175–176
  key themes for success, 158
  responding to unsatisfactory, 182–183
  rewarding good, 188–194
performance management cycle for staff, 15
performance management system, structured, 172–173
performance orientation program, 158–159
performance plan
  for recording agreed key performance indicators, 174
  revising after appraisal, 180
performance review after first 6 months, 180–181
performance standards, defining, 173–174
permanent employment versus temporary employment, 31–32
permanently incapacitated staff, managing, 278–281
person conducting a business or undertaking (PCBU), and duty of care, 251
personal attributes, asking about in interviews, 54
personal information on employees, collecting, 231–232
personal leave
  avoiding back-filling employees, 115
  and awards, 95
  cashing out, 114
  compassionate leave, 116
  entitlement to and costs of, 114
  for full-time employees, 28
  NES provisions, 70–72
  planning for emergencies, 115–116
personal questions in interviews, risks of, 54
personal relationships with staff, 7–8
personal value and wage rates, 196
personality clashes, conflict resulting from, 204
philosophy of business stated in staff handbook, 163

poor work performance
  and conflict, 204
  dealing with, 182–184
portable long service leave, agencies administering, 122
position descriptions. *See also* job descriptions
  creating, 36–40
potential employees, definition, 48
power struggles and conflict, 204
pre-existing injuries or illness and anti-discrimination law, 56–57
pregnancy and discrimination, 66–67
pressure and workplace rights, 228–229
primary purpose of job, describing, 37
prior service of transferring employee, recognising, 334–335
Privacy Act 1988, 150, 231
privacy in internet and social media use, 167–168
privacy of personal information collected by businesses, 150
Privacy Principles, 150
private use of business vehicles, providing for, 191
pro rata long service leave payment at termination, 291
productivity loss while training replacement employee, 113
profitability of staff
  assessing, 12
  effect of employing more, 24–25
prospective employees, discrimination against, 223–224
psychological injuries and workers compensation, 272–273
public holidays, NES provisions for, 76–79
purpose in motivation, 342–343

qualifications, allowances for employees with, 102–103
qualifying period for new staff, 180–181
qualifying periods for transferring staff, 335
qualitative risk analysis matrix, 258
quality performance measurement, 178

Queensland
agency administering portable long service
leave scheme in, 122
definition of deemed worker in, 269
definition of worker in, 267
duty of care in, 251
long service leave provision, 120
National Employment Standards (NES) in, 62
payroll tax and thresholds in, 124
pro rata long service leave payment in, 291

• R •

Racial Discrimination Act 1975, 206
rating systems on scorecard, 44–45
real cost ready reckoner for staff
employment, 134–136
reasonable additional hours, 104
reasonable adjustments to workplace,
relevance to interviews, 55–56
reasonable business grounds for refusing
flexible work request, 65
reasonable management practice and
bullying, 240–241
reasonably practical action on health and
safety, 252
reckless behaviour, exclusion from workers
compensation, 272
recruitment checklist, 339–340
redeployment to alternative positions during
business change, 328
redundancy notices, NES provisions for, 79–82
redundancy
genuine, 305
voluntary, 327–329
redundancy pay
and employment contracts, 326
exemptions for small business, 325–326
prescribed, 325
rules for, 81–82
and superannuation, 131
refresher training on bullying and
harassment, 245
rehabilitation after workplace injury, 273
remuneration of staff
elements considered part of ordinary pay
rate, 119
introduction to, 16–17

resignation notice
in employment contracts, 287
giving, 286
when not required, 288
resignation period, working or not during,
288–289
responsibilities of job, describing, 37–38
results performance measurement, 178
results test for determining whether
independent contractor, 31
return to work after injury, planning, 273–275
return to work (RTW) coordinator,
appointing, 274
return to work (RTW) decision-making flow
chart, 280
return to work (RTW) plans, designing
individual, 274–275
return to work (RTW) policy, implementing,
274
revenue from staff
comparing with costs, 22–23
increasing by adding, 24
reverse onus of proof, 228
risk
evaluating, 257–259
identifying, 256–257
treating, 259–260
risk management
definition, 256
introduction to, 19
risk-management measures, 260–261
rolling-up award allowances, 103, 187–188
rules of engagement for staff, 163–166

• S •

Safe Work Australia, 250
salaries. *See also* wages
definition of, 124
salary sacrifice arrangements
as reward for good work, 190
tax impact of, 192–193
scorecard for decision, 10, 44–46
seasonal employment and resignation notice,
288
selection criteria
deciding, 10–11
form for creation of, 43

selection criteria *(continued)*
  in redundancy, 326–329
  versus job description, 42–44
  weightings for, 45–46
selection procedure, 12–13
self, not paying before others, 351
self-managed conflict resolution, 210–211
serious misconduct
  definition, 307, 309
  and *Fair Work Act 2009*, 308
  notice periods for, 80
setting-off award allowances, 103
Sex Discrimination Act 1984, 206, 238
Sex Discrimination Act 1998, 223
sexual harassment. *See also* harassment
  defining, 238–239
shift loadings in modern awards, 103–104
short list of suitable candidates
  creating, 48–49
  questions for, 49
skills and experience, recognising for pay
    rises, 186, 188
small business, definition, 306
small business employer, definition, 81
Small Business Fair Dismissal Code, 299–300
  features of, 305–307, 309
Small Business Superannuation Clearing
    House, 134
social media, acceptable use policy,
    167–168
South Australia
  agency administering portable long service
    leave scheme in, 122
  definition of deemed worker in, 269
  definition of worker in, 267
  duty of care in, 2551
  long service leave provision, 120
  National Employment Standards (NES) in, 62
  payroll tax and thresholds in, 124
  pro rata long service leave payment in, 291
special maternity leave, 67
special national minimum wage 1 and 2, 101
special skills, allowances for employees with,
    102–103
spent convictions and discrimination, 57
spill and fill procedure, 327
spreadsheet ready reckoner for total
    employment cost, 134–136

staff. *See also* employees
  assessing profitability of, 12
  behaviour standards for, 163–164
  calculating investment in, 22–25
  collecting personal information on, 231–232
  consulting about changes to business, 97
  consulting on OH&S, 262
  dress codes for, 165
  duty of care by, 254
  increasing revenue by adding, 24
  motivation sources, 342–343
  motivation using pay rates, 189
  performance management cycle for, 15
  ready reckoner for calculating costs of
    employment, 134–136
  reasons for employing, 8–10
  remunerating, 16–17
  sleeping with, 351
  sources of, 12–13
staff handbook in welcome pack, 157
staff orientation (induction) process, 156–162
  checklist for, 159–161
  evaluation form, 161–162
staff performance measurement, 176–178
statutory formula method for calculating car
    fringe benefits tax, 126
statutory laws, effect on common law, 141
strategic performance management, 172
structure of business, outlining, 9–10
substituting public holidays, 77–78
success, celebrating, 343–344
suitability assessment of staff, 181
suitability versus disability, 233–235
suitable duties after incapacitation, 277
superannuation
  contributions at termination, 294
  mandatory contributions, 98–99
Superannuation Charge Act 1992, 98
superannuation funds, employees' right of
    choice, 132–133
*Superannuation Guarantee (Administration)
    Act 1992*, 98
superannuation guarantee contributions
  amount and frequency to 2019, 129–132
  eligibility of employers for, 131–132
  exceptions and inclusions to ordinary
    earnings rules, 130–131
  quarterly cut-off dates, 132

Superannuation Industry (Supervision) Act 1993, 98

Superannuation (Resolution of Complaints) Act 1993, 98

superannuation standard choice form, in welcome pack, 156

• T •

Tasmania
  agency administering portable long service leavescheme in, 122
  anti-discrimination laws in, 57–58
  definition of deemed worker in, 269
  definition of worker in, 268
  duty of care in, 251
  long service leave provision, 120
  National Employment Standards (NES) in, 62
  payroll tax and thresholds in, 124
  pro rata long service leave payment in, 291
tax file number declaration form in welcome pack, 156
taxation of eligible termination payments (ETPs), 291–294
templates for employment contracts, 143–147
temporary employment
  and awards, 92
  versus permanent employment, 31–32
termination of employment
  apprentices and trainees, 107–108
  at initiative of employer, 302
  notice by employee, 286
  required notice period, 324–325
  unlawful, 318
termination of employment notices, NES provisions for, 79–82
termination payments, summary, 290
terms and conditions in employment contracts, 142–143
terms of employment
  express, 139
  implied, 140
third-party interventions in conflict resolution, 215–217
time off in lieu of overtime payment (TOIL), 105
time off work, making up, 95
timely rewards, effect on performance, 175

total cost (TC), calculation of, 23
total employment cost (TEC), ready reckoner for, 134–136
total revenue (TR), definition, 23
trainees
  periods of training, 80–81
  and resignation notices, 288
  terms and conditions of work for, 105–109
training agreements for apprentices and trainees, 108–109
training and induction in occupational health and safety, 255
transferring employees and qualifying periods, 335
transitional amounts, 109

• U •

undue influence and workplace rights, 228–229
unfair dismissal
  appeals against, 314
  definition, 301–305
  employees not protected from, 301
  employees protected from, 300
  resolving disputes, 309–314
  in Western Australia, 315
unfair dismissal claims
  avoiding, 283
  settling during conciliation, 310–311
unfair dismissal compensation and superannuation, 131
unfulfilled expectations and conflict, 203
unjust dismissal, criteria for, 303–304
unjustifiable hardship, exemption under anti-discrimination law, 235
unlawful discrimination at work
  summary, 220–221
  when not applicable, 317–318
unlawful dismissal, definition, 317–318
unlawful termination of employment, 318
unpaid parental leave
  and continuity of service, 68
  costs of, 112–113
unreasonable dismissal, criteria for, 303–304
unreasonable management practice and bullying, 240–241

unsatisfactory work performance, responding to, 182–183
unsuccessful job candidates, feedback to, 50

• V •

values of business in staff handbook, 163
variable costs (VC), definition, 23
Victoria
  agency administering portable long service leave scheme in, 122
  definition of deemed worker in, 270
  definition of worker in, 268
  duty of care in, 250
  long service leave provision, 120
  National Employment Standards (NES) in, 62
  payroll tax and thresholds in, 124
  pro rata long service leave payment in, 291
volition in resolving conflict, 209
voluntary emergency management activity, 72–73
voluntary redundancy, 327–329

• W •

wage-work bargain, definition, 171
wages. *See also* salaries
  apprentices and trainees, 107
  competing in market for, 194–196
  definition of, 124
  modern award transitional provisions for, 109
  negotiations with unhappy staff, 196–197
warnings on poor performance, 182
weekly hours of work (NES), averaging, 63–64
weightings for selection criteria, 45–46
welcome pack for new staff, contents of, 156–157
welcoming new employees, 340
Western Australia
  agency administering portable long service leave scheme in, 122
  definition of deemed worker in, 270

definition of worker in, 268
duty of care in, 250
long service leave provision, 120
payroll tax and thresholds in, 124
pro rata long service leave payment in, 291
special features of employment in, 83–86
unfair dismissal in, 315–316
Western Australian Industrial Relations Commission (WAIRC), 315
wilful behaviour, exclusion from workers compensation, 271
win-win outcomes in wage negotiations, 197
withdrawing in conflict resolution, 212
withholding monies owed at termination, 294–295
work value and wage rates, 196
workers, definitions in states and territories, 267–268
workers compensation, responsibilities of business owner, 266
workers compensation insurance, costs of, 122–123
workers compensation payments and superannuation, 131
work flow design
  components of, 26–27
  using, 9–10
working hours, deciding on, 33–34
working out employment, 80–81
working on public holidays, 78–79
working through conflicts with employees, 210–211
workplace behaviour, policies for, 17–19
Workplace Health and Safety Act, Model, 250, 251, 253
workplace health and safety regulation pyramid, 263
workplace injuries
  defining, 270–271
  disputing claims of, 277–278
  must occur, 271–272
workplace rights
  dangers with, 227–229
  understanding, 224–225, 226
  and unlawful dismissal, 317

About the Author

Paul Maguire operates his own business management consultancy — Maguire Consulting — and is the owner of the online human resources management advice service for small to medium enterprises, employeerelationsonline.com.au.

Born in Melbourne, Australia, Paul graduated in 1982 from the University of Melbourne with a bachelor of commerce, majoring in economics, economic history and psychology. He commenced his working career as an archivist with the Victorian Public Record Office and then went on to various roles working in public policy in state government. It was while on secondment to the Public Service Association that Paul developed his lifelong interest in human resource management and employee relations. After obtaining a post-graduate diploma in employment and labour relations law from the University of Melbourne in 1992 Paul set about a career in human resources management and employee relations advice, advocacy and representation.

Seeing an opportunity in the market and keen to do things his way, Paul established his consultancy in 2000 with the aim of building a business that would provide practical, clear and no-nonsense advice to growing small and medium enterprises. Paul has worked closely with industry and professional employer associations over the past ten years, and has particular interest and expertise in employee relations advice, salary benchmarking, small business development, workforce development, regulatory compliance, advocacy and enterprise bargaining. Paul's clients operate throughout Australia in retail, ICT, construction, manufacturing, professional, human services, hospitality, health and employment services.

Drawing on his considerable knowledge and experience with commercial, not-for-profit and government enterprises, Paul continues to work closely with his clients, offering quality advice based on a thorough understanding of their businesses. Paul likes developing working relationships that are personal and believes he provides advice above and beyond the narrowly focused service promised by larger business management consultancies.

Paul has a son in his early twenties and lives with his partner, Jane, in Melbourne. Paul would love to hear from readers of this book. Visit his website (maguire.com.au) for more information and to get in touch.

Author's Acknowledgements

The idea for this book came about shortly after I had been speaking at the Australian National Small Business Summit in Melbourne on the challenges that small business employers face with ever-increasing complex regulation of employment. Clare Dowdell at Wiley Publishing asked me if I would be interested in writing a book that would assist small business employers in understanding and applying really practical human resource management methods in their businesses with their own staff. This was an opportunity that I welcomed.

Writing a comprehensive guide on human resource management from the start of an employment relationship through to its inevitable end is not an easy task. I'm really grateful to a strong network of experts and researchers (all of who run their own small businesses) who were able to assist me in gathering and organising information, verifying facts or otherwise offering wise counsel on how best to present the material throughout the book. In particular, I would like to acknowledge the contribution of Peta Nowacki, an experienced lawyer and specialist on the topics of equal employment opportunity, anti-discrimination, workplace rights, conflict resolution and prevention of workplace bullying. Carolyn McConnell of CKL Bookkeeping and her husband, Steve McConnell, an accountant and taxation specialist, cast expert eyes over the chapters explaining superannuation, salary sacrifice, fringe benefits and taxation. Kevin Egan provided the technical review to ensure accuracy on all of the factual information.

At Wiley, Clare Dowdell was especially persuasive in keeping me focused on writing when other demands were drawing me away from this project, and Danielle Karvess, project editor, provided encouragement to complete the work. Charlotte Duff did a sterling job in editing.

The topics I could have covered in this theme of managing people are endless. I hope you enjoy the topics that I have chosen to write about in this book.

Publisher's Acknowledgements

We're proud of this book; please send us your comments through our online registration form located at `dummies.custhelp.com`.

Some of the people who helped bring this book to market include the following:

Acquisitions, Editorial and Media Development

Project Editor: Charlotte Duff

Acquisitions Editor: Clare Dowdell

Editorial Manager: Dani Karvess

Production

Graphics: diacriTech

Technical Reviewer: Kevin Egan

Proofreader: Catherine Spedding

Indexer: Don Jordan, Antipodes Indexing

The author and publisher would like to thank the following copyright holders, organisations and individuals for their permission to reproduce copyright material in this book:

- **Cover image:** © iStockphoto.com/Rubberball

- **Page 240 to 241:** Information about reasonable versus unreasonable management practice © Commonwealth of Australia 2012

Every effort has been made to trace the ownership of copyright material. Information that enables the publisher to rectify any error or omission in subsequent editions is welcome. In such cases, please contact the Legal Services section of John Wiley & Sons Australia, Ltd.

Business & Investing

MYOB Software FOR DUMMIES
Making Everything Easier! 7th Australian Edition

Learn to:
- Get to grips with payroll
- Create your Business Activity Statements
- Take advantage of the latest features of MYOB, including working in 'the cloud'
- Grow your business!

Veechi Curtis
Author of QuickBooks For Dummies, Bookkeeping For Dummies and Small Business For Dummies

978-1-74216-998-9
$45.00

Small Business FOR DUMMIES
Making Everything Easier! 4th Australian & New Zealand Edition

Learn to:
- Plan for profit and maintain a healthy cash flow
- Grow a loyal customer base
- Put together a killer marketing plan
- Maximise your online presence
- Find and retain great staff

Veechi Curtis
Author of MYOB Software For Dummies, QuickBooks For Dummies and Bookkeeping For Dummies

978-1-118-22280-5
$39.95

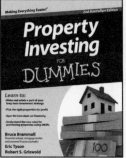

Property Investing FOR DUMMIES
Making Everything Easier! 2nd Australian Edition

Learn to:
- Make real estate a part of your long-term investment strategy
- Pick the right properties for profit
- Spot the best deals on financing
- Understand the new rules for purchasing properties using SMSFs

Bruce Brammall
Financial adviser, mortgage broker and personal finance journalist
Eric Tyson
Robert S. Griswold

978-1-118-39670-4
$39.95

Tax for Australians FOR DUMMIES
Making Everything Easier! Tax Year 2013-2014

Learn to:
- Lodge your tax return and enjoy your refund
- Keep on top of changes to the rules
- Maximise your small business tax bill
- Make the most of tax-free investing and super

Jimmy B. Prince
Tax professional and business educator

978-0-73030-584-2
$24.95

Bookkeeping FOR DUMMIES
Making Everything Easier! Australian & New Zealand Edition

Learn to:
- Get to grips with bookkeeping basics
- Record business transactions correctly
- Manage employee payroll and discipline GST
- Create financial statements

Veechi Curtis
Author of Small Business For Dummies, MYOB Software For Dummies and QuickBooks™ For Dummies
Lynley Averis
MYOB Your Business trainer
Forewords by Matthew Addison
Executive Director, Institute of Certified Bookkeepers

978-1-74216-971-2
$39.95

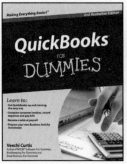

QuickBooks FOR DUMMIES
Making Everything Easier! 2nd Australian Edition

Learn to:
- Get QuickBooks up and running the easy way
- Generate customer invoices, record expenses and pay bills
- Become a whiz at payroll
- Prepare your own Business Activity Statements

Veechi Curtis
Author of MYOB Software For Dummies, Bookkeeping For Dummies and Small Business For Dummies

978-1-74246-896-9
$39.95

Xero FOR DUMMIES
Making Everything Easier!

Learn to:
- Do your accounting online anywhere, anytime
- Reduce data entry with automatic bank feeds
- Use dashboards to track your business performance in real-time
- Create and send invoices via your mobile devices

Heather Smith
Xero Certified Advisor and Chartered Certified Accountant
Foreword by Rod Drury
CEO of Xero

978-1-11857-255-9
$34.95

DIY Super FOR DUMMIES
Making Everything Easier! 2nd Australian Edition

Learn to:
- Set up and run your self-managed super fund
- Pay yourself a pension from your SMSF
- Create a tax-free retirement

SuperGuide.com.au

Trish Power
Link & Cass. Experts, Professional Writing and Editing), Co-founder of SuperGuide.com.au

978-0-73037-807-5
$29.95

Reference

English Grammar FOR DUMMIES
Making Everything Easier! 2nd Australian Edition

Learn to:
- Improve your writing and editing
- Understand and apply grammar rules
- Avoid common errors
- Correct grammar with style

Wendy M Anderson
Author, editor and educator
Geraldine Woods
Lesley J Ward

978-1-118-49327-4
$34.95

Solving Cryptic Crosswords FOR DUMMIES
Making Everything Easier!

Learn to:
- Solve different kinds of cryptic crossword clues
- Graduate from easy to medium to difficult cryptic crosswords
- Keep your brain fit and healthy
- Complete cryptic crosswords with confidence!

Denise Sutherland
Author of Cryptic Crosswords and Word Searches For Dummies

978-1-118-30525-6
$19.95

Cryptic Crosswords FOR DUMMIES
Making Everything Easier!

Learn to:
- Tackle over 50 easy, medium and difficult cryptic crosswords
- Exercise your brain and think differently
- Complete cryptic crosswords with confidence!

Denise Sutherland
Author of Solving Cryptic Crosswords for Dummies and Word Searches For Dummies

978-1-118-30521-8
$12.95

Passing Exams FOR DUMMIES
Making Everything Easier! 2nd Edition

Learn to:
- Understand what motivates you and how you learn best
- Condense course notes into study notes that work
- Dramatically enhance your retention with simple memory techniques
- Unlock your potential and improve your grades!

Patrick Sherratt
Author, speaker and trainer with Peninsula Ltd.

978-0-7303-0442-5
$24.95

Order today! Contact your Wiley sales representative.

Available in print and e-book formats.

For Dummies is a registered trademark of Wiley Publishing Australia Pty Ltd

A Wiley Brand